PAUL OL

S

A̲ ̲ ̲ ̲ ̲ ̲ ̲ ̲ ̲ ̲ ̲ Blues
Tradition

MW00478347

A DA CAPO PAPERBACK

Library of Congress Cataloging in Publication Data

Oliver, Paul.
  Screening the blues: aspects of the blues tradition / Paul Oliver.
      p.   cm. — (A Da Capo paperback)
  Reprint. Originally published: London: Cassell, 1968.
  Discography: p.
  Includes index.
  ISBN 0-306-80344-5
  1. Blues (Music) — History and criticism. I. Title.
ML3521.045   1989
573 — dc19   88-34291
                                                                  CIP

All ephemera and historic photographs are from the Paul Oliver
Collection. All photographs 1960 and later are copyright
Paul Oliver.

This Da Capo Press paperback edition of *Screening the Blues* is an
unabridged republication of the edition published in London in
1968, supplemented with illustrations supplied by the author. This
edition is reprinted by arrangement with Paul Oliver.

© Paul Oliver 1968

Published by Da Capo Press, Inc.
A Subsidiary of Plenum Publishing Corporation
233 Spring Street, New York, N.Y. 10013

All Rights Reserved

Manufactured in the United States of America

CONTENTS

ACKNOWLEDGEMENTS

Some of the following chapters have appeared in jazz periodicals and have been expanded with additional material and further examples. 'Preaching the Blues' is based on a number of short features which were included in the original 'Screening the Blues' series which appeared in *Jazz Monthly* from March 1960 to April 1961. 'The Santy Claus Crave' first appeared in *Music Mirror* for December 1955 and 'The Forty-Fours' is developed from 'Blues and Views No. 3' in *Music Mirror* for November 1955. Both 'Preaching the Blues' and 'The Forty-Fours' extend themes raised in *Conversation with the Blues*, while 'Policy Blues' and 'The Blue Blues' enlarge subjects touched upon in *Blues Fell This Morning*. 'Policy Blues' was originally written for *Jazz* for March 1963 and 'The Blue Blues' was prepared for intended publication in a proposed collection of various writings on censorship in the arts. To the editors of these periodicals I wish to extend my thanks.

For his technical advice and painstaking transcriptions for 'The Forty-Fours', I am greatly indebted to Donald Kincaid. I am particularly grateful to Trevor Huyton, Bob Koester, Mack McCormick and Pete Russell for the unissued, and unexpurgated, test pressings in their collections quoted in 'The Blue Blues' and extend my warm thanks to the following collectors and writers for their continued interest and for making available many references and recordings: Robert Dixon, Paul Garon, John Godrich, Archie Green, Bob Groom—who also kindly read the manuscript and made many helpful suggestions—Karl Gert zur Heide, John Holt, Mike Ledbitter, Simon Napier, Ian Ross, Tony Russell, Francis Smith and Max Vreede. I would also like to thank the many other collectors, who, in various ways, have also given me valuable help.

I am again greatly appreciative of the help given me by Miss M. D. Jarvis and the Mechanical-Copyright Protection Society in attempting to trace possible holders of copyright. Every effort has been made to obtain permission to quote extracts from copyright blues and songs. If, by an oversight, any quotations appear here which are in copyright and for which permission to quote has not been obtained, I would like to extend my sincere apologies. I am grateful to the following music publishing companies for permitting me to use the blues and songs listed alphabetically below. A copyright sign © appears at the end of each of these texts which may be located by the Index of Blues and Song Titles, page 278.

Cherry Red (Pete Johnson, Joe Turner). Copyright MCA Music, New York and Leeds Music Limited, London. Used by permission.

Christmas Mornin' Blues (Henri Johnson). Copyright 1927 Mayfair Music Corp. Used by permission of Edwin H. Morris & Company Ltd.

Coffee Blues (John Hurt). Copyright 1964 Wynwood Music Company. All rights reserved. Used by permission.

Dirty Dozens (unexpurgated) (Hopkins, McCormick). Copyright 1960 Mack McCormick. All rights reserved. Used by permission.

Dirty Dozen, The Original (unexpurgated) (Rufus Perryman). Copyright Koester Music 1956. Used by permission.

Dirty Mother For You (Roosevelt Sykes). Copyright MCA Music, New York and Leeds Music Limited, London. Used by permission.

Down on Pennsylvania Avenue (Delaney). Copyright MCA Music, New York and B. Feldman & Co. Ltd, London. Used by permission.

Hallelujah Joe Ain't Preachin' No Mo' (Morand). Copyright MCA Music, New York and Leeds Music Limited, London. Used by permission.

I Don't Know (Willie Mabon, J. Thomas). Used by special permission of the publisher. Copyright 1953 by Republic Music Corp., 18 East 48th St, New York, New York 10017.

Joe Louis and John Henry (John L. Williamson). Copyright MCA Music, New York and Leeds Music Limited, London. Used by permission.

Mean Tight Mama (Razaf). Copyright B. Feldman and Company Ltd. Used by permission.

King Joe (*Joe Louis Blues*) (Count Basie, Richard Wright). Copyright 1941 and 1942 Bregman, Vocco and Conn Inc. Used by permission of Bregman, Vocco & Conn, Ltd.

Kitchen Man (Razaf). Copyright B. Feldman and Company Ltd. Used by permission.

Lifeboat Blues (Walter Davis). Copyright Southern Music Publishing Company Ltd. Used by permission.

Louisiana Blues (Muddy Waters). Copyright 1959 Arc Music Corp. Used by permission of the publishers, Jewel Music Pub. Co. Ltd.

Merry Christmas (Robert Nighthawk). Copyright Campbell Connelly & Co. Ltd. Used by permission.

My Handy Man (Razaf). Copyright Edwin H. Morris & Company Inc., New York. Used by permission. Extracts from the lyrics reproduced by permission of Lawrence Wright Music Co. Ltd, London, and J. Albert & Son Pty, Ltd, Sidney.

My Man O' War (Razaf). Copyright. Extracts from the lyrics reproduced by permission of Lawrence Wright Music Co. Ltd, London.

My Starter Won't Work (West). Copyright Excellorec Music Company and Edward Kassner Music Company Ltd. Used by permission.

Noted Rider Blues (Huddie Ledbetter). Copyright Kensington Music Ltd. Used by permission.

Oh Didn't He Ramble (Will Handy). Copyright Edward B. Marks Music Corporation and Southern Music Publishing Company Ltd. Used by permission.

Preaching the Blues (Bessie Smith). Copyright 1927, 1954/5 Empress Music Inc. and Frank Music Company Ltd. Used by permission.

Preachin' the Blues (Eddie Son House). Copyright Son Dick Music Co. Used by permission.

Rooster Blues (West). Copyright Excellorec Music Company and Edward Kassner Music Company Ltd. Used by permission.

Spoonful (Willie Dixon). Copyright 1960 Arc Music Corp. Used by permission of the publishers, Jewel Music Pub. Co. Ltd.

30–20 Blues (Willie Kelly). Copyright Southern Music Publishing Company. Used by permission.

Vicksburg Blues (Little Brother Montgomery). Words and music copyright Parnes Music Ltd. Used by permission.

My thanks are also due to the following who have given permission for extended quotations from the books listed:

Music on My Mind by Willie the Lion Smith and George Hoefer. Copyright 1964. Reprinted by permission of the publishers, MacGibbon & Kee Ltd.

The Poetry of the Blues by Samuel Charters. Copyright 1963. Reprinted by permission of the publishers, Oak Publications Inc.

Really the Blues by Milton Mezzrow and Bernard Wolfe. Copyright 1946 by Random House. Reprinted by permission of Harold Matson Inc. and A. D. Peters & Co.

Mister Jelly Roll by Alan Lomax. Copyright 1952. Reprinted by permission of the publishers, Cassell and Company Ltd.

I am especially grateful to the editorial department of Cassell & Co. for their help and constructive suggestions. And my special thanks go to my wife for her untiring assistance, her patience, and her unending supply of black coffee.

SCREENING THE BLUES: AN INTRODUCTION

Now that the blues is a major influence on the words, the tunes and the structure of the songs of the 'beat groups' and in the Top Twenty pops, it is hard to think of it as a music which was the province solely of the Negro in America. In an age of mass communications the blues was nurtured in the farms and settlements of the South, reached maturity in the ghettoes of the Northern cities and emerged to become a dominant influence on the popular music of the world. No folk music has ever had so dramatic a history nor, ultimately, so widespread a distribution. At the beginning of this century, when the birth cries of the blues were just being heard, the musicologist Henry Edward Krehbiel made a definition of folk-song. He wrote:

'Folksong is not popular song in the sense in which the word is most frequently used, but the song of the folk; not only the song of the people but, in a strict sense, the song created by the people. It is a body of poetry and music which has come into existence without the influence of conscious art, as a spontaneous utterance, filled with characteristics of rhythm, form and melody which are traceable, more or less clearly, to racial (or national) temperament, modes of life, climatic and political conditions, geographical environment and language. Some of these elements, the spiritual, are elusive, but others can be determined and classified.'[1]

In many ways the blues was different from the song forms that Krehbiel studied and it is possible that he would not have recognized it as folk-song, or would have deplored it, as did many of his contemporary writers on the subject, as an indication of the decline in Negro music. But by his own definition, which has scarcely been bettered, the blues was, and is today, one of the last great bodies of folk-song; perhaps the last that will ever emerge before the folk communities are finally absorbed.

Blues is a folk music, but a special one which has been subject to pressures peculiar to the situation of the Negro in the United States, having developed during the period when the status of the Negro was changing and having evolved in the years of migration and conflict. Charles S. Johnson, writing in the early 'thirties, stressed the importance of habitat to a folk culture and its essentially local nature. 'The folk are not to be identified with the peasant who has left the soil to live and work in the city. Such peoples constitute what might be described as the "populus" or, better still, the "proletariat",' he wrote.

I

To Johnson 'the blues . . . are the natural idiom of the Negro proletarian, just as the "spirituals" have been, and to a very considerable
extent still are, the natural expression of the mind and mood of the
plantation Negro. The distinction between the folk of the villages and
the open country and the proletarians or populus of the city is expressed
and symbolized in the difference between the folk-song and the popular
ballad, the spirituals and the blues.'[2]

Looking back, more than three decades later, it is evident that the
blues has been the property not only of the 'proletarian' of the city
but of the folk Negro of the country also. It is evident too, on examination, that the divisions between the song idioms are not so simply
divided between urban and rural cultures and that the sacred and secular
forms are not the respective property of the village and the city Negroes.
Comparisons made between blues of various dates within that period
make it clear that the music has undergone considerable change overall,
although certain singers have retained qualities of blues expression
which are sometimes associated with a particular era or with a specific
locality. Yet within the music as a whole certain threads may be traced
which weave through the total fabric giving the tensile strength of a
living tradition. Not easily defined, these traditional threads are more
than the twelve-bar structure, the three-chord progression, the three-line
stanza, which are generally termed the 'traditional blues'.

The blues has become a folk music that has freed itself of the limitations of a confined locale, partly through the migration of Negroes
in its most fruitful years, but mainly through the accident of history
which saw its simultaneous evolution with the perfection of recording
techniques. With the advent of recorded blues in the early 'twenties,
a corpus of music was uniquely documented in unparalleled quantity
and this is a factor which cannot be over-emphasized. If, as a result of
recording, there was an inevitable 'influence of conscious art', there
was also within the various types of Race music, a cross-fertilization of
traditions and ideas, of lyrics and music which have been continually enriched by the creative inventiveness of individual singers and musicians.

Blues is not the music of recorded singers only. It originated without
the benefit of the phonograph and would probably have continued to
evolve without it. But recording is a fact of blues history and its influence has been immense. Through the blues record the lower-class
Negro was able to hear the voice of his counterpart from a thousand
miles away; hear him and feel a bond of sympathy which no other

2

medium could impart at such a personal level. Few radio stations were beaming with Negro audiences in mind when the blues first appeared on record and those that did had small catchment areas. Some featured blues singers, a matter of prestige for the artists involved, but the importance of their transmissions could not compare with recording. Negro newspapers were always active vehicles of protest and their power in shaping opinion is considerable. Many Northern newspapers publish editions in several cities and gain distribution widely through the Negro world but their concern has been for protest on the one hand and 'improvement' on the other. For the Negro in Tuscaloosa, Alabama or Yazoo City, Mississippi, the blues record afforded the first real opportunity of contact through a mass medium with others of his social status. Men from his own community sang on record in the company with others from Cleveland, Ohio or Gary, Indiana and the purchaser shared the blues with them all. In the recent history of the Negro in the United States recorded blues is a significant phenomenon.

Newspapers could only reach the literate, radio stations beamed locally only; records had a greater potential as a communication medium. Their direct impact on the senses made a positive impression and they could be played again and again, repeating their message in every playing. There is an abundance of evidence to show that records were learned by heart by other singers and by people with no aspirations to singing—in itself an indication of the extent to which they were played. Today, old 78s come in extremes of conditions: unplayed when they have reached collectors from the stockists' shelves and well worn when they have been obtained by house-to-house hunting. Other conditions reflect the popularity of singer or song, and some, grey on one side and 'mint' on the other, betray hard service in a juke-box.

Unfortunately, the collectors of blues records, who have conducted all too thorough and successful searches for records in Negro districts, have done a major disservice to research. No aspect of blues study has been more neglected than that of the relationship of the singer to his audience, either in person or on record. Charles Keil's recent *Urban Blues* has examined the rapport between singer and audience in 'soul' singing and the more deliberate stage presentation of modern blues professionals but the tastes of Negro audiences in the 'twenties and 'thirties, the popularity of individual singers and the appeal of particular types of blues in various strata of Negro communities, were totally undocumented.[3] Careful study of the records in Negro homes, their age, wear, artists, types and themes represented, would have done much to illumine this area, but the wilful gleaning of blues records by determined collectors has done irreparable damage to any future attempt to undertake such research. Only the trade stickers on the labels of a few records remain to give an indication of their distribution—a Spikes Brothers sticker with a Central Avenue, Los Angeles, address on a Jim Jackson record, or a Big Maceo disc with a sticker for a Dowling Street, Houston, music bar.

Against the incidence of records to be found in music shops and by the phonograph must be placed the availability of the records themselves and the types of music represented at a given point in time. The recording of Negro folk-song, blues and popular music has had a history which has inverted the general conception of its phases of evolution. The more sophisticated types of vaudeville entertainment were to be heard on wax before the Southern rural blues, while the more primitive examples of field cries, hollers and work songs, of children's game songs and unaccompanied blues were only heard on record in the rarest of instances. These were not commercially available until after the Second World War, when they appeared on labels and Library of Congress issues which could not have reached the culture that produced them. But too much stress can be laid on this; for a considerable period many forms of Negro song and music existed side by side and were available to, and enjoyed by, many Negroes with impartiality. That there was a market for the vaudeville blues before they ever appeared on record was well demonstrated by the remarkable response to Mamie Smith's first sides, which reportedly sold 75,000 copies in the first month after release.[4]

Nor were the records sold only in the Northern cities. Late in 1922 the Okeh records of Mamie Smith were already widely distributed by the General Phonograph Corporation. Scott Brothers in Milwaukee; Goldman and Wolf, and the Crampton Drug Company in Pittsburgh; the Melody Music Shop on Hastings and the East Detroit Music House on Gratiot in Detroit; and Chicago distributors, including the Vendome Music Shop on 31st Street and the Economy Phonograph Repair Shop on State, handled the records. But farther south, the Past Time Music Company was one of a number in St Louis, the Scoville Music Store one of a couple in Cleveland's Negro district, and D. M. Craft Company in Indianapolis, the Trotter Furniture Company in Knoxville, and others in Wellsville, Ohio, Poor Fork, Kentucky and as far south as

Bessemer, Alabama, were all stocked with Mamie Smith's first releases.[5] In the ensuing months more stores carried Race records, specially pressed for the Negro market, handling Okeh, Paramount and eventually, Brunswick, Vocalion, Columbia and many lesser label issues. They were bought from the Metropolitan Music Company in Chattanooga, Tennessee, the St Louis Music Company, the Artophone Corporation in Memphis, E. E. Forbes and Sons Piano Company in Birmingham, Alabama, and from others in Atlanta, Dallas, Houston, Jackson, New Orleans and throughout the South.[6]

Handled under various guises, the Paramount records of the Wisconsin Chair Company, under the trade name of the National School Equipment Company, were sold from suitcases and wagons and through local agents, and Race records from jazz to vaudeville to rural blues reached the remotest districts. Some indication of the effectiveness of their sales may be obtained from Charles S. Johnson's study of eight remote rural communities in Macon County, Alabama. Working in the first years of the 'thirties he made an intensive sociological study of 612 Negro families in these settlements: 'There are no radios, but 76 families had victrolas, bought on the instalment plan from agents in the community. There was but one banjo in the entire 612 families. . . . There were twenty-one organs and three pianos in the families, and most of these were out of repair; but playing provides some amusement. Both the organs and the pianos were in the homes of owners.'[7] There is no doubt that the agents would have ensured that a supply of records was available and playing recorded examples may well have been the inducement used to encourage some thirteen per cent. of these impoverished families without radios to purchase phonographs. Johnson did not record the nature of the records purchased but the issue of Race records by this time was almost universal among record companies and a cross-section of musical forms can be assumed from the observations of Odum and Johnson.

By the mid-'twenties these writers had already noted 'the processes of borrowing, combining, changing and misunderstanding through which formal material often goes when it gets into the hands of the common folk'.[8] In 1939, it was possible for Muriel Davis Longini to write of the 'Folk Songs of Chicago Negroes' and to cite many songs which had been derived from records. Her notes were not always strictly accurate and doubtless reflected the information given her by the singers from whom she collected. *Black Snake Blues* was attributed, as was *Milk Cow Blues*, 'to Big Boy Fuller, a blind boy' rather than to Blind Boy Fuller, or the authors of the blues, Blind Lemon Jefferson and Kokomo Arnold.[9] Her informants were revealing, through the error, the influence of blues on record. Muriel Longini observed pertinently that 'a Chicago song's similarity to its earlier southern version depends on its method of conveyance. Carried to its northern hearers by gramophone, the verses will remain intact until local or personal modifications are made.'[10] Many years after, field recordings made in Alabama by Harold Courlander and Frederic Ramsey Jr of singers like Horace Sprott and Rich Amerson showed the influence of Jefferson and Fuller in direct quotations from their records.

This interplay was important in the folk process in the second and third quarters of this century, but it poses many problems. 'It is doubtful,' warned Odum and Johnson, 'whether the history of song affords a parallel to the American situation with regard to the blues. Here we have a phenomenon of a type of folk song becoming a great fad and being exploited in every conceivable form; of hundreds of blues, some of which are based directly upon folk productions being distributed literally by the millions among the American people; and the Negro's assimilation of these blues into his everyday song life. What the effects of these processes are going to be, one can only surmise. One thing is certain, however, and that is that the student of Negro song tomorrow will have to know what was on the phonograph records of today before he may dare speak of origins.'[11]

Odum's and Johnson's words were prophetic; the more so because at the time of their writing in 1925, none of the foregoing singers mentioned—Fuller, Jefferson, Arnold for instance—had yet appeared on record. At this time many of the most important and influential voices in the blues were still known only to their immediate friends and acquaintances—Charley Patton, Frank Stokes, Tommy Johnson, Peetie Wheatstraw, Leroy Carr were unknown names to recording. The process of putting the blues on wax was in its infancy. And yet, by this time, Odum and Johnson concluded that the combined sales of three Race companies 'alone amount to five or six million records annually'. These companies apparently included Okeh and Columbia but not the all-important Paramount label.

Five or six million Race records sold annually at a time when the total Negro population in the United States was only double that amount meant that a very large proportion of the Negro world must have been hearing the music; a single record could be familiar in the lives of half a dozen people and many a young Negro grew up with the phonograph blues always in his ears. The colossal output indicates irrefutably the important part played by the gramophone in the spread of Negro musical culture and gives some indication of its potential strength in directing and forming Negro taste.

In itself the estimated number of sales is not sufficient evidence on which to base any conclusions on the extent of this influence. Viewed from the age of the 'golden disc' and the 'million seller', such a figure could represent a mere handful of issues. Sales of this scale were occasionally achieved in the 'twenties and 'thirties, but in folk music they were unusual. Proportionately, a sale of a hundred thousand records to the Negro market could be compared with a million seller in the potential tenfold white market. An over-simplification which could only be established with accuracy if the exact relationship between the Negro and white purchasing public were known, this assumption could be supported by off-setting the number of Negroes who could not afford to purchase blues records against the proportion of the white market which would not be interested in popular music of any kind.

Blues records were not cheap: although the ARC labels sold for only 25c in the 'thirties the Columbia Race series of a decade before sold at the considerable sum of 75c each. This high price did not deter sales of over 20,000 for the more popular Bessie Smith issues and sales from 8–10,000 of the most obscure country blues items. Sales of blues issues of several hundred thousand have been claimed, but only in the case of the Columbia issues have comprehensive figures been compiled and an analysis made of the types of music represented. Dan Mahony's work gives an idea of the proportion of blues issues represented within the Columbia Race series. According to his classifications, city and country blues singers together accounted for 47 per cent. of the total. Religious releases amounted to 17·7 per cent. of the series and there were nearly as many in the categories of vaudeville and instrumental music. Though not entirely representative as a Race record label, having a high proportion of the so-called 'classic', or as Mahony groups them, 'city' singers, the overall proportion of blues to the other categories is fairly typical. Blues recordings accounted for nearly half the total output in the series in the 'twenties whereas religious issues, including those by solo evangelists and jubilee groups, totalled only a fraction over a sixth of the number.[12]

According to the reckoning of Robert M. W. Dixon there were, in the score of years preceding 1942, approximately 19,300 known titles of recordings in the Race categories, of which some 70 per cent. were issued. Of the titles made for commercial release some 16,100 were listed, of which 2,600 were not issued. The balance of predominantly unissued recordings, 3,200, was made for the Archives of Folk Music in the Library of Congress.[13] At a rough estimate, something in the region of 10,000 blues titles were recorded in the period, which included the critical Depression years when there were very few issues of Race records at all. Comparable figures are not as yet available for the recordings made in the subsequent quarter-century but it is likely that the number of blues and gospel recordings made in this period exceeds the earlier tally.

Painstaking discographical work has resulted in the extensive documentation of the pre-war blues issues and the post-war period is currently receiving the same attention.[14] Research is complicated by the nature of the activities of the companies. Before the war there were relatively few companies which controlled the majority of Race issues. As an extreme example, Banner, Conqueror, Melotone, Oriole, Perfect, Romeo and sometimes Vocalion and Domino issues, were often made of a single recording, the group of labels being controlled by one concern, the American Record Company. Small labels, such as Polk or the mail order Montgomery Ward company, were rare and, though the trading and pooling of recordings between companies was extremely complex, the number of recordings was finite and largely preserved in company files and catalogues. In the post-war years a large number of small and independent companies sprang up throughout the United States. Many of these had only a handful of releases, kept poor if any documentary files and used casual methods of distribution. Of these companies specializing in blues and gospel releases many were Negro-owned, marking a further distinction between the issues of the earlier and later periods, the short-lived Black Patti and Merrit companies of the 'twenties being exceptional in this respect.

Those factors which complicate discographical research are precisely the ones which have affected the dispersal of blues in recent years. In the 'twenties and 'thirties location recordings in the South were made at intervals by Northern-based companies. In later years Southern companies were in a position to record local talent while the greater proportion of small, Negro-owned concerns permitted direct contact with the blues-producing community. Confusing the dissemination of the blues further was the growth in the 1950s of radio stations which beamed directly to Negro audiences, exploiting their potential market. Accompanying their playing of records with witty 'jive' patter which in itself attracted audiences, the Negro disc-jockeys played blues and gospel releases from local radio stations for hours at a stretch. The local blues which independent companies could record was often influenced by the latest issues from Chicago-situated firms played over the radio networks. Direct communication media reduced the miles and the time-lag in the conveyance of new blues compositions and styles.

Today the blues is threatened by pressures of mass media and commercial exploitation which may obliterate its character as a music form. On the one hand the blues has been absorbed by popular music throughout the world with consequent damage to its identity; on the other, the blues has itself absorbed the modes of expression of the Church until the qualities of each have been submerged in soul music, which exploits the intensity of expression of religious song, the form and instrumental character of the blues and the maudlin sentiments of pop music. Facile but skilful imitation by young white singers has further obscured the individuality of the blues and it seems likely that the future of the blues as 'the song of the folk', as a 'spontaneous utterance, filled with characteristics of rhythm, form and melody' is likely to be a brief one. No longer 'without the influence of conscious art' the blues may become a self-conscious art music and as such survive in a new form, but its days as a folk music may be numbered.

Robert Redfield, whose *Tepoztlán, A Mexican Village* was the inspiration for Charles S. Johnson's comments on the blues, defined 'the folk' as people who 'enjoy a common stock of tradition; they are the carriers of a culture. This culture preserves its continuity from generation to generation without depending upon the printed page. Moreover such a culture is local; the folk has a habitat. And finally, the folk peoples are country peoples. If folk lore is encountered in the cities it is never in a robust condition, but always diminishing, always a vestige.'[15] Mass communication through recording, and later through radio, spread the culture of the blues beyond the local definition until the whole Negro world was its habitat. Recordings extended the range of oral transmission of the blues while the movement of country folk to the cities did not necessarily result in the weakening of the idiom. For a period, at any rate, the blues matched the change of environment with a change of its nature which resulted in a music that was in some senses more, rather than less, robust. Yet it must be conceded that in the long run blues suffered from the levelling-out of character of which recording and radio were the primary causes. Whatever the outcome of the present confused state of the music, it is clear that mass media and the commercial interests that have inspired their exploitation of blues, will have played a large part in determining its fate. This ultimately disturbing fact must not be permitted to obscure the beneficial aspects of the long history of recording. The extent of the recording of Race, and indeed other American folk musics, was considerable over a long period. Active talent scouts, perspicacious company managers, effective assessment of the Negro market and equally effective distribution methods devised in order to reach it, together contributed to an extensive coverage of blues, if not in its earliest phases, at least in the years of its growth and dissemination.

No folk music collectors were as aware of the music being created by the Negro in modern times as were the record company representatives, and no collectors were as assiduous in tracking it down. After more than forty-five years of recording, the body of material collected has no parallel as a basis for comparative study. No system of musical notation can compare with the phonograph record as a basis for discussion. Phonophotography and voice-prints may give an accurate translation of certain characteristics of the voice in graphic form and there is much room for the use of these methods in blues study, but qualities of expression, timbre, pitch, intonation, inflection, stress and meaning are preserved together in the record as in no other way.[16] As evidence of the values of sound and technique among individual singers and instrumentalists two, three and four decades ago it is unique. With all its limitations, the blues on record remains the most valuable documentation of the evolution of a folk music in a modern society.

Any conclusions based on the screening of blues recording must be tempered by considerations as to whether the image of the blues revealed is an accurate one. Within the catalogues the disproportionate representation of artists casts doubt on this; against the names of a Tampa Red, a Big Bill Broonzy, a Roosevelt Sykes whose issued records number a few hundred apiece, must be placed those of a Freezone or an Emma Wright who are each known by a single issued title alone.[17] In spite of the extensive discographies of a number of singers and until the advent of the long-playing record, which came late to Negro homes, the average number of sides made by a singer was probably around a dozen. In the recollections of blues singers are the names of numberless others whose work remains unrecorded and among them are many whose reputations are a matter of legend. Even as an indication of the number of blues singers, records must remain an inaccurate gauge. Of those singers represented many would have been affected by the socio-economic factors which conditioned whether they were recorded at all. The infrequency of field-recording trips, the great distances between recording centres, the temperaments of the artists and many other considerations outlined elsewhere, combine to determine arbitrarily the quality and character of the music available now.

In content the blues, like any folk music, reflects in part the society which produced it. But to what extent does recorded blues give an accurate picture of the culture-producing society and the experience of a minority group within the larger social context? Is the content of recorded blues a comprehensive anthology of the blues as sung in all conditions? Too little research has been done on the blues in the field for any reasonable conclusions to be drawn here; documentary collections of early blues are very few and since recording have been little developed. Can it be assumed that the blues contained no appeals for racial solidarity, no protests at discrimination, no inflammatory outbursts, no burning declarations against lynching? On record there is virtually no direct evidence of outspoken protest and such text collections as there are give fragmentary hints only. But this may be an indication of the problems encountered by the collector in obtaining uninhibited songs that have not been modified for his ears. It is now probably too late for any such material to be reclaimed in quantity and substantial protest blues, if they ever existed, may never be available. On record the blues singer may have acted as his own censor, or the company executives may have frustrated the recording or prevented the release, of any such songs. From recordings whose content is representative of other areas of Negro life it seems that the blues singer is often content to state a fact of his experience rather than to protest about it. But it is also possible that allusion, symbol and the employment of concealing imagery may have enabled him to give covert expression to prohibited material.

If protest themes are expressed in a deliberately obscure language of concealment in the blues, it follows that the audience for whom it is intended must be the possessor of the key to the meaning, for without some means of mutually comprehensible, but otherwise indecipherable, language, communication through recording would fail. This would imply the employment of traditional vehicles of expression, shared between singer and audience. Even if protest themes do exist it is still evident that there are many other aspects of Negro life which the blues does not illumine. Though there are some Negro intellectuals who are interested in the blues, the blues singers are singularly disinterested in them. Essentially it is of the working class among coloured people; middle-class Negroes neither figure in, nor show any concern for, the blues. Whole areas of experience and perception do not appear in the songs; there are only the slightest passing references to children; family life is represented more by its disintegration than by its preservation; appreciation of scenic beauty seldom extends beyond the cliché, 'Don't the moon look lonesome shining through the trees ?'; national events and successes are seldom recorded; political comment is to be found in a handful of blues, Jim Crow laws and poll taxes hardly at all. Of the Civil Rights movement, of Freedom marches, of anti-segregation demonstrations and lunch-counter sit-ins, Black Muslims and Black Power, the blues says nothing.

With these limitations in content, it is obvious that no historical study of the coloured people in the United States, even in the twentieth century, can be made through the blues. It was not the intention of *Blues Fell This Morning* to attempt such a history but rather to relate the content of the blues on record to those aspects of the socio-economic background of society which it represented.[18] In Krehbiel's terms it attempted to examine to some extent the 'racial temperament, modes of life, climatic and political conditions, geographical environment and language' of the blues. As space would not permit proportional representation of the themes of the blues in such a study it could be prone to special pleading, while the possibility remains that the blues singer does not live the life that he describes, that much of the content of the blues is an unwitting distortion of black society through self-delusion or wishful thinking. Acknowledging these possibilities, it was hoped that through recorded monologues, taped as far as possible under conditions of free association and without direction, 'some of these elements, the spiritual', which Krehbiel noted as being elusive, might be revealed through the words and the reflections of the singers themselves. *Conversation with the Blues* was compiled from such documentary recordings of the speech of blues singers, not with the intention of writing blues history but rather with the intention of compiling the singer's own commentary on that history and the part that he played in it.[19] As a mirror of contemporary Negro society the blues may offer a distorted image and, as a mirror of his role within the blues, the singer's observations may be no less subjective. But that the blues is sung at all, let alone so widely, and that the blues singer considers himself within a tradition, is itself not without significance.

'And blues have been goin' on for centuries and centuries, and the blues was written years and centuries ago—they was always here,' declared Boogie Woogie Red with an ill-defined but none the less certain sense of a blues history and tradition.[20] Now over forty, he has lived all his life from the age of two in Detroit. A third-generation blues artist, he had no clear conception of the beginnings of the blues but he had a conscious awareness of being a carrier of a culture and of sharing a common stock of tradition with the other bluesmen of Detroit. He was virtually 'unknown' except to the city folk of his habitat, having had no records issued under his own name and having played for much of his life in the shadow of a celebrated singer, John Lee Hooker. But major artists and minor do not differ greatly in their views of the blues. Their differences lie rather in relative stature. Fame in the blues, as in other spheres, is fickle and is often linked with commercial success. The truly major artist, whether he is celebrated on record or only in the esteem of his fellow singers, is one who brings a creative genius to the blues tradition.

For blues has a tradition. Perhaps the music is now in decline but it has enjoyed a life-span long enough to establish a tradition of its own, comparable with that of say, the Dutch school of painting, whose artists, from the generation of the 1590s to the generation of the 1620s anticipated those of the blues by exactly three hundred years. In a period of unprecedented acceleration of social, technological, economic and cultural changes, the blues has changed too. But though it has been altered by the differing environments which gave it birth and modified by the social climates in which it has flourished, those constants, the elements of tradition within the music, relate it to the folk forms that preceded it and establish links between the various categories that have been discerned in its development.

Apart from the crude classifications of country blues, city blues and classic blues which are so broad in their implications and so poorly distinguished as to be worthless for any practical purposes of analysis, the most frequently applied categorization of blues singers is by state or region of origin. Mississippi Blues, Atlanta Blues, Texas Blues, East Coast Blues and similar categories have been used, sometimes in conjunction with the broader groupings. These categories, with identifying characteristics, have been advanced by such writers as Pete Welding, Samuel B. Charters and Charles Keil.[21] Mississippi singers and guitarists have been identified as being rough and stark, narrow in their melodic range, strong in their emphasis on the rhythm and given to the use of speech patterns in their vocals. Keil gives Bukka White, Son House, Robert Johnson, early Muddy Waters and John Lee Hooker as exemplary of the Mississippi Delta Blues. Blind Lemon Jefferson, Texas Alexander, Mance Lipscomb, and Lightnin' Hopkins he associates with the single-string guitar, relaxed vocals and 'light' texture of the Texas region to which Welding ascribes deliberate and sophisticated delivery and a 'lean, open, long-lined sound'. The choice of singers and instrumentalists to represent these areas spans two or three generations and the implication of such a classification is of a tradition identifiable with the territory. Further and more detailed discussion has revolved around the identification of Clarksdale, Mississippi, and Southern Mississippi traditional styles.

Although such discussion is undertaken without any agreement having been reached on what is meant by 'style' in the context, it can be assumed that it is a consideration of the manner of expression in instrumental or vocal rather than of the content. Though such styles may be the result of the dominance of a particularly strong personality or the deliberate imitation by others of a talented artist, they may also be the result of collective creation on the part of a number of artists whose exchange of ideas and mannerisms result in the emergence of a clearly defined character of music. Assimilation by subsequent artists lays the tradition, if by tradition one means the aesthetic attributes that are based on the cumulative experience of the group or that are perpetuated through prolonged usage.

Tradition in the blues seen in terms of regional styles has received considerable attention, often at the expense of other aspects. The main concern of this book is the consideration of some of these other aspects. Any discussion of styles within the blues must be based on the premise that many elements are common to them all and are sufficient in number and recognizable enough to make subdivision as the basis for argument practicable. But rigid classification in an art form builds in error, forcing the rejection of items which do not fall into the compartments constructed. This is as true of blues as it is of any other area of study and it is necessary, in seeking common elements of the blues tradition, to trace them where applicable across the boundaries of style, local or regional.

Strongest of the traditional elements in the blues is the three-line stanza and the twelve-bar form. Rare in any music before the late nineteenth century, this structure is to be found in isolated cases in the spirituals and has been noted on occasion in other folk musics. As a basis for a whole cultural expression, however, it was unique to the blues until its recent widespread adoption by commercialized popular music. Though this familiar form is prevalent it is not by any means the only one used by blues singers. 'The blues is a feeling,' says many a blues singer and, if he most frequently chooses the traditional twelve-bar, three-line pattern in which to express himself, he will also use other structures. Songs and verse patterns of eight-bar, sixteen-bar and other lengths and in two, four, five, eight and other numbers of lines in the stanzas are by no means uncommon; they are blues in feeling if not blues in the narrowest structural definition. If blues is considered more in terms of what blues singers choose to sing and less according to the strict application of the twelve-bar definition, the form becomes open-ended. Blues singers may show a preference for the traditional three-line stanza but they draw upon other song types also and, in doing so, frequently reveal the strength of other traditional fibres within the main stem of their music.

Older Negro folk-song forms than the blues, such as the ballads or the spirituals, have influenced the later song which still contains some elements in common with them. Other aspects of Race music, minstrel songs and vaudeville songs among them, have also left their mark on the blues and these various types may be found to be shared by singers of widely differing character and of various regions, styles and traditions. In the chapter on 'The Blue Blues', some of the structural forms used by blues singers are classified and their use by different types of singers is discussed. Many of them are survivals from a pre-blues period whose tradition is strong enough to persist, in some cases, to the present. One of the characteristics of such songs, which distinguishes them from the blues in its most representative forms, is the importance attached to the traditional verse sequence and the total song composition.

15

Variations in *Duncan and Brady, Railroad Bill, John Henry, Wade in the Water, Two Wings* or *My God Is a Rock in a Weary Land* arise from individual interpretation and errors through the process of transmission and committing to memory. The words may change and the tunes slightly alter but essentially the songs retain their identity at the core. Superficially, the blues is an endless succession of personalized verses on a simple structure, modelled and remodelled by each singer according to his needs. Improvisation is endemic in the blues and this aspect has been stressed in writing on the subject which has appeared in books on jazz. Blues singers pride themselves on their ability to 'rhyme up a song' but they do not consider this an essential requirement of their music. A blues singer is prepared to use the tune of one blues for the basis of his composition of another: *Betty and Dupree*, in fact, makes the transition from ballad to blues when it loses its singularity and becomes the melodic setting for Robert Johnson's *From Four until Late* or Brownie McGhee's *Diamond Ring*. One blues tune is adapted by many singers and the theme may be taken up by piano or guitar, string band or harmonica. So Charlie Davenport's *Cow Cow Blues* becomes Louise Johnson's *On the Wall* and Cripple Clarence Lofton's *Streamline Train*; it makes the transition from piano to guitar and mandolin when it is played by Bo Carter and Charlie McCoy as *That Lonesome Train Took My Baby Away* and *Jackson Stomp* and it becomes a harmonic solo by Cow Cow Davenport's namesake, Jed Davenport. Over the space of thirty-odd years the tune became the basis of many other blues and train interpretations, retaining some of its identifiable instrumental features but becoming the setting for new blues vocals. In monologues transcribed in *Conversation with the Blues*, Little Brother Montgomery and Roosevelt Sykes described the genesis of a blues instrumental. How this passed into the tradition and became, through the meeting of other melodic tributaries, a stream which carried other vocal themes is pursued in the chapter on 'The Forty-Fours'.

In this and other instances the melodic line or instrumental accompaniment becomes the vehicle for new verse compositions. A closer link with the ballads may be found in those blues which are recalled and performed according to a traditional sequence even though their form is essentially of the twelve bar. *See See Rider, Ain't Nobody's Business What I Do, Sail on, Little Girl Sail on, Sloppy Drunk, Diggin' My Potatoes* and many others are blues 'standards' known to every blues singer. Some, like *Hesitating Blues*, are obscure in origin; others, like

Shady Lane, are traceable, perhaps, to their source—in this case probably Leroy Carr. Through the popularity of recording, some traditional blues of this kind have become linked to the names and even the manner of delivery of individual singers. They need not necessarily be the composers—Jimmy Witherspoon is generally associated with *Ain't Nobody's Business* which was first recorded before he was born. Blind Lemon Jefferson's *One Dime Blues* and Charlie McFadden's *Groceries on the Shelf*, Bessie Smith's *Backwater Blues* and Bumble Bee Slim's *Hey, Lawdy Mama*, Bukka White's *Shake 'Em on Down* and Big Joe Williams's, *Baby, Please Don't Go*, Sonny Boy Williamson's *Good Morning School Girl* and Big Boy Crudup's *Mean Old Frisco*, Robert Lockwood's *Take a Little Walk with Me* and Jimmy Rodger's *That's All Right* are some of the blues which can be said to have passed into the tradition, though several of them are sung in a manner fixed by the recording of the singer mentioned. Others have had verses altered, even the subjects changed, but the elements of the original song remain in sufficient evidence for the root to be clear. Many of these are narrative blues which tell a story that the blues singer may relate to an experience of his own. Leroy Carr's *Prison Bound* or Curtis Jones's *Lonesome Bedroom Blues* might be instanced as blues which lend themselves to personalized adaptation on the part of the singer, becoming ballads in some attributes while remaining blues in feeling and form. Blues that follow the role of the ballads in recording an epic event or the deeds of a folk hero are exceptionally rare. What happens to the blues when it attempts to record heroic deeds? In the chapter on 'Joe Louis and John Henry', an isolated instance of the ballad-type theme, perpetuated by blues singers within the blues idiom, offers an opportunity for further defining the blues tradition by studying one of the exceptions.

More often it is a verse of the blues rather than the whole blues composition which survives in a traditional sense, to be drawn upon by various artists as it suits a particular context. Again, the single verses are sometimes identified with individual singers, as:

Sittin' here wonderin', will a match-box hold my clo's? (2)*
I ain't got so many matches but I got so far to go,[22]

* Lines marked with (2) are sung twice. In some instances a word or two may be interpolated or omitted in the second line, for example, 'Ooh, well, well', or 'baby', but only where the change affects the sense has the repeat line been quoted in full.

which is associated with the influential Blind Lemon Jefferson, or:

I've got the blues before sunrise, with the tears standin' in my eyes, (2)
It's such a miserable feelin', a feelin' I do despise,[23]

which is linked with the name of Leroy Carr. Carr was apparently the composer of the blues from which this verse comes, *Blues Before Sunrise*, but Jefferson, though he used the 'match-box' verse as a personal trade-mark, may have derived it from an earlier source. Gertrude (Ma) Rainey had already used the image in her *Lost Wandering Blues:*

Lord, I stand here wondering, will a match-box hold my clothes ?[24]

She may have heard Blind Lemon sing the verse in person, or both may have absorbed it from traditional usage. The poetic imagery and the universality of the verses make them applicable to many blues on the subjects of migration and loneliness. It is not easy to determine who first sang:

The blues is a lowdown achin' heart disease, (2)
It's like consumption, killin' you by degrees,

but it had been in text collections long before Ida Cox put together a number of folk verses to make her recording of *Blues Ain't Nothin' Else But*. And who was the source of:

I'm goin' to the river, take my rocker chair, (2)
If the blues overtake me, gonna rock away from here,

which has had a life of more than fifty years ?[25]
Verses like these impress by their vividness and by their succinct expression, in two iambic pentameters, of a human situation or as an epigrammatic comment on common experience. Often a single line rather than a verse reappears in numerous contexts; sometimes even a single phrase. Maverick lines that move from blues to blues are given new rhymes and new meaning by their juxtaposition with other ideas, while they retain the quality of surprise. A startling image, a telling phrase, is heard, learned and adapted. A wealth of associative meanings are carried in such lines as, 'My heart struck sorrow and the tears come

rolling down', 'I been down so long, it seems like up to me', 'If you don't like my peaches, please don't shake my tree', 'If the blues was whisky I'd stay drunk all the time', 'I got the blues so bad I can feel them in the dark', 'Everyone who smile in your face ain't a friend to you', or 'If you don't think I'm sinking, look what a hole I'm in', and they are drawn upon freely by singers who find in the traditional words the summation of their thoughts. Such 'floating verses' and maverick lines, which move restlessly from blues to blues, are to be found in all types of Race music; often the blues has borrowed them from other song types wherein they originally occurred. In the chapters, 'Preaching the Blues', 'The Santy Claus Crave' and 'The Forty-Fours' numerous examples are instanced of these traditional vehicles which have been remodelled repeatedly to fit variations on a few basic themes.

Much of the effectiveness of these migrant lines and verses depends on the subtleties of interpretation which they offer.

> The sun's gonna shine in my back-door some day
> My back-door some day . . . mmm,
> The sun's gonna shine in my back-door some day,
> And the wind's gonna change, gonn' blow my blues away,[26]

runs one celebrated verse which appears in Tommy Johnson's *Maggie Campbell*, from which this variant is taken, the Memphis Jug Band's *KC Moan*, Big Bill Broonzy's *The Sun Gonna Shine in My Backdoor Some Day* and countless other blues. But, one may ask, what is the exact meaning of the verse? Why should the sun shine one day in the back-door—is it because the sun usually shines in the front-door? Is it because the sun normally shines on a closed door and the song implies that the door is open and the occupant gone? Or does it imply that the dark recesses of the interior are at last illumined in some complex metaphor of good fortune? Is the emphasis on the *back*-door an allusion to the illicit lover, the 'back-door man' of so many blues, or is the singer himself the back-door man who has left for good? Does the front-door at last face *north*, when the sun shines in the back, suggesting that the singer has migrated to a more liberal, if less warm, Northern climate? And what is the wind of change that is going to blow away the blues—merely changing circumstances? good luck? Or is the line a subtler one with overtones of eventual racial equality and the dispersal of the conditions that cause the blues? Clearly the verse has a special appeal for blues singers, if its frequency is any indication. Perhaps it is the poetry of the lines alone that attracts, but it is equally likely that they carry some weight of meaning which is now only half-consciously understood. A change of context can alter the emphasis of the words and the interpretation of their meaning.

Through transmission to new blues, traditional words can acquire new significance and can retain their vitality and freshness when the applications are apt or original. In the mouths of less gifted singers, they provide ready-made phrases which can trigger off responses from their listeners. For it seems that certain words, verses, even whole blues, may have code implications which can be interpreted by the blues audience in safety. Through them, taboo themes may find expression, whether sexual, racial or related to illicit behaviour. In the chapter 'Policy Blues' the deliberate use of code references is examined to show how traditional terms—in this case, number combinations—can act in a closed society where their meaning can be understood by those within the group while remaining confusingly obscure to those outside it. In a period of tension and in conditions of some oppression, such devices strengthen the group and the individual's sense of identity within it. In this way the blues has become an important medium which has the potential to shape opinion, colour ideas and mould attitudes within the Negro community. And through the coded forms of blues verses it may give expression to those attitudes. This aspect is discussed in the chapter on 'The Blue Blues' where certain traditional songs on record would appear to perform a special role. But this is not to argue that the influence exerted by traditional words and themes was necessarily beneficial; to a certain extent the blues may have contributed to the delay in the Negro's active demand for civil rights, fixing traditional attitudes along with traditional modes of expression. Whether for good or ill, either in the history of a folk music or in the history of the folk communities, it is a fact of the blues and as such, deserves study.

If the Negro has been stereotyped it is also true that he creates his own stereotypes of himself. The Negro who acts out these stereotypes before whites is accused of 'Uncle Tomism' but in the relative privacy of the group he may still do so, unwittingly accepting the negative values that have been attributed to him. Accused of shiftlessness he can become shiftless, accused of a lack of independence he may be reluctant to accept responsibility. One of the damaging aspects of tradition is that it is resistant to change, and attitudes formulated in the nineteenth century, through traditional verses, may be sustained well into the twentieth, as the examples in 'Preaching the Blues' may show. Here are tired, outmoded concepts unnecessarily perpetuated, though below their surface meaning there may lie others of a symbolic nature. So the blues singer may continue to deplore the 'cruel ole fireman, mean ole engineer' who will not let him ride on a freight train, long after the steam locomotives have ceased to run. The fireman and the engineer remain effective as symbols of deliberate obstruction and their rejection of the singer in his attempt to ride the train continues as a symbol of frustrated ambition long after its effective use in narrative. It is the use of such symbols underlying the more obvious usages which give to many of the examples in 'The Blue Blues' their strength of impact.

Railroads, as was shown in *Blues Fell This Morning*, have been a powerful symbol in Negro folk-lore since the *ante-bellum* years of slavery.[27] Figuring prominently in spirituals and ballads, they have provided an unending stream of blues since the earliest noted examples. Though other subjects may have declined, blues about railroads still figure in the work of most singers. Symbolic of migration, power, escape, the locomotives have also served as an important sexual symbol. It is no coincidence that the 'play' in the 'numbers game'—explained in the chapter on 'Policy Blues'—for 'railroad cars' is 4–44, that the plays for 'locomotive' or for 'railroad' are both 4–11–44 and that the play for the male generative organs is likewise 4–11–44. That $4 \times 11 = 44$ is no doubt one of the additional reasons for the popularity of *The Forty-Four Blues* as a theme, indicating the complex web of associations within the blues tradition. Initials and numbers are popular with blues singers and though their sources are from aspects of their experience— travelling on railroads—the C & A, IC, KC, B & O, T & P, L & N, and so on; working on federal or other projects—the CCC, PWA, CWA, WPA; or on the numbered highways, one may speculate on the possibility that propitious combinations for letters and numerals also linger in the folk memory. Apart from the obvious fact that Highway 51 is a major northbound migratory route from Mississippi, is the appeal of the theme also something to do with 51 as the play for 'woman and man' or 61 as the play for 'drunken man'?

Whereas the railroads have a long history in Negro song, the highway theme seems to have been developed with the blues or with migration; or indeed, the blues were born from migration. It seems to have been Roosevelt Sykes's *Highway 61 Blues* made in 1932 which initiated the theme, inspiring no less than three versions by Jack Kelly the following year. 1933 also saw Sonny Scott's *Highway No. 2* and two years later Big Joe Williams made *49 Highway* of which Freddie Spruell also made a version. In turn came Joe McCoy's *Highway 61*, Walter Davis's *13 Highway*, Son Bonds's *80 Highway*, Lowell Fulson's *Highway 99* and innumerable versions of Curtis Jones's *Highway 51* by singers as varied as Tommy McClennan, Jazz Gillum, Smoky Hogg and Stickhorse Hammond. As a subject the highway seems to have had little precedent in the 'twenties and recorded blues has created its own traditional theme. Highways, nevertheless, are a constant in Negro environment in rural America, as are also the 'streets' which preceded them in the blues of urban singers of the 'twenties. Some themes in the blues reflect the recurrence of events which have affected the lives of singers and which may do so again, but which are of less specific interest in the periods when the subject is dormant. Thus the theme of floods is most meaningful when it appears at the time of flooding, or as a direct result of it. Those instances cited in *Blues Fell This Morning* which illustrated the subject of floods—Memphis Minnie's *When the Levee Breaks*, Blind Lemon Jefferson's *Risin' High Water Blues*, *The Flood Blues* by Sippie Wallace, *The Mississippi Flood Blues* by Joe Pullum, Barbecue Bob's *Mississippi Heavy Water Blues* and Lonnie Johnson's *Flood Water Blues*—were probably sufficient to show that the compositions made reference to a persistent phenomenon that brings misery perennially to thousands of Negroes, but they could not show the number of blues which have been concerned with it. Among those excluded were Big Bill Broonzy's *Terrible Flood Blues*, Casey Bill's *Flood Water Blues*, Carl Martin's *High Water Flood Blues*, Ivy Smith's *Southern High Water*, Charley Patton's six-minute blues *High Water Everywhere*, Ruby Gowdy's *Florida Flood*, Barbecue Bob's *Mississippi Low Levee Blues*, Lonnie Johnson's *Broken Levee Blues* and, more recently, Larry Davis's *Texas Flood*.

Examination of these recorded examples would reveal the degree to which some were original compositions recording specific events while others were reinterpretations of earlier blues. It would show which singers were concerned personally with their subject matter and further analysis might reveal whether some artists had an obsessive interest in a theme or were merely repeating past successes; why, for instance, Lonnie Johnson should record *Flood Water Blues*, *South Bound Water*, *Backwater Blues*, *Broken Levee Blues*, *Sleepy Water Blues* and three versions of *Falling Rain Blues* in the space of a dozen years? Lonnie Johnson was undoubtedly more interested in the related themes of heavy rainfall and inundation than in any other subject of social or environmental interest. Among blues of this type the theme of flooding is prominent yet spoliation of crops or, in fact, the whole process of cultivation of cotton, is very rarely the subject of blues, even though cotton cultivation and picking has figured in the lives of most blues singers. Much remains to be done in the study of the themes chosen by blues singers for their compositions and 'The Santy Claus Crave' is one recurrent subject which was not mentioned in *Blues Fell This Morning*.

To respectable, middle-class, church-going Negroes, blues is often considered evil music; the devil's music that beguiles the listener and leads him to damnation. Blues about liquor and the 'whisky-head man', about prostitution, gambling, vagrancy and intended violence, figure in the work of singers of all generations. Undoubtedly the blues acts as a catalyst at times, the singer dispersing his anger or the irresponsibility of his intentions through the blues. The prevalence of some themes may indicate a particular function of the music, acting as a release for discharged energies which might otherwise seek more dangerous outlets. Blues does not offer a true picture of Negro society but it does afford in some details an image of some aspects of it. And, even if the picture is sometimes a distorted one, there are few aspects of traditional blues which do not have relevance to some aspect of Negro life. Certainly the blues is temporal and its values worldly; and many blues singers reviewing their careers are disturbed by the fact. The singer who has once been 'in the world' and now 'done changed' and joined the Church is a familiar figure in blues annals. In *Conversation with the Blues* some of the views of blues singers, occasionally conflicting, were transcribed on the subject of the Church and religious observance.[28] Their uneasiness suggests that the blues singers' view of the Church is not the direct antithesis of the church-goers' view of the blues and, in 'Preaching the Blues', there is evidence of traditional stereotypes surviving in blues which touch on religion.

There is no doubt that the church members have good reason for regarding the blues with abhorrence, given the strictures of Negro religious sects, for the pleasures of the flesh predominate above all other aspects of life and experience in the work of blues singers. Since the earliest recorded examples of Race music, sexual themes have figured prominently in the work of most singers, sometimes to the exclusion of any other subject. Any discussion of the blues tradition must ultimately revolve around this libidinous hub of the music. For all its pervasiveness it has received very little critical attention and those comments that have been made on the sexual content of the blues may themselves now be open to scrutiny. Any examination of the titles and content of blues singers' discographies will reveal the repeated appearance of *Whip It to a Jelly*, *What's That Smells Like Gravy?* *Somebody's Been Using That Thing*, *Let Me Play with Your Poodle*, *Shake It Down*, *Hair Parted in the Middle*, *Let Me Squeeze Your Lemon*, *Jackass for Sale* and countless other songs whose meanings were thinly camouflaged in metaphors and symbols which presented few problems in unravelling. Many of these passed into the language of the folk to become traditional images and the songs became the common property of many singers. It may be argued that by no means all of them were blues according to a strict definition, but there is little question that they were sung, and sung frequently, by blues singers of all types. Under 'Problems of Classification' in the chapter on 'The Blue Blues', the blues and song types of sexual content are analysed as an introduction to a discussion on the traditional element of song, verse, image and other aspects of transmission which cut across the customary stylistic classifications of the blues.

In no area is the investigation of tradition in the blues rendered more difficult than in the field of sexual song for, in spite of the profusion of recordings, the dearth of documentation in text collections or from the folk communities frustrates comparative study. There is evidence from the comparison of recorded songs that many of them have a longer history than the standardized blues forms, but deductions have to be made on the limited references available. This applies no less to the blues and songs of the recording period, for an active censorship seems to have been applied to blues of sexual content. Comparison of songs on record with unissued and privately recorded examples gives some indication of the wealth of material which has been withheld and the areas in which future research might profitably be made, examples of the traditional songs *Sweet Patunia*, *Shave 'Em Dry*, *Dirty Mother Fuyer* and *The Dirty Dozens* being examined at some length.

Blues on sexual themes show all the aspects of the blues tradition discussed here but as a subject they would appear to have an importance to the Negro unequalled to any other. To observers it is evident that sexual and near-pornographic blues have superseded most others in the past decade. Though some may regret the passing of blues which are concerned with other facets of Negro life and experience, this development may be of no small significance. Screening the blues for the elements that have shaped its tradition may in turn yield some valuable pointers to the ways in which a folk idiom changes with its society. In a period when the Negro's 'racial temperament, modes of life, climatic and political conditions, geographical environment and language' are altering radically under the militant direction of a new generation of leaders and at a time when a disc-jockey's catch-phrase of 'Burn, baby, burn!' becomes a battle-cry, the end of some blues traditions and the emphasis on new forms could be a barometer of the increasing pressures on society.

1 THE SANTY CLAUS CRAVE

In the windows of the fashionable Fifth Avenue stores the rock salt lies in thick chunks amongst the Harris tweeds, Scotch whisky and shooting sticks. Imitation frost sparkles on the lingerie and pairs of thick socks vie with the leather gloves for the place of honour on the pine branches. There are kneeling children too, candles in hands, gazing at a single star and white plaster reindeer gallop across paper sheets of midnight blue. From the scores of Christmas trees in Times Square are festooned chains of coloured lights and banners float across the streets. Over all, the rubicund face of Santa smiles benignly and his head nods to the rhythm of a score of clockwork motors. Santa Claus appears again on the glossy backs of lush magazines still smelling invitingly of the printer's ink. He is depicted pausing in his rapid consumption of a crate of Coca-Cola to rub the Scandinavian locks of the boy and girl in night attire, snuggled beside him. But Santa is in danger of being overworked in his brief season—though doubtless it will stand him in good stead during the lay-off period. Within the covers he is helping the family with the home movie show, looking through an instrument at stereoscopic pictures or stealing a glance across the page at the brand new automobile, wrapped in cellophane and tied with a pink bow, which a teenage company director has bought for the wife and kids. This is a world of coloured faces—white faces coloured with the healthy rose-pink induced by a snowball fight and a proprietary brand of night-cap. But the only Negro face that brings a darker hue to the pages of this issue in the Season of Goodwill is that of an aged and liveried footman whose eyebrows and wisps of cotton-wool at his temples are as white as his teeth. A balloon above his head declares, 'Ole Massa used to say gib 'em a ham fo Christmas.... Sho do make you believe in Santa Claus.'[1]

Christmas belongs to white and coloured alike and, if the stores in Lennox Avenue are not as extravagant in their seasonable displays and if their loudspeakers are not endlessly dreaming of a white Christmas, the festival still means as much in the Negro section as in any other. It is a time of goodwill, of present-giving, and of family gathering, as important in the dog-trot cabin as it is in the tenements along the tracks; for Christmas is as impatiently awaited by the Negro child as it is by his lighter-skinned counterpart.

'Little children all gets so happy on a Christmas day,' recalled Leadbelly, 'when they gets Christmas-comin' they have their own way. I had a li'l boy come to see me on a Christmas day, an' I heard my mama say, "Son, Christmas is coming." So I grabbed the li'l boy by the hand and went out in my papa's field on the highes' hill he had in his field, an' I said, "Listen, I don't see no Christmas, do you?" He says, "No, I don't see no Christmas." We come back to the house and tol' my mama. We says, "Mama, we don't see no Christmas." She says, "Well, it's comin'." ' Then he swung into a dance song of the simple, endless pattern so common in the South to which there is no limit to the verses which can be added, and to which the children and their parents can dance whilst they have the energy in their bodies and the strength in their legs:

(All lines repeat)
Think I heard my mammy say it's Christmas Day,
Think I heard my pappy say it's Christmas Day,
Ole Santy Claus is a movin' in on Christmas Day,
Chicken crows at midnight on a Christmas Day.
Children all gets so happy on Christmas Day,
Children gets out in the yard and swing on Christmas Day.
Children all so happy on a Christmas Day,
Everybody gets happy on a Christmas Day. . . .
I see that Santy Claus comin'. Here he is right now!
Oh children is a-walkin' on a Christmas Day,
All children is a-talkin' on a Christmas Day.
Children all be so happy on a Christmas Day,
Good Lord I get so happy on a Christmas Day. . . .[2]

For the Negro, Christmas has a deep-rooted significance beyond that of the religious meaning of the celebration itself: a more worldly one which has none the less firmly established itself in his folkways. Since far back in slavery Christmas has signified a rest, a break in the year's routine which no other festival affords, providing an opportunity for a man to be with his family and, for a brief period at any rate, for a relaxation of the rigorous monotony of rural labour. Travelling in Texas in 1843, William Bollaert, an Englishman from Liverpool, observed in his diary on Christmas Day, 'At this time of the year the Negroes have their week's holiday. Bedecked out in their best, they visit each other, the evening ending in singing and dancing.' After attending the candy-pullings, the quadrilles and cotillions of the white populace, he noted on the last day of the year that 'the Negroes of this

27

vicinity had their Christmas Ball'. Held in an unfinished store building, 'it was late ere all had arrived, many of them having come several
miles. It was a "subscription" ball and the unfortunate Negro who could
not raise two bits (about 1s.) was not admitted at the commencement
of the ball. Gladness sparkled in his eye, decorum or carriage forgotten,
every limb would be in movement, the truly joyous and hearty laugh
would resound through the room and the yagh! yagh! as finale truly
indicative of the Nigger.'[3]

The feasting and dancing with which Christmas was greeted was
recalled by one ex-slave, Cato, from Alabama, 'Christmas was the big
day. Presents for everybody, and the baking and preparing went on for
days. The little ones and the big ones were glad, 'specially the nigger
mens, 'count of plenty of good whiskey. Massa Cal got the best whiskey
for his niggers. We used to have frolics, too. Some niggers had fiddles
and played the reels, and niggers love to dance and sing and eat.'[4]
There may have been a change of venue—a Harlem cellar dive for the
'quarters' and a jazz band instead of the fiddles, but there was probably
little difference in kind and certainly in spirit at the Christmas ball
described by Bessie Smith more than four-score years later:

Christmas comes but once a year,
And to me it brings good cheer and to everyone
Who loves wine and beer.

Happy New Year is after that,
Happy I'll be that is a fact,
That is why—I like to hear:
Folks I say, that Christmas is here.

Christmas bells will ring real soon,
Even in the afternoon,
There'll be a chimes bell ring at the Christmas ball.

Everyone must watch their step,
Else they'll lose their rest,
Everybody full of pep at the Christmas ball.

Grab your partner once and all,
Keep on dancin' round the hall,

And there's no one to fall,
Don't you dare to stall.

If your partner don't act fair,
Don't worry there's some more over there,
Pickin' up cheer everywhere, at the Christmas ball.[5]

Negro slaves, who had embraced Christianity in one of the variants taught by the evangelists of the various sects who worked among them, saw in their teachings the promise of salvation after suffering on earth. Few could fail to have been disillusioned by the disparity between the teachings of the Church and the practices of the slave owners and, though Christmas was traditionally a period of relaxation on the plantations, another veteran slave could note, not without a certain wry humour, the avarice of his master even at this time:

'All the Christmas we had was Old Master would kill a hog and give us a piece of pork. We thought that was something, and the way Christmas lasted was 'cording to the big sweet-gum backlog what the slaves would cut and put in the fireplace. When that burned out, the Christmas was over. So you know we all keeps a-looking the whole year round for the biggest sweet gum we could find. When we just couldn't find the sweet gum, we git oak, but it wouldn't last long enough, 'bout three days on average, when we didn't have to work. Old Master he sure pile on them pine knots, gitting that Christmas over so we could git back to work. We had a few little games we play, like Peep Squirrel Peep, You Can't Catch Me, and such like. We didn't know nothing 'bout no New Year's Day or holidays 'cept Christmas.'[6]

Many of the habits and customs of slavery continued after the Emancipation and those of the Christmas festivities in particular persisted, not least in their secular aspects. Negro spirituals and subsequently, gospel songs, derived their content from a wide span of Biblical stories, but it would seem that the Nativity as a theme is far less frequent than those that refer in one form or another to death and Resurrection. A large proportion of both spirituals and gospel songs refer to 'the other side', to 'crossing the river', to 'the other shore', using simple euphemisms about the time when 'the train comes along' and 'when I lay my burden down'. More specifically, they sing that

Jesus Is a Dying Bed-Maker, call on *Jesus, Make Up My Dying Bed*, rejoice in the time *When I Make My Vacation in Heaven* and call on others to *Come on, Let's Go to Heaven*. Joyful in the prospect of life after death as so many gospel songs are, they do not eclipse the Nativity theme but they do appear to take marked precedence over it. Until an adequate examination of modern gospel songs has been made and careful analysis of their content undertaken it is not appropriate to draw firm conclusions from the circumstantial evidence of their recorded output. Yet it would seem likely that the Negro could find less reason for rejoicing in the Nativity than in the Resurrection: joyful acceptance into Heaven rather than rejoicing over birth into this world might well reflect the sufferings of his own experience.

Though Christmas was celebrated as a religious festival and was always of major importance to the God-fearing members of the church community, the impression gained from nineteenth-century writings reporting Negro festivities at Christmas suggests that it was the material aspects of present-giving, feasting, drinking and dancing that were most enthusiastically observed. This, at any rate, was the view of the Negro leader and educationalist, Booker T. Washington, whose first year at Tuskegee in 1881 terminated with a Christmas in which the carousals of the coloured people in the country impressed him as much as did the poverty of a large proportion of the celebrants. At Christmas in slavery times he noted, 'The male members of the race, and often the female members, were expected to get drunk. . . . There was widespread hilarity and a free use of guns, pistols and powder generally. The sacredness of the season seemed to have been wholly lost sight of.'[7] He observed that 'in the majority of cases there was nothing in the cabin to be seen of the coming of the Saviour'. Instead there was held a 'frolic' on the plantation. 'This meant a kind of rough dance, where there was likely to be a good deal of whiskey used, and where there might be some shooting or cutting with razors.'[8]

The duality of Christmas as a religious and secular festival remained. 'Christmas,' wrote Julia Peterkin in Georgia, is 'the bright crown of the year, [it] is a religious festival but it also marks the year's end and is a time for fun and feasting as well as for worship and prayer. It is not one short day, but a long week of jubilation that begins Christmas Eve morning and lasts through New Year's night. Even time pauses to rest "in de Christmas" for a span of happy days and nights lying between joys and sorrows of the year left behind and those of the New Year ahead.'[9]

Though Decoration Day features in many blues no festival is so frequently represented as Christmas. It might be said, in broad generalization, that the blues singer rejoices in his folk-songs—his dance songs, play-party and game songs, ballads and stomps—and declares his sorrow, anguish, dissatisfaction and anxieties in the blues. It is not surprising, therefore, to find that 'the joys and sorrows of the year' feature prominently in the blues, and that it is the secular aspects of Christmas with which the blues singer is mainly concerned. The loneliness of the single, the widowed and the forsaken constitute the main theme. When Julia Peterkin was living on a Georgia plantation, Blind Lemon Jefferson, up from Texas, was singing in Chicago:

(*Spoken*) Oh mama, this is going to be a hard winter—look how it's
  snowing. . . . Baby won't you hear me moan?
I woke up the day 'fore Christmas, mama won't you hear me moan, (2)
If you take me back baby I'll get you anything you need.

I had a good time, baby give me just one more. (2)
I wanna taste that lovin' like you have never did before.

Mama if I did you wrong, I'm just as sorry as I can be, (2)
. . . Mmmmm . . . sorry as I can be,
Just the day before Christmas mama, please come back to me.

Mama turned me down on this Christmas Eve, (2)
I cried about you so hard it wetted my overcoat sleeve.

Just the day before Christmas let me bring your present tonight, (2)
I wanna be your Santa Claus even if my whiskers ain't white.[10]

Warnings to the sinner who may miss the Christmas festival figure in the sermons of a number of Negro preachers on record. Reverend J. M. Gates seems to have been particularly concerned with the theme. *Where Will You Be on Christmas Day?* he asked. *Will the Coffin Be Your Santa Claus?* and *You May Be Alive or Dead, Christmas Day* were admonishments which he developed vigorously to constitute the subjects of some of his sermons. In common with other 'fire and brimstone' preachers he uttered awful warnings to those who spent Christmas in pleasurable pursuits. 'When we think of the Twenty-uh-

Fifth of December we are expectin' a great day, for on that day it is
said that Jesus was born,' he preached.

Uh—but we' celebratin' Christmas wrong from the way I look at
the matter—shootin' off fireworks, cussin' and dancin', raisin' all
other kinds of sand . . . uh—Death may be your Santa Claus!

Those of you who are lookin' after the little folks and tellin' 'em
that Santa Claus is comin' to see 'em, an' little boys tellin' their
mothers and fathers to tell ole Santa to bring me a li'l pistol—that
same li'l gun may bring death into that boy's home—Death may be
his Santa Claus.

Little girl is sayin' to her mother and father to tell the Santa
Claus to bring me a li'l ol' deck of cards so I can play seven-up
in the park—but while that li'l girl plays, Death may be her
Santa Claus!

All of you that had prepared to take an auto trip and now fixin'
your old tyres and gettin' your spares ready and your automobiles
overhauled—Death may be *your* Santa Claus.

All of you who are decoratin' your rooms and gettin' ready for an
all-night dance—Death may be your Santa Claus! Death is on your
track and is gonna overtake you after a while—Death may be your
Santa Claus![11]

His arguments may have been confused but his congregations could
read his message clearly—retribution for the wicked might be most
terrible for those who sin at Christmas. Separation from a partner who
spent Christmas in a prison is the theme of Victoria Spivey's *Christmas
Mornin' Blues*. Her image of the man for whom 'death will be his Santa
Claus' would appear to be a direct reference to the Reverend Gates's
recording, *Death Might Be Your Santa Claus*, made the previous year:

Woke up Christmas mornin' went out to get the mornin' mail, (2)
A letter sent from Georgia, the postage mark 'Atlanta jail'.

In a mean ole jailhouse because he broke them Georgy laws, (2)
New Year he won't be out because death will be his Santa Claus.

My man's so deep in trouble, the white folks couldn't get him free, (2)
He stole a hawg—the charges was murder in the first degree.

I ain't never had a Christmas with trouble like this before, (2)
Them bells is like death bells and hard luck is knockin' at my door.

Next Christmas I won't be here to get this bad news,
I won't be here to get this Christmas bad news,
Just mark on my tombstone I died with the Christmas mornin'
    blues.[12] ©

Specifically related to the subject of Victoria Spivey's song was
Leroy Carr's *Christmas in Jail—Ain't That a Pain?*, a blues which
inspired Reverend Gates to reply within months with *Did You Spend
Christmas Day in Jail?* The theme apparently won its converts for he
repeated it five years later in his sermon *Will You Have Your Christmas
Dinner in Jail?* But the condition of the lonely and ill whether in jail
or confined in the tenement cell did not need the preacher's moralizing
to make its point, as Blind Blake's *Lonesome Christmas Blues* illustrates:

This is December, the last month in the year, (2)
Twenty-fourth day and Christmas is almost here.

Last Christmas mornin' I was standin' in the jailhouse cell, (2)
And this Christmas I'm sick and can't get well.

I'm lying in my bed watching the snow-flakes fall, (2)
Worried in mind 'cause I ain't got no baby at all.[13]

Typically, there is not a hint of repentance, of any thoughts on the
significance of Christmas or of any reasons for his having been in
jail in Blind Blake's blues. It was the blues of a man for whom the
religious connotations of Christmas appear to have had no significance.
This was an attitude taken a stage further by Elzadie Robinson, whose
The Santy Claus Crave was recorded in 1927 within a month of Victoria
Spivey's *Christmas Mornin' Blues*. It was, in effect, a prayer, a prayer
directed not to God but to a deity personified by Santa Claus. For
all her references to 'prayin' to the Lord above' it was Santa Claus
whom she entreated to hear her 'lonesome plea':

Santa Claus, please hear my lonesome plea, (2)
Don't bring me nothing for Christmas but my daddy back to me.

You know I loved you daddy, that's why we couldn't get along, (2)
But some day you'll be sorry that you ever done me wrong.

Well Lord, it's Christmas time, and I want to see Santy Claus, (2)
If you don't bring my daddy I swear I'll break all the laws.

Oh please, Santy Claus, Santy Claus, Santy Claus,
Santy Claus, I'm down on my bended knees,
I'm praying to the Lord above for my old-time used-to-be.

When you hear the church bells tonin' you know your mama's
        gone, (2)
Just because old Santa Claus left my man at another woman's
        home.[14]

Too late for issue in time for Christmas, Elzadie Robinson's blues
appeared in 1928. Her company, Paramount, attempted a more timely
topical issue with Blind Lemon Jefferson's *Christmas Eve Blues*,
quoted above, which was recorded in August that year together with
Happy New Year Blues as its backing and advertised in good time for
dealers to order for the festive season. It was billed as a 'rip-snorting
hit' but perhaps Paramount were a little uneasy at the growing atheistic
tendency in the blues. At any rate, their *Dealers' Supplement* late that
fall advertised well over a score of 'Christmas, Spiritual and Sermon
Records That Are Dependable Sales Producers' with the warning to
the dealers that they 'Should Be in Your Stocks Now'—in time for
the Christmas rush.

A number of other blues were recorded in the period, which, though
they did not refer to Santa Claus, were clearly related to Elzadie
Robinson's composition. The 'pleading' chorus was addressed by Jack
Ranger to a 'thievin' man':

Thievin' man, please hear my lonesome plea, (2)
Now I'm beggin' you for my baby, down on my bended knee.

Now I cried for mercy, I don't know what mercy means, (2)
Now if it means any good, Lord have mercy on me.[15]

The second verse quoted suggests an appeal to God rather than to the 'thievin' man'. Another variant, by King Solomon Hill, is apparently an appeal for divine intervention and strengthens the impression that Santa Claus is, in other blues, a God-substitute.

At last, at last, down on my bended knee, (2)
I'm worried 'bout my baby, bring her back to me.

You know I love my baby, that's why we can't get along, (2)
Look like everything I do, somethin' going on wrong.

Oooh—down on my bended knee, (2)
I'm worried 'bout my baby, bring her back to me.

I can see the sun a-shinin', leaves shakin' on the trees, (2)
I got a letter from my Dinah, my baby's packed her trunk to leave.

Mmm . . . mmm . . . hear my lonesome plea, (2)
I'm worried 'bout my baby, down on my bended knee.[16]

There remains the possibility that both Robinson's and Hill's blues emanate from a common folk source, but there seems little doubt that many other blues on the Santa Claus theme were modelled on Elzadie's record. Many of them employed the 'Santy Claus, Santy Claus' incantation which her blues featured, supported by the sombre piano played by Bob Call. Another pianist, Walter Davis, recorded a version—*Santa Claus*—in July 1935 which was closely patterned on hers. The first four verses were sung in identical order but the repetition of the 'Santy Claus' plea was extended to six times. Another, more original, version was recorded in 1937 by Black Ace (B. K. Turner) who accompanied himself with brilliant slide guitar playing and who made of the song a totally personal expression for himself:

Santy Claus, what is you going to bring? (2)
If you don't bring my baby don't bring me a doggone thing.

You know I love her Santa Claus, why don't you bring her home,
   (2)
If you bring her back to me I'll never do her wrong.

Oh Lord, it's Christmas time and I want to see ole Santa Claus, (2)
I asked my baby will she come home Christmas? She says, 'Go
 and see ole Santy Claus.'

Oh please, Santy Claus, Santy Claus, Santy Claus,
Santy Claus, my eyes is almost blind,
I'll be lookin' for you Christmas mornin' before I lose my mind.

I'm gonna buy me a shepherd dog and keep him at my door, (2)
And teach him to follow my baby everywhere she goes.[17]

The basic theme of these blues is that of loneliness at Christmas but
not all of them implore 'Santa Claus' to bring back the partner. Mary
Harris in her *No Christmas Blues* makes a self-pitying statement of her
lack of company, but asks no one for help:

Here comes Christmas, everybody is glad to see, (2)
It don't mean a thing because Santa Claus won't come to me.

Here comes Christmas, my good man has left me all alone, (2)
I know I won't have nothin' so I'll be glad when Christmas is gone.

Here comes Christmas and I began to feel so blue, (2)
If I would tell you my troubles I know you'd be worried too.

If I had a good man I could have me a Christmas tree, (2)
But since I'm a poor girl, Santa Claus don't care for me.[18]

Few other recording sessions could have been so dominated by one
theme as this one for Decca on 31 October 1935. It would be pleasant
to think that each singer was inspired by the others to create a blues
on the same subject but at this date, with Christmas two months away,
it is more likely that it was a deliberate promotional device by Mayo
Williams. Charley Jordan played guitar and Peetie Wheatstraw the
piano at the session which also included Mary Harris and Verdi Lee as
blues singers. Verdi Lee sang *Christmas Tree Blues* after Jordan had
made a single title, *Christmas, Christmas Blues*. After two more items by
Lee, Mary Harris made her *No Christmas Blues* and *Happy New Year
Blues* accompanied by Jordan and Wheatstraw. Finally Peetie came

forward to record his own *Santa Claus Blues* into which he incorporated the Christmas tree motif:

Christmas almost here, what are you gonna do for me? (2)
Am I goin' have a present, ooh well, well on your Christmas tree?

I begin to worry, when it's almost Christmas time, (2)
Now you know I worry to myself, ooh well that I'm goin' be left
  behind.

Seems at Christmas, you made Santa Claus come to me, (2)
And you didn't hang my stocking ooh, well on your Christmas tree.

If I don't get a present this Christmas, babe I don't see the reason
  why, (2)
Because you know now I don't never ask, ooh well for Santa Claus
  to pass me by.[19]

In his blues Peetie Wheatstraw makes no appeal to Santa Claus but addresses his woman in less abstract terms. In a final verse he assumes the role himself, concluding, 'if you don't change your ways, ooh well baby, I ain't gon' be your Santa Claus', while throughout there is a certain innuendo. Stemming in part from Elzadie Robinson's blues, though at many stages removed, Jack Dupree combined the elements of *The Santy Claus Crave* with those of Peetie Wheatstraw's *Santa Claus Blues* in his own recording under the latter title:

Well it's Christmas time and I want to see Santa Claus, (2)
If he don't bring me nothin', bring my baby back to me.

Santy Claus, Santy Claus, what wrong have I done? (2)
Well here on Christmas day, I'm the only one.

I'm gonna hang my stocking on my baby's Christmas tree, (2)
So when Christmas mornin' come, ooh well, well, she'll fill my
  stockin' for me.

(*Spoken*) Play them Christmas for me. . . .
Christmas day here I'm all alone. . . .
Yes, yes, I wonder do my baby think of me?

It's Christmas day, here I am all alone, (2)
With my head hung down, ooh well, well and I don't have a lonely
   dime.

I'm gonna call my baby, call her on the phone, (2)
Tell her she went away and left me, ooh well, well on Christmas day
   all alone.

Santy Claus, Santy Claus, don't want no singin' for me, (2)
All I want is something real, ooh well, well that I can really enjoy.[20]

Though his exclamations of 'Ooh well, well' proclaim his debt to
Peetie Wheatstraw neither his delivery, his words nor his playing are
derivative. He creates a new blues from the raw material of two rich
seams within the idiom. A number of blues tap the same source, in-
corporating original ideas of the individual singers but sharing many
elements of a common tradition: Walter Davis's *Santa Claus Blues*,
Tampa Red's *Christmas and New Year's Blues*, Bumble Bee Slim's
Christmas and No Santa Claus and its original backing *Santa Claus
Bring Me a Woman*. Roosevelt Sykes's *Let Me Hang My Stocking on
Your Christmas Tree* developed the obvious sexual implications of the
metaphor that appears in Peetie Wheatstraw's composition. This had
been the basis of a ribald and witty vaudeville exchange recorded by
Butterbeans and Susie, *Papa Ain't No Santa Claus (Mama Ain't No
Christmas Tree)*. Made in 1930 it was the last title they were to record
for more than thirty years:

Butterbeans. Now each night you keep me out of doors,
Susie. Well, you sure ain't gonna get my key.
B. Why, why?
S. Well now pay me for my goods and you can get your fill,
B. Well, let me know what I'm buyin' and I certainly will.
S. Why?
B. 'Cause papa ain't no Santa Claus,
S. And your mama sure ain't no Christmas tree.
B. Look here, I said papa ain't no Santa Claus,
S. And your mama sure ain't no Christmas tree, no sir!
B. Now Sue, you know I don't pay no money down,
S. And I do business strictly COD.

B. Well, there's a lot of chocolates on the stall,
S. But where can you get good chocs free?
B. Anywhere! Anywhere!
S. Well now, in my market I don't put no samples out!
B. Well, you know it ain't New Year so let me know what's it's all
about.
'Cause papa ain't no Santa Claus,
S. And your mama sure ain't no Christmas tree! Play it boy,
B. All last summer, you were runnin' with Brother Bill,
Now this mornin' you come up askin' for a Christmas gift,
Now papa ain't no Santa Claus,
S. And your mama sure ain't no Christmas tree, no sir![21]

Rejecting the suggestion that he is Susie's 'Santa Claus', Butterbeans
nevertheless plays on the notion that the man who brings gifts to his
woman is performing that role. This was the specific reference in Blind
Lemon Jefferson's closing verse in his *Christmas Eve Blues* already
quoted. In popular song this had its antecedent in Irving Jones's and
Maxwell Silver's composition, *You Must Think I'm Santa Claus*,
published as early as 1904, to which Lil McClintock's song, recorded
in 1930, *Don't Think I'm Santa Claus*, may well have been a counterpart.
Lil McClintock, though he recorded only four titles, would appear to
have been of the same generation and character as such songsters as
Jim Jackson and Henry Thomas, whom he somewhat resembled in
repertoire and delivery. Like them he mixed fragments of songs to
make a whole for the recording and his *Don't Think I'm Santa Claus*
had a 'coon song' refrain which suggests a nineteenth-century, and
most probably, white origin. The verse might well have come from the
same period:

Please don't think that I'm Santa Claus,
'Cause Christmas comes everyday,
You can hear them sleigh-bells a-ringin' out,
If you turns 'em around this-away.
You need not think that I'm a human being,
It's nothin' but a fraud,
'Cause I bring you a present ever' once in a while,
Don't think I'm Santa Claus.
          Lindy, Lindy, you sweeter than sugar cane,

Oh Lindy, Lindy, say you'll be mine,
While the moon am shinin',
And my heart am a-twinin',
Meet me dear little Lindy,
By the watermelon vine.[22]

Recording a few years later in 1938, Bo Carter gave a new twist to the theme by obscurely hinting that Santa Claus was neither himself nor his lover but an unspecified sexual symbol:

Now I'm gonna use your Santa Claus several different ways,
I'm gonna use your Santa Claus baby both night and day,
  Baby, please let your Santa Claus come down the chimney to
    me tonight,
  Because I believe what Santa Claus gonna bring me will just
    suit my appetite.

Now if you let your Santa Claus come to me one time,
I'll pay your Santa Claus two dollars and one dime,
  Baby, please let your Santa Claus come down the chimney to
    me tonight,
  Because I believe what Santa Claus gonna bring me will just
    suit my appetite.[23]

Though many blues on the Christmas theme use its accessories as opportunities for sexual metaphor, some are more personally involved in the festival itself. Occasionally they reflect a specific circumstance, as Lonnie Johnson's wartime blues which in terms warm, but not mawkish, expresses the regrets of a man unable to keep Christmas with his wife:

Christmas Eve mornin' baby I was on my way back home to you, (2)
It was your love that kept me fighting, kept me safe the whole war
  through.

It seems a long time since I been fightin' the Japs 'cross the deep
  blue sea, (2)
Yes that's why I'm so glad darlin', to have a li'l wife love still
  waitin' for me.

It's so great to have you darlin' to have a li'l wife like you, (2)
My three brothers couldn't make it but they say Happy New Year
  to you.[24]

A similar tenderness of sentiment is to be found in a recent recording
by Robert Nighthawk which rather engagingly, and singularly, uses a
traditional greeting for the title of *Merry Christmas*:

Merry Christmas pretty baby, I'm so glad that you back home, (2)
I guess that's the reason why I'm so glad I can still call you my
  own.

Yes, I'm so glad my darlin' to have a sweet li'l girl like you,
Yes, I'm so glad my darlin' to have a sweet li'l thing like you,
I guess that's the reason why I am so glad I got someone to come
  home to.[25] ©

It is the strength of the blues that as an art it regenerates itself;
the singers continually draw from traditional resources to create anew
and they invest in old and familiar themes fragments of their own
experience which impart to them a refreshing individuality. The almost
invariable subject of the Christmas blues is that of the lonely or forsaken man or woman; few have any other references and there is never
a suggestion that 'Christmas is a time for children'. There are almost
no hints that it is a religious festival, but when there are, as in a line of
Sonny Boy's Christmas Blues, the singer introduces them in a typically
oblique way. Sonny Boy Williamson No. 2, the 'original' Sonny Boy
as he insisted to his death, was always a hard drinker:

Got some mighty sad news and I ain't got nothin' to say,
I heard some mighty sad news and I don't have nothin' to say,
My baby left me, started me to drinkin' on Christmas Day.

Lord, I tried to fetch religion but the Devil would not let me pray,
Lord, I tried to fetch religion boys, but the Devil he will not let
  me pray,
That's why I gotta stay drunk boys all day Christmas Day.

(*Spoken*) Oooh . . . on a Christmas Day. You know that's one day
I hate to have the blues; you know when she walked out and left
me she give 'em to me, so I have to drink 'em all. I don't even
have a Christmas tree in my house unless she comes home, but if
she do happen to come home I will enjoy this Christmas.

Yes, run here baby and let me tell you what I got to say,
Please, please run here darlin' and let daddy tell you what he got to
    say,
Unless'n you come back to me I'll be drunk all day Christmas Day.[26]

Often the minutiae rather than the broad narrative makes a blues
convincingly authentic and if 'I hung my head and cried' is a blues
cliché Louis Hayes makes it convincing in context:

Well it's Christmas time, it's Christmas time and everybody's going
    away, (2)
Now well it hurts me so bad my baby's goin' away to stay.

My baby's got her suitcase packed and her trunk is already gone, (2)
And I'm a lonesome man, done gone a long way from home.

When my baby left for the station I was walkin' right by her side,
    (2)
Now when she got on the train y'know I hung my head and cried.

Now when the train left the station, y'know my heart begin to
    swell, (2)
'Cause it was takin' the one Lord, that I love so well.[27]

Christmas may have lost much of its meaning and commercialization
destroyed the simplicity of its message; it may have become a secular
feast rather than a religious festival, but it is treated with unsentimental
realism in the blues. In the stormy expression of human relationships
which predominate, the Christmas theme allows room for tenderness
and mutual dependence. Although the succession of threats, beatings,
infidelities and sexual bouts, which are in the blues the evidence of the
uncertainties and unrest within the Negro community, are still present,
the symbolic significance of Christmas does enter their content. Gentle-

ness and affection, and the pain of loneliness find their place in the
Christmas blues, even for an essentially contemporary singer like
Jimmy McCracklin. Perhaps it is not surprising after all, that his
Christmas Time not only summarizes all other blues on the subject, but
reflects, too, the observations made by William Bollaert more than a
century ago:

Christmas time is here, let's party all night long,
I know you know Christmas can't last too long,
Right now, Christmas is here and everywhere, and everywhere.

Some people waiting for tomorrow, some celebratin' somehow else,
I'm not waiting on tomorrow, let tomorrow speak for itself,
Because now Christmas is here and everywhere, and everywhere.

Jingle bells was ringing, Christmas lights is everywhere,
I know the world is celebrating baby, 'cause it only comes once a
    year,
And right now Christmas is here and everywhere, everywhere,
Right now, Christmas is here and everywhere.

Every day seems like Christmas as long as I am with you,
To me it's just another day, I often feel, the way I do,
Your love mean more to me in a way, than a holiday.

So long as we're together and holidays have passed and gone,
Now just because it's past Christmas, why should I keep alone,
Your love mean more to me in a way, than a holiday.

I know it's Christmas time baby, and a time to celebrate,
And while we can't be together why should we go separate ways?
Your love mean more to me in a way, than a holiday . . . a
    holiday. (2)[28]

Between two churches on West Lake Street, Chicago, is a narrow, lurching entrance to a rooming-house. Thumb-tacked to the jamb a cardboard notice, crudely penned and signed by 'Ruby', requests:

PLEASE DON'T KICK THE DOOR IN

It seems to have been written in the same hand as the notice curling sadly in the adjacent window which proclaims:

GREAT REVIVAL NOW IN PROGRESS

Both have an air of resignation. Ruby doubtless knows that her door will soon yield again, and perhaps for the last time, to an impetuous boot; the church elders are unlikely to expect many new converts. But there is a certain realistic defiance in both signs, offering some sort of challenge to the dismal conditions of the long, dirty street with its cracked sidewalks and wind-whipped shreds of newspaper.

At night the paint-starved woodwork, the bug-infested cracks, the thick layers of smuts and dust, are less evident; the lights from the joints glow and the neon crucifixes shine pink in the shop-front windows of the store-front churches. A door swings open and one may hear the shouts and laughter of a jostling crowd packed solid to the far end of the smoke-filled interior, where a dimly perceived blues band thunders with amplifiers turned up to maximum volume and the lead singer roars hoarsely into a hand-held microphone, mere inches from his closest listeners. Another door may open on a scene no less intense, as a gospel quartet, with frenzied gestures and heads thrown back, stir a small but exultant congregation to irrational ecstasy. Sacred and secular are found side by side on West Lake and however different the avowed purposes of the church and the blues joint, to the observer the heady mixture of music and emotion to be found in each has much in common. Exhilarating and elemental, the music transports the gathering from the meanness and poverty beyond the doors.

In the joints of West Lake—Sylvio's, Ruby Gatewood's and a host of small, unassuming clubs, singers like Big Bill Broonzy, Kokomo Arnold, Sonny Boy Williamson, Jazz Gillum, Muddy Waters or Memphis Minnie have entertained in the past, and in these places or their successors, Howling Wolf, Homesick James or J. B. Hutto may work today. Their frontages are small, the width of a shop, and standardized Cola signs and swinging notices draw attention to the 'taverns'. A montage of beer advertisements—rainbow-hued, block-typed cardboard bills, hand-scrawled signs announcing the function 'Tonite' and crude window repairs fashioned from wood and hardboard, are the indications of the blues joint which runs for two or three rooms back into the row. Next door, or a few doors down, the store-front church presents a not too dissimilar appearance, with the same awkwardly painted notices attracting the eye. But here the montage is one of Biblical texts, gothic-type inscriptions, prints of *The Last Supper*, troughs of plastic flowers, gilt crosses and purple draperies. Incongruously, the Cola signs are to be seen here also, bringing in a humble revenue for the church; the visiting gospel choirs and groups, the pastors and preachers for the week, are announced in terms and letters much like those outside the blues club. Inside, the main room of the shop has been converted into a chapel with bentwood chairs, or sometimes old pews, placed in rows before the draped altar, the fretwork lectern, the illuminated cross and the large letters that state once again that this is the 'Greater Bethel', the 'Trinity', or the 'Mount Calvary Church'. Walking down West Lake one passes the 'Bethlehem Temple of God in Christ' and the 'Bethlehem Junior of God in Christ' right next door. Adjacent is the 'Primitive Baptist House'; the 'Christ Whosoever Will', the 'Original Church of God, Sanctified' and the 'Corinthian Church of Christ' follow in succession.

'It is only when we are within the walls of our churches that we are wholly ourselves, that we keep alive a sense of our personalities in relation to the total world in which we live, that we maintain a quiet and constant communion with all that is deepest in us. Our going to church of a Sunday is like placing one's ear to another's chest to hear the unquenchable murmur of the human heart. In our collective out-pourings of song and prayer, the fluid emotions of others make us feel the strength in ourselves,' wrote Richard Wright.[1] His words expressed the comfort and support that membership of a church gives to the Negro women, who 'keep thousands of Little Bethels and Pilgrims and Calvary's and White Rocks and Good Hopes and Mount Olives going with their nickels and dimes'.[2] Women are the mainstay of the Negro church; their menfolk seek and find a similar strength and solidarity in participation in the juke joints and blues clubs. Or did. Today, the ferment in Negro lives is reflected in the churches and the joints and in the music of both. The churches continue to attract new adherents on the one hand while disappointing by their failure, in many instances, to take an effective lead in the demand for civil rights. While the churches

45

have borrowed the instrumentation and the dress of many of the younger blues singers, together with many of their musical characteristics, a reverse process has taken place where the blues has met and merged with gospel music. Whatever the convictions of the church member to the observer, the distinction between gospel music and the most recent development of blues and rock 'n roll—soul—is one of content rather than style. And even this is a suspect distinction, for the appeal of the soul singer is that he presents the blues as a quasi-religious experience, trading on the emotions of his listeners and using the heart-tearing techniques of the gospel singer to get a secular message home. 'Soul' is not an idle term.

This meeting of religious and secular idioms and the studied borrowing of the language of the Church in contemporary song is perhaps indicative of many aspects of the current social situation. It may represent a more specific unity in Negro life as a whole which has whittled away the demarcation barrier between the adjacent store-fronts of church and joint. It may also be indicative of a diminishing faith in the power of the Church to meet the problems of the day. And it is clearly the result of deliberate exploitation commercially of song styles, as the pace gathers in the race to produce new tricks for rapid consumption on record, radio and television. The rapid assimilation of rhythm and blues, rock 'n roll, the Tamla-Motown sound and the techniques of the gospel singer, by popular music, English beat groups, American college students and enthusiastic groups from Warsaw to Tokyo, has accelerated the process in the mid-'sixties. It may be unwise to cherish the sanguine view that this merging of characteristics and widespread popularity of once totally Negro idioms presages integration as a fact. But it is, in itself a fact and it clearly distinguishes the music of the 'sixties from that of the four decades which preceded it.

In the past, the attitude of the Church to the singer of 'Devil songs' was clear and inflexible. 'When she was singin' them blues I told her—she was pavin' her way to Hell,' said Emma Williams of her daughter, the blues singer Mary Johnson, firmly expressing the church member's view. It was one shared by a number of blues singers assailed by doubts about their way of life. 'A man who's singin' the blues—I think it's a sin because it cause other people to sin,' said Lil Son Jackson who gave up his 'fast life' and the blues to join the Church. Other blues singers think with John Lee Hooker that 'when spirituals was born it was born on the blues side'—that the spirituals expressed the personal unhappi-

46

ness and sorrow that is so often the source of the blues. And some, feeling no guilt at singing the blues and in doing so defying the doctrine of the strict Negro churches, echo the comment of Henry Townsend, 'If I sing the blues and tell the truth, what have I done? What have I committed? I haven't lied.'[3]

Most blues singers, if they considered the morality of the blues at all, might well take the latter line of argument. But their views on the subject have seldom been noted and for their opinions on religion, on the Church, on their personal, moral values only their blues recordings provided any indication in past decades. Musically the blues and the spirituals, or the spirituals' successor, the gospel song, may have stemmed from common sources. But in the recording era, though they shared on occasion similar instrumentation and voices, they were separate and distinct. There is no confusing the gospel song and the blues of the 'thirties or 'forties musically speaking and their content was emphatically divided. Gospel songs did not express secular ideas and the use of secular imagery—of trains, for instance—was for purely religious instruction. In content and sentiment the blues appears as the creation of singers who have set themselves aside from the Church; who have accepted worldly values and have expressed them sometimes objectively, sometimes with cynicism, and seldom with any ethical or moral considerations. What then, is the image of the Church as presented in the blues? What are the attitudes to religion which the blues has expressed in the past? Has the blues singer had anything pertinent to say about the teachings of the Negro Church, about its influence or its song before they reached his soul?

Vividly illustrating the traditional attitude of the blues singer to religion was Texas Alexander's *Justice Blues*. It is significant that, if the title suggested any ethical standards, they did not appear in the lyrics of the blues itself:

When you see a woman with a cigarette in her hand, (2)
You may choose her husband for a milky man.

Take me out of this bottom before the high water rise, (2)
You know I ain't no Christian and I don't want to be baptized.

I cried, 'Lord, My Father, Lord, Thy kingdom come, (2)
Give me back my woman and Thy will be done.'

47

I never been to Heaven, people but I've been told, (2)
Oh Lord, the women up there got they mouths chock-full of gold.

I'm gonna build me a Heaven, have a kingdom of my own, (2)
Where these brownskin woman can cluster round my throne.[4]

Sardonically humorous, his words are those of a man who claimed no religious convictions; they manifestly proclaim his disregard for the beliefs, the prayers, the symbol and the ritual of the Church. His work was consistent and he did not record any gospel songs to confound the impression of a man totally uninvolved in Church doctrine. The words could have been completely original, a blunt statement of Alexander's cynicism. But the final verse, at any rate, echoed one that was in general currency. A form of it had appeared in the recording entitled *Preachin' the Blues* made by Son House some four years before. In an angry, at times rasping, voice not too far removed from those of the exhorting preachers themselves, Son House railed against an unnamed preacher to the accompaniment of his plangent guitar, whooping and moaning under the vibrating bottleneck on his finger:

Oh, I'm gonna get me religion, I'm gonna join the Baptist Church,
(2)
Oh, I'm gonna be a Baptist preacher and I sure won't have to work.

I'm gonna preach these blues an' I want everybody to shout,
Ooo . . . oh, I want everybody to shout,
I'm gonna do like a prisoner, I'm gonna roll my time on out.

Oh, in my room, I bow down to pray, (2)
But the blues came along and blowed my spirit away.

Ooh, I'd've had religion on this very day, (2)
But the womens and whisky well they would not let me pray.

Ooh, I wish I had me a Heaven of my own (great Godawmighty),
Eeeh . . . heh a Heaven of my own,
Then I would give all my women a long, long, happy home.[5] ©

On the evidence of the recording, Son House was as disillusioned as was Texas Alexander. He had, in fact, been raised in a religious family and had shunned the blues until manhood, 'I was brought up in church and I started preaching before I started this junk.' He was induced, he said, to take a drink or two and he 'got in a little bad company'. As he explained it, 'I began to wonder, now how can I stand up in the pulpit and preach to them, tell them how to live, and quick as I dismiss the congregation and I see ain't nobody looking and I'm doing the same thing. I says I got to do something, 'cause I can't hold God in one hand and the Devil in the other one.'

Son House decided to quit the pulpit and resolved, when he recorded, to name his composition *Preachin' Blues* because, he told Julius Lester, 'I'm preaching on this side and the blues on that side. I says, well, I'll just put them together and name it *Preachin' Blues*.'[6] The composition was not entirely original, however. Al Wilson has reported that he was attracted to the playing of one James McCoy and, after attempting to play a couple of his tunes, 'his interest shifted to two other songs he had heard McCoy doing. These two were none other than *My Black Mama* and *Preachin' Blues*'. He acknowledged the debt and stated that 'the first chorus lyric on *Preachin' Blues* is James McCoy's and [I] took it from there'.[7]

Son House's song did not preach a blues counterpart to a sermon, did not present an ethical, non-religious argument in blues terms and did not preach a sermon for the Devil. Its verses, of varying character, suggest that it strung together a number of ideas and probably part-traditional blues stanzas. One, at any rate, stemmed from McCoy, one was shared in part with Texas Alexander, and one subsequently inspired Robert Johnson's own *Preaching Blues*. It ran:

Y' know I met the Blues this mornin' walkin' jest like a man.
Oooh . . . walkin' just like a man,
I said, 'Good mornin' Blues, give me your right hand.'[8]

In itself it probably derived from earlier stanzas for the personification of a Blues, with whom greetings were exchanged, was already popular. Here the verse does not seem particularly in context and Son House's blues has not the coherence of Texas Alexander's song or of Hi-Henry Brown's *Preacher Blues*. This was made in 1932 and extended the criticism of a preacher, essayed by House in a single verse, to the whole song:

If you want to hear a preacher curse,
Bake bread sweet mama, and save him the crust.
    Oooh, if you want to hear a preacher curse,
    Says, bake bread sweet mama, ooh, and save him the crust.

Preacher in the pulpit, Bible in his hand,
Sister in the corner cryin', 'There's my man!' *(repeat stanza)*

Preacher come to your house yesterday to rest his hat,
Next day he want to know, 'Sister, where your husband at?'
  (repeat stanza)

Come in here and shut my door,
Want you to preach a text for me, preach like you did before,
    Come in here and please shut my door,
    Want you to preach a text for me, preach just like you did
    before.[9]

Though the words were humorous there was little humour in Hi-Henry Brown's delivery which was deep, rough-textured and with an intonation that suggests there was some truth in the narration of the misdemeanours of the preacher. But if this was so, some specific references, even perhaps a thinly disguised name, could be expected. The first verse does hint at some experience of a minister's duplicity but the subsequent verses conform to a pattern long delineated in popular Negro ballads and minstrel songs. A couple of years before, a Texas singer, Coley Jones, had recorded an entertaining example of the type of parody which was popular in minstrel and medicine shows. Coley Jones led a string band in Dallas which performed for both white and coloured audiences and which 'serenaded' in the streets. His repertoire included a number of songs from before the turn of the century and his technique, naïvely modelled on that of the vaudeville stage, was ideally suited to comic narrative songs of the type which included *The Elders He's My Man*:

Now my pappy was a deacon in a little, small church,
Way down South where I was born.
Sisters used to come from ten or twelve miles every night,
While those big meetings was goin' on.

One night pa got in preachin',
And forgot, and left the sermon out.
Sister Fullbosom over there in the Amen Corner,
Mad anyhow, she let all them secrets leak out.
She hollered, 'Sisters and brothers, thoroughly understand,
The Elder he's my man.
Now I don't mind you goin' out to talk to Elders occasionally,
But nix on standing out there holdin' his hand.
I washes hard both day and night,
Catch you off with that Elder we gonna have a miserable fight,
Do you hear me? Sisters and brothers, thoroughly understand,
The Elder he's my man.'[10]

Mild though the narrative was, it gained its point from Sister Full-bosom's letting 'all them secrets leak out' revealing that the preacher had been 'carrying on' with one of the congregation without the knowledge of the rest. This is a frequent theme in Negro songs which often dwell on the alleged failings of the preacher. Another string band, the Mississippi Sheiks, featured similar material to that of Coley Jones at times but, with the blues singer Bo Carter as its principal singer, there was a greater emphasis on blues-inclined songs. In a structure much favoured by the Mississippi Sheiks, Bo Carter and Walter Vincson added to the preachers' list of misdemeanours:

Well the preacher used to preach to try to save our souls,
But now he preaches just to buy jelly roll.
   Well he calls that religion, he calls that religion,
   He calls that religion, but I know he's going to Hell when he
      dies.

Went from the church last night fast as I could be,
That ole preacher was tryin' to take my wife from me,
   Well he calls that religion etc.

He will swear he's meetin' God's command,
Has women fussin' and fightin' all over the land,
   Then he calls that religion etc.

They reckon the people stop goin' to church,
They know the preacher's tryin' to do too much,
    But still he calls that religion etc.

Old Deacon Johnson was a preachin' king,
They caught him round the house tryin' to shake that thing,
    Well he calls that religion etc.[11]

What Gunnar Myrdal termed 'the often faltering economic and sexual morals of the preachers' are widely commented upon both within and outside the Negro church.[12] Looking to the preacher for guidance in his personal life and turning to him as a leader in local affairs, the church member is the more disillusioned when the minister reveals human weaknesses that run counter to his teachings. In mock generosity a Chicago singer, Rob Robinson, in 1932, made allowances for the preacher's vacillations. 'The preacher must get some sometime,' he sang to the accompaniment of the youthful Meade Lux Lewis who was to become one of the most celebrated of the pianists of the boogie-woogie craze of the late 'thirties. Robinson's song was an excuse for making further accusations at the expense of the unidentified minister, with incest implicit in one verse:

The preacher must get some sometime,
Where and whenever he can,
The preacher must get some sometime,
Just like any other man.

    Brother John, make no mistake,
    I takes a little gin for my stomach ache.
The preacher must get some sometime,
Where and whenever he can,
The preacher must get some sometime,
Just like any other man.

    I found his little sister all alone,
    With her little silk pyjamas on,
The preacher must get some sometime etc.

Now I ain't tryin' to hand you no bluff,
But don't blame me for wantin' this stuff.
The preacher must get some sometime etc.

Now she sells that stuff in her negligée
And it was doggone good, I must say.
The preacher must get some sometime,
Just like any other man.[13]

In the Negro church of whatsoever denomination the Fundamentalist preaching lays emphasis on sin and the Devil and, though card-playing, back-biting, drinking, dancing and singing the blues are all sinful occupations, sexual behaviour constitutes, under various guises, the main theme of the preachers' sermons. 'The emphasis upon sex,' wrote Franklin Frazier, 'is, of course, a reflection of the sex pattern among the lower class. Since the lower-class churches are attended largely by women, many of whom are deserted or have other irregular marital relations, the church helps to accommodate the women of this class to their fate.'[14] In the 'lower-class' churches the services are marked by extreme demonstrations of emotional fervour, deliberately fostered by the preachers, whose exhortations provoke ecstatic responses from members of the congregation. That these are often sublimated expressions of sexual ecstasy there seems little doubt and the abandonment of those who 'get happy' and 'roll in the aisles' permits them freedom from the inhibitions that the strictures of the church demand in their private lives. Both in country and urban churches 'holy dancing', 'rolling in sheets', 'spirit possessions', self-induced trance states, tearing of clothes and other physical expressions of religious fervour are commonplace. Though in general the sincerity of the religious feeling and expression on the part of the 'members' is not in question, its sexual sublimation is apparent to the observer of the sisters, the deacons and even the elders who participate in the demonstrations. Hambone Willie Newbern, a fine, though little recorded blues singer, who worked for many years in the Memphis area, sang a parody which probably had medicine-show origins:

Nobody knows what the good deacon's doin',
I declare when the lights was out,
I ain't no fortune teller but I declare I know,
Just what I'm talkin' about.

There was one ole brother by the name of Mose,
Got so happy he pulled off all his clothes—why?
    Nobody knows what the good deacon's doin',
    I declare when the lights go out etc.

There was one ole sister by the name of Yern,
Shamed to tell you brother what that sister was doin' . . . sssh!
    Nobody knows what the good deacon's doin' etc.

There was one ole sister named Sister Green,
Jumped up and doin' the shimmy, Lord you ain't never seen.
    Nobody knows what the good deacon's doin',
    I declare while the lights was out.[15]

'A hard preacher,' explained Louis E. Lomax, a Negro with close
associations with the Baptist church, 'was a man who could, somehow,
keep unity and understanding in his church. To do this the minister had
to know the Baptist Discipline, Roberts' Rules of Order and the Holy
Bible almost from memory. He had to cajole some members, pray with
others: much of his time was spent outwitting love-starved widows in
his congregation, particularly those with money or who had influence
with some of the brothers on the "deacon" board. Having mastered all
this, the Negro Baptist minister had his troubles. His only recourse was
the pulpit on Sunday morning; there his mission was clear: he must
preach love into the congregation by scaring the hell out of them.'[16]
Though the ministers in the more organized churches are ordained, the
majority have 'got religion' by receiving the 'call' to preach. Many have
had little formal education and Mays and Nicholson reported in 1933
that only some forty per cent. of Negro preachers had got beyond the
lowest grades in school.[17] The popularity of the small store-front
church with a following numbering a score or two members has enabled
charlatans to exploit the faith of the congregations, giving grounds for
the cynicism of many Negro songs. The double standards of members
of the congregations are likewise a frequent theme and, smarting perhaps
under the condemnation of the more self-righteous members, a number
of singers have directed their criticism at the behaviour of the sisters
and the deacons of the churches.

Hollerin' church bells on one Sunday mornin', (2)
Some dirty deacon come and stole my good gal and gone,[18]

sang George Noble in 1935. But his verse was not original; it had appeared earlier in the singing of Kokomo Arnold and was apparently based on a traditional song lying in the transitional forms between the minstrel and ballad songs and the blues. It was recorded in one version, by Luke Jordan in 1927:

> Say the church bells ringing,
> Secretary's singing,
> Preacher's preachin',
> Can you hear the sisters shout?
> Childrens in the cornfield,
> Mama's tryin' to learn that song,
> And that lowdown dirty deacon,
> Done stole my gal and gone.

His song continued with other verses that were to be found in the more standard blues including the bragging lines familiar in blues:

> I did more for you woman,
> Than the Good Lord ever done;
> I bought you good hair,
> The Lord never give you none.[19]

In the blues many of the attitudes expressed in earlier song forms and often the verses or phrases themselves appear to have been continued. Often they reflect opinions which are prevalent in the society as a whole and the preacher as a butt for jokes and criticism found in songs directly relates to the view of the preacher often found within the group. 'The Cayton-Warner Research staff collected thousands of random comments during the Depression years,' wrote Cayton and Drake. 'The most striking thing about these comments was the prevalence of grumbling against preachers and the Church—a habit found among members and non-members alike.' Among the major criticisms that they listed were that 'church is a racket', 'ministers don't practice what they preach', and the 'church places too much emphasis upon money'. They noted in particular that 'during the Depression the charge that the church was a "racket" was encountered everywhere in Bronzeville'; they gave many examples of opinions expressed to the effect that 'the preachers want to line their pockets with gold' and had similar doubts as to the honesty and integrity of the church leaders.[20]

The rapacity and immorality of the preachers, real or imagined, is the subject of folk stories in many countries and cultures. This is no less true of the folk-lore of the American Negro than it is of Balkan, Nordic of Anglo-Saxon folk-lore. The folk tales stress their foibles in traditional terms, and the folk-songs, while making some allowance for human weaknesses in the preachers, share the same target.[21] But it seems likely also that as a butt of folk humour the preacher has been substituted for the 'nigger' of the minstrel show, whose cunning, artfulness and unreliability were age-old stereotypes of the Negro. Especially in those songs and stories which have been absorbed or borrowed from the white traditions, the transfer of the butt from the 'nigger' to the 'preacher' seems a natural one.

> Some folks say that a nigger won't steal,
> But I caught two in my cornfield,

ran a familiar, frequently cited verse. More than a hundred years ago it was collected in the Georgia Sea Islands as part of a slave song giving warning of the 'paddy rollers', the patrols who curtailed the movements of Negroes in the South:

> O some tell me that a nigger won't steal,
> But I've seen a nigger in my cornfield,
> O run, nigger, run, for the patrol will catch you,
> O run, nigger, run, for 'tis almost day.[22]

A characteristic shift had already taken place when Lafcadio Hearn collected the words from a Negro roustabout on the Cincinnati levee some fifteen years later in 1876:

> Some folks say that a rebel can't steal,
> I found twenty in my cornfiel',
> Sich pullin' of shucks an' tearin' of corn!
> Nebber saw the like since I was born.

Known as *Shiloh* or as *Limber Jim*, the song, wrote Hearn, was 'very profane and some of it not quite fit to print'.[23] Several of its verses reappeared in many songs collected in subsequent years, by Dorothy

Scarborough in *Jim Crack Corn* or Howard Odum in *Raise a Rukus Tonight*, for instance. At an indeterminate date the stanzas already quoted became associated with the song generally known as *You Shall Be Free*, 'a more sophisticated development of Negro folk-music, with only a suggestion of the spiritual in the background', in Sigmund Spaeth's words.[24] Howard Odum, who collected the song early in this century and published it in 1911, stated that it 'was originally adapted from a religious song *Mourner, You Shall Be Free*'.[25] This would appear to be the song given in one verse by Roark Bradford as:

You shall be free, po' moaner, (3)
When Sweet God set you free.[26]

In its secular forms it was widespread in its distribution and Dorothy Scarborough quoted many variants under different titles collected by her informants in several states. Elizabeth Dickinson in Birmingham, Alabama, gave the 'You shall be free, mourners' refrain to *There Was an Old Nigger, His Name Was Dr Peck*; while Harriet Fitts in the same state collected it as *Ain't No Use O' My Workin' So Hard*. In Texas it was variously collected as *Ole Marse John*; *Pore Mournah*, or by Mrs Bartlett as *Po' Mona*. Mrs Bartlett's version included the chorus:

Po' Mona, you shall be free,
Gooba-looba, Nigger, you shall be free.
Keep a-shoutin', Nigger, you shall be free,
When the good Lawd sets you free,

which was followed by the familiar lines beginning, 'Some folks say that niggers don't steal'.[27]

In an exhaustive study of Negro folk-songs Newman Ivey White published some fifteen song fragments with the *Po' Mourner* and *You Shall Be Free* refrains. Several of these were collected in or near Auburn, Alabama, in the period 1915–16 by a number of student informants. Others came from adjacent counties and from North Carolina, Florida, Tennessee and Louisiana, confirming that the song was widely known among Negroes. Under the title *Some Folks Say* he listed in addition five versions of the 'cornfield' refrain collected in Alabama and traced the song to a verse in *Negro Singers' Own Book c.* 1846. In two Alabama manuscripts the themes were joined to make a new song.[28]

A dozen years later, the medicine-show singer, Frank Stokes, chose it for his first recording, abbreviated to *You Shall*. Perhaps the Paramount Company was deterred by the implications of the full title. Stokes, too, may have been alive to the sensibilities of his listeners, for there was a further shift in the target of the song:

Well some folks say that a preacher won't steal,
I caught about eleven in a watermelon field,
Just a cuttin' and slidin', couldn't stand up fine,
They was eatin' stalks most all the time:
They's hungry, they'd rob you, brother—yeah,
They was cryin', 'Don't rob me!'
Don't rob you . . . watermelons, yeah.

You see that preacher behind a log,
His finger on the trigger, his eye on a hog,
The hog says (grunt), the gun says 'zip',
He jumped upon the hog with all his grip,
He had pork chops, yeah,
And neckbones, and spareribs . . . yeah,
Now when the Good Lord sets you free.

Now when I first moved to Memphis, Tennessee,
I was crazy about the preachers as I could be,
I went on the front porch just a-walkin' about,
Invite the preacher over to my house,
He washed his face, combed his head,
Next thing he want to do was slip in my bed,
I caught him by the head, man, kicked him out the door,
Don't allow no preachers in my house no more.
Don't like 'em; they'll rob you,
Take your daughter, take your wife from you,
Take your chickens, take your money,
They'll rob you, yeah. . . .[29]

But when Howard Odum collected the song the words still ran:

Great big nigger, settin' on a log,
One eye on trigger, one eye on hog. . . .[30]

Medicine-show singer of an older generation though he was, Frank Stokes was alive to the blues and included in his repertoire a number of songs which were mainly drawn from an older tradition. Fragments of his verses survived in the singing and in the blues of younger singers and Madlyn Davis, essentially a blues singer, used the traditional theme in her recording of *Too Black Bad* the following year. Under the name of 'Red Hot Shakin' Davis' and accompanied by Georgia Tom on piano and Tampa Red on guitar, she sang a fragmentary, blues version of the song:

Now some folks say that a preacher won't steal,
But I caught a preacher in my daddy's field,
Hey, and that's my way,
And that's my way,
And it's too black bad.

Now one had the sack, the other had the wool,
If that ain't stealin' boys, I'd like to know,
Oh, now that's my way etc.

(*Spoken*) Hey, whip that thing down to the bricks, boys.

Now here come my father with his gun,
You ought to see them preachers run,
Oooh, now that's my way etc.[31]

Though the song did not take the customary blues verse form Madlyn Davis placed her *Too Black Bad* on the twelve-bar structure, extending her refrain lines to complete the sequence. A little over two years later, the song appeared again in a more complete, though rather less original, synthesis with the blues. Kansas Joe and Memphis Minnie were the recording names of Joe and Minnie McCoy, whose *Preachers Blues* was sung by Joe McCoy to their guitars. It took one of the common blues forms of couplet and refrain in which the first pair of lines are sung in the initial four bars and the refrain extended over eight. In the first verse, however, acknowledgement is made to the origins of the song by the use of two couplets which impose a sixteen-bar stanza:

Some folks say a preacher won't steal,
I caught three in my cornfield,
One had a yeller, one had a brown,
Looked over in the middle, one was gettin' down.
    Now some folks say, that a preacher won't steal,
    But he will do more stealin' than I get reg'lar meals.

I went to my house, 'bout half past ten,
Looked on my bed where that preacher had been,
    Now some folks say etc.

I been tryin' so hard to save my life,
To keep that preacher from my wife,
    Now some folks say etc.

I went out last night, came in late,
I found out where he had made his date,
    Now some folks say that a preacher won't steal,
    But he will do more stealin' than I get reg'lar meals.[32]

Madlyn Davis lays emphasis on the preacher's dishonesty and cowardice, Kansas Joe stresses his sexual propensities, all characteristics that have been ascribed to the Negro in general in the past. If the preacher could be an acceptable butt for the jibes of the singers where the references to 'niggers' were no longer palatable, Frank Stokes's recording of *You Shall*, quoted above, suggests another aspect of the process of modification which took place in the formative years of the blues, and the recording of Negro singers. His first verse ran:

Now Our Father, who art in Heaven
The preacher owes me ten dollars, he gave me seven.
Thy kingdom come, Thy will be done,
If I hadn't took the seven,
I wouldn't-a got none.
I had to fight about it,
What he owed me, my money—yeah.[33]

Hidden in a recording by the Reverend George Jones and His Congregation issued by Gennett in 1929 lay another version of the verse.

'Listen brothers, my subject is that White Mule of Sin,' spoke the Reverend Jones to his congregation and he called upon a member, 'Sister Jones, lead us in a word of prayer.' To which she replied:

Our Father, who art in Heaven,
The white man owes me ten dollars,
But I didn't get but seven.
Thy kingdom come, ah, Thy will be done,
I took that or I wouldn't-a got none. A-men.[34]

It is not without interest that 'Reverend George Jones' was in fact the blues singer John Byrd recording under a pseudonym. The fragment of social protest in a traditional verse was well obscured in the sermon of a pseudonymous blues singer turned preacher. In the age of recording the process of coating the pill as the songs reached a wider audience seems in this instance to have followed a progression from 'nigger' and 'white man' to 'preacher' and eventually the personalization of Texas Alexander's:

I cried, 'Lord, My Father, Lord, Thy kingdom come, (2)
Give me back my woman and Thy will be done.'[35]

On the subject of the preacher and his church, the blues singer in fact had remarkably little original to say. Most of his comments on the Church are couched in extremely general terms and can be traced back to firmly established stereotypes. Sometimes he uses the phrases of an older song directly, sometimes he remodels them and sometimes he borrows the attitudes they express. But specific comment on individual, identifiable figures in the Church, national or local, are lacking and the stock types of 'Deacon Jones' and 'Deacon Johnson', or merely 'preacher', pervade his references to personalities. Very rare indeed is Fats Heyden's verse:

I ain't no washfoot Baptist, and I can't do the Holy Roll, (2)
I joined Father Divine and it gave me peace that satisfies my soul.[36]

His verse illumines another aspect shunned by the blues: the complexity of the Negro Church itself. Though there are occasional references to the 'Baptist preacher' the many denominations within the

Baptist Church are nowhere indicated. By 1916 there were some three million Negroes in Baptist churches and the figure remained fairly constant until in 1936 this membership was shared by some 20,000 churches throughout the country. There were over 340,000 members of the African Methodist Episcopal Church—the AME in the Bureau of Census report for that year—and almost as many in the African Methodist Episcopal Zion Church. Fewer by a hundred thousand were the members of the Colored Methodist Episcopal—and the distinctions in the names were indicative of the splintering of the churches into separate factions. Their divisions were to be paralleled by those in the Church of God, The Church of God, The Church of God in Christ and so on, while the steady rise of the Pentecostal churches brought similar factionalism in its wake. Beside these churches must be set the cults— The Mt Sinai Holy Church of America Inc., Bishop Emmanuel Grace's United House of Prayer for All People, Prophet Cherry's 'Black Jews', the African Orthodox, Timothy Drew's Moorish Science Temple of America or the Father Divine Peace Mission Movement. And infinitely smaller, but important because of their numbers and their devout followings of tiny congregations, are the multitude of storefront churches which line the streets in the Negro areas of the main urban centres. But as a comment on the various churches, *Denomination Blues* is exceptional:

> Well, the denominations have no right to fight,
> They ought to just treat each other right,
> > But that's all, I tell you that's all,
> > But you better have Jesus, I tell you that's all.

> The Primitive Baptists they believe,
> You can't go to Heaven less'n you wash your feet,
> > But that's all etc.

> Now the Missionary Baptists, they believe,
> You go under the water, not to wash your feet,
> > But that's all etc.

> Now the African Methodists they believe the same,
> 'Cause you know denominations ain't a thing but a name,
> > But that's all etc.

Now the Holiness people, when they come in,
They said, 'Boy we can make it by livin' above sin.'
But that's all etc.[37]

Washington Phillips, a Negro evangelist, was more stringent than any blues singer in his commentary on the ritual trappings of different bodies within the Church. His song was not a blues and his criticisms were made from a Fundamentalist, religious standpoint. That the Negro churches in all their rivalry, jealousies and often strictly puritanical codes of behaviour, presented the blues singer with a rich theme for his worldly cynicism seems evident, but it is equally evident that he seldom chose to exploit it.

If one opportunity was evaded by the blues singer, another was presented in the form of parody. If the preacher could preach his sermon for God and his congregation, the blues singer could preach the blues for the Devil and those who had aligned themselves against the Church. Most preaching parodies were in comic imitation of church sermons, rather than attempts at blues parallels to religious sermons. The parody sermons, as Stith Thompson shows, are one of the more popular of folk-tale motifs and they abound in Negro folk-lore.[38] They were apparently much employed in vaudeville and minstrel entertainments and were carried to the professional stage. The celebrated entertainer, Bert Williams, featured parody sermons by 'Elder Eatmore' in his stage act and the earliest examples on record were of a similar type. Jodie Edwards, who called himself 'Butterbeans', recorded a characteristic example in 1926 which opened with a somewhat confused imitation of a deacon's address. Though he commenced by saying that he was opening with a text he made no further reference to it in the introduction or the narrative-song that followed: 'Sisters and brothers, I am opening up my text this evenin' on page 200 and O Z O. It's a certain type of brother in this house has been talkin' about the Reverend, and the brother that I am speakin' of, I don't like to throw stones at no one. But when I start to throwin' stones this evenin' I ain't gonna miss not a single brother.'

After the introduction he declared himself to be 'Deacon Bite-'Em-in-the-Back' and proceeded to 'get 'em told'—to name those who had been attacking him. He concluded:

Now I'm gonna tell you brothers somethin',
And it's a nach'l fact,
David never would have killed that lion with that brick,
If he hadn't-a bit him in the back.
Now there's old Reverend White,
A talkin' to a friend of mine;
Started to bitin' on me last week,
But I been chewin' on him a long, long time.
I'm Deacon Bite-'Em-in-the-Back,
From the tumble-down shack,
I ain't nobody's friend.[39]

It is difficult to ascertain whether Butterbeans innovated the sermon-parody song. Very probably it had been current for generations, but Butterbeans was undoubtedly instrumental in popularizing the form. At his first recording session he made *A Married Man's a Fool* which set the pattern for many subsequent 'preaching' blues. It was his third record to be issued and was as popular and as influential as the second, *A to Z Blues*:

Luther Brown was a deacon, just as wise as he could be,
He knew the Bible—I mean *backwards*—
From Revelations back to Genesee.
Now last Sunday mornin' at the church, as he's takin' the stand,
He look down upon the congregation with his Good Book in his
        hand,
Now he cast his eyes about,
And then he loudly shout: he says,
'A married man's a fool when he thinks that his wife
Don't want nobody else but him.
She will stick by you all of your life,
But the chances is mighty slim.
Now in the Good Book on page twenty-one,
"Every married woman's gwina have a little fun."
Turn over boys, read on page twenty-two,
It says, "My wife's John's wife and Henry's gal too."
Now let me tell you somethin' boys about page twenty-three,
It says, "She'll two-time you like she double-crossed me."
It says in the Good Book on page twenty-four,

"If they shimmy the first time they gonna do it some more."
Now let me tell you somethin' boys 'bout the twenty-fifth page,
Says that "backbitin' women is all the rage."
It says in the Good Book on page twenty-six,
"To keep your wife boys, you gotta mash her cream with a brick."
Now page twenty-seven, it reads like this:
"If your wife gets hungry boys give her a mouthful of fist."
Now in the Good Book on page twenty-eight,
"When you go out your front-door to work
A pinchback come in your back gate."
Now I'm closin' my sermon on page twenty-nine,
Says, "A married woman gets tired of one man all the time." '[40]

Butterbeans's song was an example of the vaudeville composition
which fed back into folk usage: nearly thirty years later Blind Willie
McTell recorded it in an Atlanta record shop with only a few minor
changes in the words. Though he chanted the quoted lines from 'the
Good Book' it appears that Butterbeans's 'sermon' was probably
adapted from a spiritual, which had employed a similar structure, to
offer a message of hope to the illiterate and point a moral by the same
means. Roark Bradford associated a song of this form with the Civil
War years putting the following verse in the mouth of 'Aunt Free':

So I reads on down to-a number three,
Oh, lonesome Jesus, won't you set me free?
Shet up my eyes and take-a my hand,
And let me fly away wid de angel band.

adding later the words 'recited in a monotone':

So when you reads on down to-a number ten:
When you kills yo' brother you's doin' a sin.[41]

That the words of a spiritual in this form were changed by the
irreverent into a mock sermon would be an almost inevitable outcome.
It is difficult now to ascertain when such a process took place but a
number of versions exist on record. Wilson Meyers's vocal to Sidney
Bechet's band recording of *Preachin' Blues* extracted a few of the 'pages'
from Luther Brown's sermon. It seems to have been Bessie Smith who
introduced the relationship of 'preaching' and 'blues', however, with

her mock sermon, *Preachin' the Blues*, the first to use the title. It was not a sermon in its entirety for it had the familiar vaudeville introduction to set the scene:

> Down in Atlanta GA,
> Under the viaduct every day,
> Drinkin' corn and hollerin', 'Hooray!'
> Piano's playin' till the break of day.
> But as I turned my head, I loudly said:
> > Preach them blues, sing them blues,
> > They certainly sound good to me.
> > I been in love for the last six months,
> > And ain't done worryin' yet.
> > Moan them blues, holler them blues,
> > Let me convert your soul. . . .

By 'convert' she made it quite clear that she 'ain't here to try to save your soul, just wanna teach you how to save your good jelly roll'. Then briefly she moved into the preaching parody, chanting her words on one chord:

> Goin' on down the line a li'l further now,
> 'There's many a po' woman down.'
> Read on down to chapter nine,
> 'Women must learn how to take their time.'
> Read on down to chapter ten,
> 'Takin' other women's men, you are doin' a sin.'
> Sing 'em, sing 'em, sing them blues,
> Let me convert your soul.

After a short piano solo by James P. Johnson, she concluded with the words:

> Now one old sister by the name of Sister Green,
> Jumps up and done the shimmy you ain't never seen.[42] ©

The brief couplet, somewhat out of context, appears to have come from the same source as Hambone Willie Newbern's *Nobody Knows What the Good Deacon Does*, quoted above. Probably this song had been in

currency at an earlier date and it could well have been Edith Wilson's
What Did Deacon Mose Do (When the Lights Went Out)? which was
recorded in 1922 but unissued.

Bessie Smith's sermon-like recitation commences at 'Read on down
to chapter nine' and assumes a general understanding on the part of her
listeners that she is purporting to read from the Bible, for at no time is
it specifically mentioned. That she commences at chapter nine suggests
that on stage she sang a much longer and fuller version which the limitations of the three-minute recording could not permit in its entirety. It
is not difficult to imagine the possibilities for ribald and topical improvised verses which the form offered, the singer 'reading on down' to each
new chapter against the stop chorus of the pianist or a full jazz band.

These were jazz-blues songs that lay between the jazz song and the
conventional blues form. Preaching imitations appealed to some jazz
trumpeters who had mastered the art of 'choking' and 'muting' their
horns to produce sounds imitative of the voice. Players like King Oliver
and Chris Kelly pioneered the 'wa-wa' technique with these imitations.
Kelly, said Danny Barker, 'should have been a preacher. But he preached
so melodiously with his horn that it was like somebody singing a song'.[43]
Such musicians as Tommy Ladnier, Bubber Miley and Cootie Williams
employed these 'vocalized' techniques which made the imitation of
sermons as effective as the mimicry of blues vocals. Reuben Reeves's
Parson Blues made in 1929 or Wingy Carpenter's *Preachin' Trumpet
Blues* of a decade later were specific examples on record.

But, apart from these parodies, blues singers seem seldom to have
sung in mock-religious manner or used preaching techniques for blues
purposes. Occasionally they used blues as a means of projecting a
religious, or quasi-religious message, but examples like Big Bill
Broonzy's *Preaching the Blues* are quite rare:

Men go to church just to hide their dirt,
And women go to church just to show their skirts,
But there's a day coming, an' it may be for you:
When Gabriel blows his trumpet,
Brother, what you gonna do?
Brother, you'd better get on your knees,
Well, and pray both night and day,
Now you may have a good time with married women,
But you may go to Hell that way.[44]

The sentiments expressed were conventional and there was nothing in Big Bill Broonzy's work at this time to suggest that it was anything more than an experiment in varying the song forms that he was using. One of the very few post-war blues to have any reference to the Church or its teaching was *Judgement Day Blues* by Roy Brown which was original also in its use of examples. It was sung to a twelve-bar blues structure though it was clearly a composed song:

Hey you back-sliders, listen t' what I have to say,
There's a day comin' soon and it's called Judgement Day.
I'm standin' and wonderin' what will I do on Judgement Day,
Well when I face St Peter, tell me what I have to say.

Well, like the preacher told the gambler, laying on his dying bed,
Instead of reading cards it's the Bible you should have read.
You got to face the situation man, you gonna have an awful time,
Yes, when Judgement Day comes around you gonna take your place
    and stand in line.

Like the rooster told the turkey just before Thanksgiving Day,
If you don't know dear brother, it's time to learn to pray.
Yes, tomorrow this time, you'll be dead golden-brown,
Yes, you better get religion, be ready when the hatchet man comes
    round.[45]

The song concluded with a recitative in mock-preaching fashion with the final warning to 'the hypocrites, you better get your business straight'. A sophisticated and often witty singer, Roy Brown was an early exponent of modern rhythm and blues and his compositions were far removed from the blues of the rural South.

As has been seen, *Preachin' the Blues* by Son House had neither a religious theme which used the blues for a vehicle, nor had it a blues theme delivered in the manner of a preacher. Rather, it was a verse sequence which expressed a number of personal attitudes to the Church and to the blues. This was the case with Robert Johnson's *Preaching Blues* which drew one verse from Son House's composition and added others from the tradition that had been on record at least since 1924 when Ida Cox made her *Blues Ain't Nothin' Else But*. Sang Johnson:

Mmm, I woke up this mornin', my blues walkin' like a man,
Woke up this mornin', my blues walkin' like a man,
Well now, Blues, give me your right hand.

And the Blues grabbed mama's chile and trowed me all upside down,
The Blues grabbed mama's child, trowed me all upside down,
'Travel on poor Bob, just cain't turn you roun'.'

The Blues, is a lowdown, shakin' chill,
Mmm . . . is a lowdown, shakin' chill,
Ain't never had 'em—hope you never will.

Says the blues is a achin' ole heart disease—hit it now—
The blues is a lowdown achin' heart disease,
Like consumption, killing me by degrees.[46]

Nowhere does Robert Johnson refer to 'preaching' in his blues and, if his title has any significance at all, it is that the Blues, personified, is paralleled to the Devil. This has some support in the curiously obsessive themes in his *Me and the Devil Blues*, *If I Had Possession over Judgement Day* and the oft-quoted *Hell-Hound on My Trail*. The former does suggest that the Devil, like the blues, may be a state of mind:

Early this mornin', when you knocked upon my door, (2)
I said, 'Hello Satan, I believe it's time to go.'

Me and the Devil was walkin' side by side, (2)
I'm gonna beat my woman until I get satisfied.

You can bury my body down by the highway side, (2)
So my ole evil spirit can get a Greyhound bus and ride.[47]

In this and other blues, the anguished, tormented spirit of Robert Johnson appears to have been deeply disturbed by a conscience battling with the lustiness of a young man who was playing his own hell with his women. It reflects the strict puritanism of the teaching of many of the Negro churches which reaches its most extreme expression in the cultist movements. Wrote Arthur Huff Fauset in his findings on such cults, 'The American Negro religious cult exercises rigid taboos over certain features of the private lives of its members, frequently reaching into the most intimate details of their private lives. Sex inhibitions are of paramount importance in most of the cult groups.'[48] What is true of the cults is true in kind, if it is not taken to such lengths, in the majority of the churches, in many of which segregation of the sexes is obligatory during worship. Sex plays a large part in the content of the sermons, but sexual innuendo is also employed by Negro preachers whose skilful titillation of their congregations probably provides a necessary release. Nevertheless, the strictures of the churches on the behaviour of their member breeds a guilt which sometimes finds passing expression in the blues. Lightnin' Hopkins, for instance, complaining that 'the way you doin' is just about to worry me to death', expressed a personal dilemma:

My mother, she's a Christian,
She been beggin' me to join the church too,
Babe, but how can I join the church and always bother wit'chu?[49]

Against the pressures of the church within the community which, in rural areas where the church is the focal point of local social life, are considerable, the decision to align oneself with the blues must be an emphatic one. Dissatisfaction with the Church and disillusion with its teachings would be likely themes for the blues under such circumstances. Sometimes there are indeed blues which express the singer's belief that the Church, or God, has failed him, though they are relatively few in number. Cautiously declaring himself to be 'just a fool', J. T. Funny Paper Smith, a Texas singer with an unusually lyrical turn of phrase that matched the easy swing of his guitar playing, sang a blues which revolved round a popular belief:

Some people tells me that God takes care of old folks and fools, (2)
But since I been livin' he must have changed his rule.

I used to ask God questions and answer that question myself, (2)
But when I was born, wonder was there any more mercy left?

Look like here of late I been cryin' both night and day, (2)
Everybody talks about me and nobody ain't treatin' me right.

You know until six months ago I hadn't prayed a prayer since God
    knows when, (2)
Now I'm askin' God every day to please forgive me for my sins.

You know this must've been the Devil I'm servin', I know it ain't
    Jesus Christ, (2)
All I ask Him is to save me, and look like He's tryin' to take my life.

I got TBs, I got LTs,
I got third degrees and Polk's Disease,
My health is gone now, left me with the sickness blues,
People, it don't seem to me that God takes care of old folks and
    fools.[50]

Funny Paper Smith's *Fool's Blues*, sung in a voice at once melan-
choly and resigned, is the statement of a man who has had his personally
held opinions confirmed by experience. More moving is Tommy
Griffin's *Dying Sinner Blues*, a simple and convincing blues which
conveys both in the words and their intonation the reproach of one who
has been deeply hurt in his personal life and his religious faith:

My baby's gone, can't come back no more, (2)
She's dead, and gone where she never been before.

Lord, oh Lord, I believe that you didn't hear me pray, (2)
I begged you so hard; still you taken my baby away.

Some people tell me, 'The dead know what the livin' do.' (2)
If that's a fact people, I know my baby's feelin' blue.

When she was livin'—never would do me wrong, (2)
But I got a mean mistreater now my baby's dead and gone.

She go out in the mornin', stay drunk all day long, (2)
And swear to her Maker she had done nothin' wrong.

She be out drinkin' whisky Lord, and her high-brown gin, (2)
If I want to have supper—I don't know where she's been.[51]

Both these examples make specific reference to what 'some people tell'—the superstitions and condensed, epigrammatic versions of religious doctrine on which much Negro Church teaching is based. In the more primitive churches and those where the preachers have received 'the call' but have had little formal education, considerable dependence is put upon a limited canon of Fundamentalist teachings illustrated by the more colourful Biblical passages, imaginatively if sometimes luridly interpreted. Some of the aphorisms are to be found in the blues though they are generally clichés both in their choice and in their application:

Please baby, cain't you see the tears come runnin' down, (2)
If you don't take me back I will have to leave this town.

Please baby, honey don't drive me from your door, (2)
Because the Good Book says, 'You gotta reap just what you sow,'[52]

is one of the most familiar. Sometimes contrite and often self-pitying verses appear in the blues where the singer regrets his 'wicked ways' and having 'broke his mammy's rule'. 'If I had listened to what my mammy said. . . .' begins many a blues verse and, while sometimes the singer has merely ignored good advice, in many instances he has led a sinful life:

I been a bad boy, mother, I didn't do the things I should, (2)
My mother always told me, 'Please do the things good.'

Mother, dear mother, please pray for my wicked soul, (2)
Lord when I die and go to Heaven, I wanna walk down those
    streets of gold.

Now I been drinkin' and gamblin', chasin' women too,
Those are the three things that you told me not to do,
I been a bad boy, mother, I didn't do the things I should,
My mother always told me, 'Son, please do the things good.'[53]

The belief that prayer will provide the solution to most problems is also frequently echoed in the blues, though it is often no more than a variation of 'Lord, have mercy, fall on my bended knees' or 'I'm down on my bended knee, saying, "Lord have mercy on me, please." ' It was this kind of entreaty which formed, as already shown, the basis of the Santa Claus invocation. Bert Mays once resorted to this formula in a blues which, in content and in structure, was otherwise rather unusual:

I got down on my knees, I had a long talk with the God above,
I cried, 'Oh Lord, Lord send me back the woman I love.' (2)[54]

Even inventive singers will revert to cliché when quoting prayers in their blues and lines like those in *Teach Me Right From Wrong* are rare. Charmingly and somewhat naïvely, Kaiser Clifton in his still unbroken youth's voice asked for guidance from God, or 'somebody', but spoiled the image by a trite concluding line:

Lord I've been a good boy, I even be goin' to Sunday school, (2)
May the Lord forgive me, and tell me what can I do.

Come here somebody and teach me right from wrong, (2)
If I done killed my baby I didn't mean no harm.[55]

As a previous verse had stated that 'she left me this morning when the clock was striking one' and there was nothing to suggest that Clifton was referring to her death, the resolution of the blues is unconvincing. Pleading to 'the good Lord' to send back a woman who has left accounts for most references to prayer in the blues. Blind Willie McTell was less hypocritical than many when he sang in his *Broke Down Engine*:

Feel like a broke down engine, mama ain't got no drivin' wheel, (2)
If you been down and lonesome, you know just how Willie McTell feels.
Well it's, 'Lawdy-Lawd, Lawdy-Lawdy-Lawd. . . .'

I been shootin' craps and gamblin', good gal and I done got broke, (2)
I done pawned my 32 Special, Lord and my clothes in soak.

I even went down to my prayin' ground, dropped on bended knees, (2)
I didn't cry for no religion, 'Lawdy give me back my good gal, please.'
But it's, 'Lawdy-Lawd, Lawdy-Lawdy-Lawd. . . .'

If you give me my baby Lawd, I won't worry you no more, (2)
You ain't got to put her in my house Lawd, only lead her to my
    door.[56]

Though the blues singer is 'dealing with the Devil' in singing his
'worldly' songs and playing his music, Willie McTell was one of the very
few who occasionally expressed a sinner's view of religion in his songs.
In his rough and surly *Southern Can Mama*, which is coarsely sexual,
he tells his woman that after he gets out of jail 'and hit the ground, your
southern can is worth twelve dollars a half a pound'. He imputes a
Biblical authority to his claims as a pimp:

Now looka here mama, let me explain you this,
You wants to get crooked, I'll even give you my fist.
Read from Revelations back to Genesee,
If you get crooked then you'll see,
Your southern can belongs to me.
Your southern can is mine, in the mornin',
Your southern can belongs to me.[57]

Many blues are aggressive in content and to canalize violence would
appear to be one of the functions of the blues. Such a combination of
violence and religious association is nevertheless unusual and it must
be acknowledged that even here, Blind Willie McTell was using a ready-
made phrase which had no real Biblical significance.

Faced with the evidence of those blues which make any reference
whatever to the Negro Church, to Christianity, to God, to the Nativity,
the Crucifixion or any other aspect of religious belief, one is mainly
impressed by the reticence of the comments. There are few blues with
religious images as striking as Walter Davis's verse in *Lifeboat Blues*:

I put my baby on a lifeboat and told her bye, bye, bye, (2)
And her eyes got full of water and she began to cry.

I tried to ship my baby in some far and distant land, (2)
But the way she looked at me people, I really don't think I can.

Now if you be my baby, you can be my boss, (2)
And I will stick closer to you than Jesus did the Cross.[58] ©

A brief reconsideration of recorded examples over several decades makes it clear that blues singers are cautious in their observations on religion. They seldom criticize any aspects of religious dogma or challenge the authority of the Church. They do not criticize or satirize the devotions of the members but confine their comments to conventional jokes concerning the behaviour of preachers and deacons. In this they merely follow a tired formula which has long been a mainstay of vaudeville, minstrel-show and medicine-show humour where the preacher's sexual behaviour, his lazy preference for preaching rather than for physical work, his duplicity, his chicken-stealing habits, his money-grasping techniques of persuasion and the alleged disparity between his sermons and his personal conduct have been the target of broad humour.

Whatever the basis in fact, and there is evidence that there is some in certain circumstances, at any rate, a conventional caricature still remains of the minister and to a lesser extent of his congregation. That this is in part rooted in jealousy, in the security which challenges the footloose pattern of life of many blues singers seem possible. And there are the echoes of white caricature of Negroes in the minstrel shows which have been transferred to a new butt. The purpose of caricature is to show by satirical exaggeration and ridicule the weakness of the target. But this is caricature which has not the courage of its intention; not *caricatura* but popular cartoon, sketched in with the crude lines of a hack draughtsman.

A close parallel exists between the minstrel-show, blackface 'nigger', banjo, watermelon, tight pants and all, and the Negro vaudeville, 'Deacon Jones'. He may thump the Bible instead of the banjo but in essence he is the same man—or cartoon figure of a man. That his creation reflects in part an earlier one within the minstrel shows and more emphatically has often been substituted for the painful caricature of the Negro seems likely in Negro entertainment. It is also possible that he has assumed a dual role, taking on some of the attributes of the white man which may have figured in a virtually secret body of Negro song. This is conjectural and much research might be needed to establish or disprove a relationship, but the evidence of a number of old songs, which have witnessed a distinct shift of emphasis in the identity of the principal character, points strongly in this direction. One thing is clear—the blues, when it has taken an attitude to the Negro ministry at all, has borrowed it often to the details of line and verse from the older traditions.

Specific criticism or comment on the multitudinous sects, cults and denominations within the Negro Church is avoided by the blues singer and he confines any attack to deliberately vague and unspecified targets. When he turns to doctrine he depends on a small number of well-worn phrases culled long ago from the Bible, from the preachers or from the quasi-religious sayings within a folk society, repeating them to make a rhyme and seldom, if ever, adding to the stock. There seems to be no evidence of serious consideration of the content of a sermon in blues nor critical evaluation of any of the Church's teaching. The glimmerings of doubt which appear in John Lee Hooker's *Burnin' Hell* derive from a verse in Son House's *My Black Mama*:

Everybody talking about that burning Hell,
Ain't no Heaven, ain't no burnin' Hell. . . .
When I die, where I go, can't nobody tell.

I says oooh . . . mmm cain't nobody tell,
Where I go, cain't nobody tell. . . .

Go down to the church house son, get down on your bended knee,
Ask Deacon Jones just to pray for me,
Well I said, ask Deacon Jones just to pray for me.

Mmm . . . Deacon Jones told me, 'Get on your knees son, repent
for your sins, let me pray for you. . . .'
Mmmm, ain't no Heaven, ain't no burnin' Hell,
When I die, cain't nobody tell, cain't nobody tell. . . .[59]

It is disappointing to find Deacon Jones reappear in this relatively unusual, if fragmentary, blues, exhorting the singer to 'get down on your bended knee'. If John Lee Hooker's blues suggests uncertainty as to a concept of life after death, it is one which he has not followed in other recordings and which stops far short of loosening any stones in the foundations of his belief. Raised in a church community and once a member of a spiritual group, he still relates the blues to spirituals; any fundamental groping at the roots of his Christian belief in his blues is still unlikely, though he has recorded no religious songs.

It is not without significance that among the singers quoted here who have been most outspoken in the expression of disillusion or disbelief—

Texas Alexander, Funny Paper Smith or Tommy Griffin—none have recorded spirituals or gospel songs. Only Alexander displayed a disregard for religion even so, projecting a picture of a totally worldly singer, one comparable to that of Doctor Clayton whose *Angels in Harlem* was the blues of an unrepentant sinner:

> I know Harlem can't be Heaven 'cause New York is right down
>   here on earth, (2)
> But it's headquarters for brownskin angels from everywhere else in
>   this world.
>
> Plain-looking women live out in the country 'cause nobody just
>   don't want 'em around, (2)
> When you find a ugly woman livin' in Harlem she's either rich, or
>   from some other town.
>
> I know blues singers don't go to Heaven 'cause Gabriel bawls 'em
>   out, (2)
> But all the good ones go to Harlem and help them angels beat it
>   out.[60]

Doctor Clayton, who lost his wife and children in a tragic fire and died an incurable alcoholic, may have had his faith destroyed; he did not record any gospel songs either.

At first glance it would seem unlikely for a blues singer to sing, much less record, religious songs, for the whole blues idiom falls in the 'sinful' class of music so rigidly defined in the Negro mind. Apparently irreconcilable, the gospel songs and the blues represent the poles of the sacred and the secular. But the evidence to the contrary is substantial enough to throw some light on the blues singers' cautious approach to religious themes.

Between the session which produced his *Southern Can Mama* and his next recording session in 1935, some eighteen months later, Blind Willie McTell may have been 'converted'; or perhaps, under pressure from the Decca Record Company, or merely for a change, he drew upon an unexpected resource of religious song. Whatever the circumstances, he recorded on 23 April a number of titles which included *I Got Religion, I'm So Glad*, which was unissued, and *Ain't It Grand to Be a Christian* with his wife, Kate McTell, which was issued under the name of 'Blind Willie'.[61] He also recorded an unissued *Let Me Play with Your Yo-Yo* on the same date, which, if it was similar to others in the same vein, was more in character with his previous recording. Subsequently he recorded blues for many years. When he was recorded in 1940 for the Library of Congress, none the less a fairly large proportion of the titles were religious ones. There are countless possible reasons why McTell chose to record a number of religious titles; the fact still remains that he did, and that his doing so is indicative of a far from unusual situation among blues singers.

Even a cursory examination of the recorded output of a large number of major blues singers reveals that a significantly high proportion were conversant with gospel songs and spirituals and included them in their repertoires. This applies to some of the most important singers who helped to shape local traditions and may point to an important relationship between the song forms. Blind Lemon Jefferson's earliest recordings under the pseudonym of Deacon L. J. Bates were *I Want to Be Like Jesus in My Heart* and *All I Want Is That Pure Religion* and, after he had a couple of dozen blues titles issued, he recorded *He Arose from the Dead* and *Where Shall I Be?* His Mississippi counterpart, Charley Patton, concluded his first session with *Lord I'm Discouraged, I'm Going Home* and, under a pseudonym, *Prayer of Death*. It was a pattern that obtained in five of his seven sessions, with Patton preaching on *You're Gonna Need Somebody When You Die* at his next, and being joined by Bertha Lee on later occasions. Mississippi John Hurt was another singer who included gospel songs—*Blessed Be the Name* and *Meeting on the Old Camp Ground*—at his first session and though these were unissued he recorded them again later that year for issue early in 1929. Another Mississippi singer, Skip James, similarly recorded gospel titles at his first appearance before the microphone, cutting *Jesus Is a Mighty Good Leader* and *Be Ready When He Comes* in anticipation of his long career preaching and travelling with a gospel quartet in Texas.

Some singers, like Sam Collins, who recorded *Lead Me All the Way* or Bo Weavil Jackson, who made *I'm on My Way to Kingdom Land*, had their blues and their gospel titles issued under their own names in both instances; others, like Louis Washington, who made *Heaven in My View* or Robert Hicks, who made *Jesus' Blood Can Make Me Whole*, had their religious items issued under their proper names and their blues titles under their more familiar pseudonyms of Tallahassee Tight and Barbecue Bob respectively. In these cases the singers had relatively few gospel titles on record but Joshua White was an artist who made as great a reputation from his many religious titles as he did from his blues, recording the former as by 'Joshua White—The Singing Christian' and the latter as by Pinewood Tom.

Among the many singers whose blues and gospel recordings fought on equal terms were the fine, rough Texas singer, Henry Thomas, who sang *When the Train Comes Along* and *Jonah in the Wilderness* with formidable conviction, and Blind Roosevelt Graves and his brother Uaroy Graves, whose *Take Your Burdens to the Lord* had the same rhythmic impetus as their *Guitar Boogie*. The latter's guitar and tambourine accompaniments were joined by Will Ezell's piano and an unknown cornet; Brother George and His Sanctified Singers was a name that hid the identity of an impressive collection of blues artists including Blind Boy Fuller, Sonny Terry and George (Oh Red) Washington. Later, after Fuller's death, Brownie McGhee recorded in his stead with the same group and under the same name. He also recorded *If I Could Hear My Mother Pray Again* under the name of 'The Tennessee Gabriel'. In Fuller's early years he had worked with Blind Gary Davis, the blind singers begging together and singing both gospel and blues. After recording his *Cross and Evil Woman Blues*, Blind Gary made his *I Am the True Vine* in July 1935 and did not record another blues for a quarter of a century, though other singers testified to the fact that he sang them.

Like many other blues singers, Blind Gary was 'converted' and devoted many years of his life to evangelism and preaching on street corners in Harlem and Brooklyn. Among others who turned to preaching were the little-recorded Rube Lacey, the great Mississippi singer Ishman Bracey and Blind Roosevelt Darby from St Louis. In his later years another St Louis singer, Walter Davis, became a preacher, repenting perhaps for the ungodly recordings that he had made for so many years. Though these men, blues singers who 'changed', were content to live in comparative obscurity as preachers, at least one religious composer of note was originally a blues singer. This was Thomas A. Dorsey who, as Georgia Tom and partner to Tampa Red, made many ribald and sophisticated recordings in the 'twenties before turning to the Church. His creative talent as a composer made him one of the most significant figures in the whole of gospel-music history though he made only a handful of recordings as a gospel singer.

Of the women singers of the 'twenties whose blues merged into jazz and vaudeville song, only a few recorded religious items at the time though a large number later joined the Church. Bessie Smith's attempts in the religious vein can be counted as failures; *On Revival Day* and *Moan, You Mourners*, the former subtitled as 'A Rhythmic Spiritual', though performed with the Bessemer Singers under the direction of James P. Johnson, sounding totally unconvincing. Quite different are *Get on Board* and *Living Humble* by Clara Smith which are gospel songs of considerable interest, finely sung. Though musically removed from accepted notions of either gospel or blues technique, being more reminiscent of the Victorian music hall, Laura Smith's *Face to Face* and *Take Me Home Heavenly Father with Thee* should be noted. Another celebrated singer of the 'twenties, Sara Martin, accompanied the blind gospel pianist, Arizona Dranes, on *John Said He Saw a Number* in June 1926 and ten months later made her own *Where Shall I Be?* and *I Am Happy with Jesus*. Her next recording was *Gonna Ramble Blues* on the same day, under the name of Sally Roberts but, when her recording career concluded the following year, she had still a long association with the Church before her as a gospel singer in Louisville. Josie Miles made a large number of recordings of blues and jazz songs in the 'twenties but, when she returned to the studios in 1928 after a three-year lapse, she had been converted to evangelism and, with *God's Warning to the Church*, she began a session as Missionary Josephine Miles. Indicative of a common characteristic among women singers, these artists were joined in the change from a career in blues to one in the Church by singers as varied as Tiny Franklin and Sippie Wallace in Detroit, Ann Cook in New Orleans, Lillian Glinn from Texas, Mary Johnson in St Louis and Martha Copeland and Bertha Idaho in the Eastern states.

Mention of the Dunham Jubilee Singers who accompanied Bessie Smith underlines the fact that the popular vocal quartets of the 'twenties, though they were on the extreme fringe of blues, frequently performed secular material, often of a blues nature though not in a blues style. As the 'Bessemer (Blues) Singers' or as the 'Dunham Jazz Singers' they concealed their identity when recording non-religious titles. Many such groups used similar camouflage; the Excelsior Quartet, which cut the earliest version of *Jelly Roll Blues* in 1921, subsequently made a miscellaneous selection of titles from *Sinners Crying, Come Here Lord* to *Roll Them Bones* in similar harmonized techniques. Typical of later groups to use both sacred and secular songs of a blues-associated nature were the Birmingham Jubilee Singers, who could follow *Four and Twenty Elders* with *Sweet Mama, Tree Top Tall*, or *Walk in Jerusalem Just Like John* with *Louisiana Bo-Bo*, dropping the 'jubilee' name where applicable. Among the most celebrated and widely recorded of the groups was the Norfolk Jubilee Quartet which, as the Norfolk Jazz Quartet, recorded very many blues titles freely mixed with their jubilee themes. And there were others following their lead, including the Monarch Jubilee Quartet from their own town of Norfolk, Virginia.

Though the gospel, or jubilee, quartets performed all their songs in harmonized style which smoothed out the differences between the blues, popular and gospel song forms, it is not uncommon for blues singers to employ very different techniques from their blues style when approaching religious songs. In general they tend to play them 'straight' and to sing them without the shading, the flattening and use of 'blue notes' which they enjoy in the blues. Singers who have been recently recorded under the more liberal circumstances of the long-playing era have demonstrated this on many occasions. Black Ace (B. K. Turner), for instance, sang *Farther Along* in a steady but emotional voice closely approaching that of many white singers; Son House, without guitar accompaniment, sang strong, forthright gospel songs like *John, the Revelator* with no blues colour and Little Brother Montgomery recorded an entire album in which his normally inventive blues piano was reduced to pedestrian church-styled accompaniment to his spirituals. Rediscovery and new recording have revealed new talents in singers like Robert Wilkins, once a blues singer, now totally committed to the Church, who has adapted his intricate guitar playing to evangelical requirements. It is the blues guitarist who plays in 'bottleneck' style who often plays a similar accompaniment in both religious and blues recordings—Bukka White, for example, whose recent *Jesus Died on the Cross to Save the World* or early *I'm in the Heavenly Way* of more than thirty years before, have the same pounding guitar, the same fierce intensity. Fred McDowell, similarly, accompanies his wife, Annie, with much the same technical fire that he uses on his blues on such titles as *Amazing Grace* or *Keep Your Lamp Trimmed and Burning*.

Keep Your Lamp Trimmed and Burning was one of the many titles made by the great evangelical singer, Blind Willie Johnson. Johnson, who made no secular recordings, had a technique of guitar playing and a powerful form of vocal delivery which was extremely influential. He probably borrowed more from blues guitarists in his handling of his music than did other players, though this is most noticeable in the non-vocal, highly impressionistic *Dark Was the Night, Cold Was the Ground* in which his low humming against moaning, sighing guitar had the deeply affecting qualities of the singing from the 'Mourner's Bench' in a Southern church. There seems some likelihood that this highly vocal form of guitar playing has strong links with the formative techniques of the blues. Its use by the 'songster' generation of singers lends support to this and such recordings as Jesse Fuller's profoundly moving, bottle-neck guitar solo, *Hark from the Tomb*, and *As Long As I Feel the Spirit* help to establish the link.

It seems likely that the gospel singers borrowed more from the blues artists than the latter did from the religious artists, at least during the 'thirties. Some gospel singers of note—Mahalia Jackson and Sister Rosetta Tharpe in particular—derived much from the blues, Mahalia Jackson always acknowledging her indebtedness to Bessie Smith's singing and Rosetta Tharpe gaining much from her experience of working with the Lucky Millinder Band. Influential as these singers were, they did much to shape the developing music which gained something of the rhythmic impetus of boogie-woogie while retaining its essential character. The form of gospel songs with their regular verse structures is distinct from the blues however and this, more than any other musical element, kept the two musics apart, for the structure of the blues in its conventional form is hardly ever echoed in gospel song.

In the majority of instances, at least on record, the blues singers who have changed places with the gospel singers have been solo artists, though some, like Skip James or John Lee Hooker, have worked with gospel groups. Blues has been, for much of its history, a solo perform-ance art and, while there are solo evangelists, there is a long tradition of collective singing in the Church. This has taken the form of preaching leading to mass singing by the congregation; of 'lining out' in which a lead singer paces a line and the congregation follows with the same line or a refrain response with a linear reply; and of the singing of the gospel choirs and quartets. Whereas the solo artists who changed from blues to gospel had only to make an adjustment in their singing style and often accompanied themselves with a simple strum, the few who moved into the world of preaching, congregational singing and gospel choirs had to make a marked change in their techniques. Reverend

George Jones, as noted earlier, was the blues singer John Byrd but this is not detectable from *That White Mule of Sin*; nor is it apparent from Hallelujah Joe's 'straining' preaching on *That Great Love* (*He's So Good to Me*), to the moaning and cries of the congregation, that he was the much-recorded blues singer Joe McCoy who had recorded *One More Greasing* just a week earlier. McCoy's sermons did not suggest that they were parodies of preaching but his conversion seems to have been short-lived. Within a year he was playing with the Harlem Hamfats, a jazz-blues band led by the New Orleans trumpeter, Herb Morand, who employed both Joe and his brother, Charlie McCoy. Joe McCoy's ability to write songs was gleefully celebrated early in 1937 with the song *Hallelujah Joe Ain't Preachin' No More* which accurately stated:

Hallelujah Joe, (Hallelujah Joe—*responses throughout*)
Ain't preachin' no mo',
Everybody thought he was true,
When he preach that song about *What You Gonna Do?*
Hallelujah Joe, ain't preachin' no mo',
He's swingin' now so he ain't gonna preach no mo'.[62] ©

The song continued with a catalogue of Joe McCoy's compositions suggesting that the church members thought he had died, until his song *Oh Red* appeared. This simple theme was their first record and made a hit for the Hamfats, securing them a Decca contract for fifty titles. They remade it at the next session when *What You Gonna Do?* was recorded and it passed quickly into popular blues currency. The following verses made reference to Joe McCoy's other songs, *Move Your Hand* and *Weed Smoker's Dream*. As its title implies, *Move Your Hand* was a suggestive item which could be interpreted as the hearer chose. Subtitled *Why Don't You Do It Now?* the song *Weed Smoker's Dream* referred to the hallucinations induced by marijuana. In spite of the apparent sincerity of *The Prodigal's Return* or *Main Key to Heaven* it seems likely that Hallelujah Joe's religious titles were more the result of contract than conversion. To the Harlem Hamfats it was clearly a huge joke.

For some blues singers, like Robert Wilkins, conversion was a major emotional and spiritual experience which changed their lives, while for others alternating between singing blues and spirituals appears to have been readily acceptable. So Son Bonds could record as Brownsville Son Bonds at his first session; as Brother Son Bonds at the next, when he made a number of religious recordings and as Son or as Son Bonds on later dates. Bearing in mind the disrepute of blues singers and the objections of the Church to their music, this must cause misgivings among some singers. It did to Lil Son Jackson who looked upon an auto- mobile accident in which he was involved as the retribution of God for his sinful ways. Robert Peter Williams, drawn continually to the Church though he has served a sentence for murder in Angola Peni- tentiary, explained, 'I jus' don't like it, jumpin' on to a spiritual after I been singin' the blues. I have to wait. Because you can't mess with the Lord and I think that's messin' him up, singing blues and spirituals both. 'Cause he made us and he knows all we do, and I know it ain't right.'[63] Other singers, like Willie Thomas who is both preacher and blues singer, contend that if the blues are honest and tell the truth they are not sinful to perform.[64] Sippie Wallace, a gospel singer, church member and a trainer of gospel choirs, has recently returned to blues singing. Her concern was not that she should be 'sinnin' before God. I know I ain't doin' that. Because spirituals and blues is just the same thing, head on'.[65] But she was concerned that her church members might not take the same view. Other blues singers show in conversation much evidence of devout feelings which do not find expression in their blues, and reveal sometimes a troubled and confused mind. In the words of Curtis Jones, never a religious performer on record or in person, 'We must all have fresh air, which is a free gift of God for all mankind to enjoy; the same as life is a free gift of God. So all of this must be the work of God. Even in my blues story I must recognize God who gave us our five senses. In our dreams when we are asleep, he is the one who talks with all of us. So many people of today think that the blues came from America, but they come all the way from that unholy city of Bablem. . . .'[66]

Some blues artists were attracted to the Church late in life, like Pete Johnson, the boogie-woogie pianist who became a devoted member after his paralysing stroke. But there were a great many who had always maintained, as did Elmore James, a close connexion with the Church although neither their performing lives, nor their records in any way suggested it. An early connexion with the Church was common to a very large number of blues singers and musicians, whose ability to play an instrument or sing at all was often due to their parents' religious associations: the mother who played the organ, the father who preached and led a gospel choir are familiar in the backgrounds of innumerable blues singers, from T-Bone Walker and Lightnin' Hopkins, Yank Rachell and Otis Spann to Chuck Berry and Junior Wells. Not only were a large number—perhaps the majority—of blues singers raised in God-fearing families, but a high proportion of them also had their first experiences of singing, and sometimes playing, in public in the churches of the South. Singers whose later careers were as varied as those of Bukka White, Sunnyland Slim, Jimmy Witherspoon, B. B. King, Magic Sam and Little George Buford commenced in this way.

It is evident that a significant number of blues singers of all periods and styles on record during the four decades of recorded examples have been raised in religious families; have started their careers in the church; have maintained some contact with religious song and have sometimes recorded little-known examples of gospel music; have been church members or have been converted to the Church; have become preachers and gospel singers, or in other ways have revealed closer connexions with Negro religious music and practice than their careers and recordings specifically as blues singers might lead one to suppose. Undoubtedly their association with the Church, erstwhile or continuous, has inhibited many singers from being more outspoken concerning religious matters. It seems that the blues singer has been satisfied to sustain his anti-theistic, irreligious front in terms of conventions of song and clichés of comment, vague, mildly humorous and unspecific. But there are many singers whose careers do not suggest any such associations and whose recordings are sufficiently worldly to accord with the popular image of the blues: Frankie Jaxon and Monkey Joe Coleman, Red Nelson and Walter Roland, Speckled Red and Buddy Moss, Lucille Bogan and Merline Johnson are just a few. Tough, laconic, bawdy and as obscene as the record companies would permit, these singers had in all probability no special regard for the Church and its members. But if this was so they still remained uncommitted in their view on record.

Perhaps an unofficial but effective censorship on the part of the record companies ensured that no direct expressions of criticism, no outrageous blasphemies likely to alienate the purchasing public or the churches themselves, were put on disc. Undoubtedly the companies had good reason in the 'twenties and 'thirties not to alienate the churches, for the sale of religious records was considerable. As Dan Mahony has shown, the sales of records by Reverend J. C. Burnett in 1926 exceeded 50,000 copies on more than one occasion and, in the single instance of *The Downfall of Nebuchadnezzar*, attained well over

80,000 sales at a time when Columbia's best-selling blues singer, Bessie Smith, was averaging around 20,000 copies of each issue.[67] But the figures also reveal that the blues and vaudeville issues exceeded the religious ones by a ratio of nearly four to one. Though the sensibilities and the purchasing power of religious bodies may have had some influence on the attitude of blues singers to the Church expressed on record, it seems unlikely that this was a major factor. The strength of the Church may well have been a more subtle influence, exerting itself on the blues singers even when, ostensibly, they had rejected it. In the Negro communities, not only of the South but in the concentrated Negro areas of the Northern cities too, the church provided the social leaders and the centre, often, of community life. It had to make many adjustments in the period of Northern migration but, by and large, the Negro populace still looked to the Church for leadership in the 'thirties and blues singers may still have shared this respect for the Church leaders even if they did not always share their teachings. In the post-war years the Church found itself losing its hold over the Negro populace, a decline in power which Gunnar Myrdal's team noted and forecast. Wrote Arnold Rose, 'As a class Negro preachers are losing influence, because they are not changing as fast as the rest of the Negro community. Young people have begun to look down on the old-fashioned Negro preacher.' He continued, 'The Negro church has been lagging ideologically too. While for a long time the protest has been rising in the Negro community, the church has, on the whole, remained conservative and accommodating. Its otherworldly outlook is itself an expression of political fatalism.'[68]

Painfully, this has also been true of the blues singers of the older generations who have likewise been conservative, accommodating and if worldly, still politically fatalistic. Current conceptions to the contrary, the blues has played little part as a vehicle of protest; fatalism has been more in its character. If the Church has lost its power, if it had largely failed for too long as an instrument of protest, the blues singer did not challenge its authority or its effectiveness. Equally conservative he fell back on banalities about the Church and its preachers and when Texas Alexander in 1934 made his *Justice Blues*, ironically he made one more contribution from which the other singers might draw. Nearly twenty years after, Wright Holmes, in a curiously titled *Alley Blues*, as un-related a title as Alexander's own, adapted his words in a confused version with borrowings from other Alexander records:

You know my mama she tol' me, eeh now mama, before the high
    water rise,
You-all know I ain't no Christian, 'cause I once have been baptized,
You know I went to the church this mornin', yes and they called
    on me to pray,
Well I fell down on my knees, on my knees, gee I forgot just what
    to say.

You know I cried, 'Lord My Father, My Jesus,'
(*Spoken*) I didn't know what I was doin'.
'That would be to Kingdom come.'
I said, 'If you got any brownskin women in Heaven, would you
    please to send Wright Holmes one,
You know I ain't never been to Heaven, but this black man have
    been told,
You know they tell me they got women up there, women up there,
Gee, with their mouths all lined with gold.'

I bet'cha I get my cream from a cream, I bet'cha I get my milk
    from a Jersey cow—all right,
I tell you I got my meat from a pig, I bet'cha you get you'rn from
    a no-good sow,
(*Spoken*) Tell the truth now darlin'.
'Cause the women I'm lovin', she's a holy woman, and she beats
    that tambourine,
Every time you let them sisters go to lovin' each other,
Ooh well boys she's the only one that will talk to me.

Now some of these days I'm gonna have me a Heaven of my own,
(*Spoken*) Lord, don't you hear, keep on appealin' to ya',
Lord, some of these days I'm gonna have me a Heaven of my own,
Have a gang of brownskin women, yeah, gonna have gals all around
    my throne.[69]

Rough and strong, with many asides and with a faultily played guitar,
Wright Holmes's blues was a mixture of traditional lines and attitudes
and occasional original images. But it was almost the swan-song of the
traditional blues singer's comments on religion in this form. The post-
war years have seen a dramatic change in the role of the Negro Church.

To a marked extent it had lost its power of leadership except for the example set by such singular figures as Reverend Adam Clayton Powell or Dr Martin Luther King. The policy of moderation advanced by Dr King and the Southern Christian Leadership Conference won support in the impending storm but the gathering clouds were darkened by the angry militants of the Black Muslim movement. On all this the blues singer made no comment: there were no blues except white folknik ones to enrich the Freedom songs, no blues to fan the flames of dissent in the Black Muslim meetings. Nor, with a few sparsely scattered exceptions, were there any more blues reiterating the old, good-natured fictions about Deacon Jones which had obscured a deep-seated regard for the Church.

As the gospel groups retreated into ever more frantic expressions of passionate singing, marked with screaming crescendoes and wild, clothes-tearing dancing, the popular and blues singers who had kept the musical forms carefully apart no longer seemed to feel the need for this implied respect. Spearheaded by singers like Little Richard Penniman, Ray Charles or B. B. King who had all at one time or another been gospel and blues singers both, the musical forms which had been held at a distance for so long were allowed to merge. The younger singers like Sam Cooke or Solomon Burke turned from gospel singing to the blues as had their predecessors—but with the difference that they took the gospel technique with them. Even the words were often secularized gospel songs and the screaming delivery, the exploitation of emotional involvement, the frenetic displays of dancing singers, the hysterical singing and frenzied, crowd-whipping declamations that had marked the performances of the young gospel groups were borrowed without qualm by the younger blues singers. The Church, it seems, had lost the mute acknowledgement of respect that lay behind the blues singers' years of reticence in comment and restraint from blasphemy, whether it arose from genuine religious feeling or mere superstition. Whatever the deterrent it no longer applied in the music; the two were no longer separate, and if the new blues singers made no reference to the Church even in conventional, traditional terms they made their disregard manifest in their deliberate borrowings from the gospel idioms.

Today, only a 'rediscovered' and a resuscitated Son House sings *Preachin' the Blues* and even he has totally forgotten the words of the blues that he once sang. *Preachin' the Blues* as a title has no meaning now when blues and religious song have so narrowed the gap that divided the forms, meeting to influence together a vast corpus of popular song. But *Preachin' the Blues*, as a title and as a theme, probably never did have any real significance. For all gospel song attempts to preach the Gospel, and all blues succeeds in preaching a gospel of blues. 'It must never be forgotten that the Negro church is fundamentally an expression of the Negro community itself,' wrote Arnold Rose.[70] His words are no less true of the blues, which in all its phases and forms and in the attitudes it takes both to its own society and society as a whole, has every bit as important a message to preach.

3 THE FORTY-FOURS

It is one of the strengths, but also one of the weaknesses of the blues that it offers to the singer or the instrumentalist of very little accomplishment a means whereby he can give some expression to his ideas. Many blues guitarists never learn to form a chord—John Lee Hooker is one who has achieved wide fame in the blues without even this degree of musical knowledge. Often it is better so; unorthodox fingering and the trial-and-error process of finding his way along the fingerboard of his guitar has given to many a blues musician a sound quality which is his own. Familiarity with the tradition itself and the sense of what sounds 'right' often guides him to the notes within the simple harmonic structure of the blues, and it is this simplicity which makes such an empirical method possible. Similarly, the habit of repeating lines has enabled singers to invent rhymes and to compose blues spontaneously and, when invention flags, a stockpile of traditional phrases, images and lines lingers in the mind to be drawn upon in order to complete a verse. With a commonplace blues tune for the melody line, a simply repeated instrumental phrase and the shadowy memory of oft-heard verses in his mind, the singer who daydreams about leaving his women can summon a logical story line with little effort:

I'm goin' away sweet mama, and your cryin' won't make me stay, (2)
'Cause the more you cry, the further you'll drive me away.

Says I'm goin' away baby and I won't be back till fall, (2)
And if the blues overtake me, I won't be back at all.

I'm goin' away baby, to wear you off my mind, (2)
'Cause you keep me bothered, worried all the time.

One of these mornings baby, an' it won't be long, (2)
I'm gonna catch the first thing smokin' and down the road I'm
  goin'.

These words come from no special blues, but from a hundred, or a thousand. They are typical of the vast reservoir of blues resources and have been tapped by innumerable minor singers and major singers alike. For the minor singer with small creative talent they are an indispensable substitute for original thought; for the more inventive bluesman they are sometimes too easy a solution for the verse problems posed by his own song. Blues singers like Blind Willie McTell or Furry Lewis, Walter Davis or Bumble Bee Slim, Ida Cox or Merline Johnson, Johnny Shines or Little Walter, who have proved by their other work their talents for composing blues on new themes with novel images, all use the ready-made verses and lines in some of their blues. But in these instances the measure of their abilities is to be found in the ways in which old and familiar lines may be re-employed in their compositions to take on new meaning.

Often the words appeal by the vividness of the images they evoke or the neatness of the phrasing in summing up a number of associated ideas in a single iambic pentameter. When the singer says that his women comes with 'a handful of gimme, a mouthful of much obliged' he conveys at once a picture of greed as succinct as any in the blues. 'I looked at my pillow where my baby used to lay'; 'when I leave your town you can pin *crêpe* on your door'; 'I asked her for water, and she gave me gasoline'; 'stay with me baby and I will turn your money green'; 'I got a big fat mama, with the meat shakin' on her bones'; 'thirty days in jail with my back turned to the wall'; 'Death Valley is half-way to my home'; 'Baby you may never see my smilin' face again'; 'I'm goin' to write a letter, mail it in the air'; 'so cold in China, the birds can't hardly sing'—these and scores of other lines appear in numerous blues. They focus attention with their novelty, with the dramatic situation expressed in a sentence, or sometimes by their very obscurity.

Though little attempt has been made to study the genealogy of blues verses, it seems likely that many of them stem from other song sources which pre-date the blues. Ben Harney's *You've Been a Good Old Wagon, but You've Done Broke Down* has its echoes in a number of blues lines and dates from 1896. The many blues on the telephone theme probably stem from Charles Harris's *Hello, Central, Give Me Heaven* which, though sentimental in the extreme, initiated a number of other songs on the *Hello, Central* theme in the early years of this century. Pieces of homespun philosophy or unabashed moralizing have a way of surviving in the blues where the familiar phrases crop up with small but significant changes of emphasis: one such is *You Never Miss the Water till the Well Runs Dry* which was copyrighted as a song as early as 1874. But if the meaning is modified and the moral diminished, the sense still remains intact in these instances of the influence of popular song on blues lyrics. Sometimes, in the process of using traditional material, the singer may sacrifice some degree of sense. 'My home ain't here, it's way out in the West; yes, in the Smoky Mountains where the eagle builds his nest,' sings Jack Dupree and many another singer who presumably had the Rocky Mountains in mind. 'Back to the land of California, sweet home Chicago' was the confusing geography which Robert Johnson ascribed to the traditional *Sweet Home Chicago* version of *Kokomo Blues*.

Clearly it is the music of the phrase rather than the meaning which frequently attracts. The obscure line 'smokes like lightning, shines like gold' could well evoke the image of a thunderbolt. It seems to have been a favourite line of Tommy Johnson's and is often associated with his *Big Road Blues* though it does not occur in his recording of the blues. Some singers would have learned it at first hand from Johnson, while others would have acquired it from later recordings of this extremely influential blues. In the process of transference, shifts of image take place. Kokomo Arnold employs the hearse theme of *Big Road Blues* in *Stop, Look and Listen* singing, 'Well it smokes like lightnin', bare wood shines like gold.' It is still uncertain what 'smokes' in his version. Lightnin' Hopkins, in his *Cooling Board*, gives the theme a more logical framework by evoking a dramatic image of a lightning flash illuminating the coffin. 'That night it thundered, thundered and lightnin', velvet shines like gold' was his interpretation. Howling Wolf typically sang his version with great intensity and almost complete obliteration of the sense. But it must be admitted that his 'smokestack lightnin', shinin' just like gold' is a striking phrase which could be applied to a train. Howling Wolf is reported to have been taught by Charley Patton and it may have been a line from Patton's *Moon Going Down*, ' 'cause the smoke stack's black an' the bell it shine like—bell it shine like—bell it shine like gold', which he had imperfectly learned. Sung to the same tune as *Big Road Blues*, Patton's *Moon Going Down* may have been Johnson's inspiration or they may have both stemmed from an earlier source.

These versions on a Tommy Johnson blues emphasize another aspect of the blues tradition. As blues depends for much of its effect on the individuality of the singers, the outstanding personalities from Blind Lemon Jefferson to B. B. King have registered by their singular techniques. Often they are remembered particularly by a certain vocal or instrumental trademark: Joe Pullum's high-pitched 'black gal, black gal, what makes your nappy head so hard?' for example, or the falsetto, deliberate and mannered, which Tommy Johnson used when he sang

Big Road Blues, *Cool Drink of Water Blues* or a variant. Even Lightnin' Hopkins sang *Cooling Board* quoted above with something of Johnson's inflexion, though his personal style is marked.

In such instances the tradition is directly traceable to a single singer whose personal inventiveness and song treatment has shaped the song for the future. But this is not necessarily the end of the trail; in some instances the singer with whom the song is associated is himself the originator; in others he has been the skilful organizer of material that is already traditional. Leroy Carr, for example, is associated with the blues *How Long, How Long* although earlier versions of it are known by Ida Cox and Papa Charlie Jackson. Carr gave it a special quality which 'fixed' the blues in his style of singing and playing. Big Maceo similarly is recalled best for his *Worried Life Blues* which has been copied by innumerable singers including a note-for-note imitation by Ray Charles. But the song derives from Sleepy John Estes's *Someday Baby* and has probably a much longer history. *Trouble in Mind*, composed by Richard M. Jones but associated with Bertha Chippie Hill; *Key to the Highway*, probably composed by Big Bill Broonzy though linked with Jazz Gillum; Bukka White's *Shake 'Em on Down*; Jimmy Rodgers's *That's All Right*; Ray Charles's *Do What I Say* or Jimmy Witherspoon's *Ain't Nobody's Bizness If I Do* are blues which have become traditionally associated with these artists and generally performed in their styles though they are often older—the last-named was current before 'Spoon was born.

It is noticeable that the majority of these blues have distinctive tunes, either as instrumental or vocal lines, or both. Interestingly, although the form is far less common than the familiar twelve-bar, three-line structure of the majority of blues, the eight-bar, two-line themes predominate among the more memorable themes. Some of these identifiable blues tunes have been applied to other words, serving as the basis of several blues. *Baby, Please Don't Go*, generally associated with the singer Big Joe Williams when in this form, is also the basis of a much older Southern rural song, *Another Man Done Gone*, and appears again as *I'm Gonna Walk Your Log*. Again, *Kokomo Blues*, as *Original Kokomo Blues* linked with Kokomo Arnold, is known in a great many variants: *Sweet Home Chicago*, *Pokino Blues*, *Eleven Light City* and *Red Cross Store* among them. The latter song arises from a slight melodic shift leading to another chain of songs within the blues idiom. These are some of the facets of the workings of traditional repertoires of words and verses, themes and tunes in the blues; in some cases a number of them are to be found together. Such is the case with *The Forty-Fours*, a blues tradition in which the patterns of continuity in the idiom can be seen.

'I come on up to Tallulah, Louisiana, and then the 1922 high water ran up the side of Louisiana and then I came over—I come over to Vicksburg. That's where I started playing—at 1014 Washington Street for Zack Lewis,' explained Little Brother Montgomery when I asked him how he first came to play the theme of *The Forty-Fours* or, as he called it, the *Vicksburg Blues*. 'That's where I met Ernest Johnson, he was three years older than me and he was playing at Addie's Place on Mulberry Street. Well I played there and that's where we originated these numbers like *Vicksburg Blues*, *44 Blues* and things like that.'[1]

Eurreal Montgomery did not claim exclusive credit for composing the theme. Among the people that he mentioned who played the tune in its formative period were Johnny Eager, or Yega; Nub-Handed Son Crooks, or Cooks; 'a man they called Friday' who was apparently a different pianist from Friday Ford who worked in the Belzoni-Jackson area; Ernest Johnson and his cousin, Big Brother Robert Johnson. In a letter to Karl Gert zur Heide, Little Brother Montgomery revealed that Ernest Johnson's cousin was not the famous young Mississippi guitarist, Robert Johnson: 'Now Robert Johnson—Big Brother—played violin and piano. He died in 1925, he fell dead at the railroad station in Jackson, Miss., the Illinois station. His home was Canton, Miss. Ernest Johnson was his first cousin. His home was Durant, Miss. Robert was older than me and Ernest.'

On the tune which these men developed Little Brother Montgomery commented, 'It's a blues, it's a barrelhouse, honky-tonk blues. People danced by that, did the shimmy by that. It's a thing we just steady made up; you could keep addin' to it.' From this it appears that originally *The Forty-Fours* was a piano piece for dancing. The shimmy dances, though depending on undulating movements of the body which shook the heavily fringed shift dresses of the period, were not necessarily fast. The sensuous 'snake-hip' movements of the shimmy or the shuffle of the 'slow drag' would have been effective at the medium tempo of the tune.

If *The Forty-Fours* began as a dance tune it probably had no words initially, and this is supported by Roosevelt Sykes's assertion that there were no lyrics to the tune when he first heard it. But when he recorded his '*44*' *Blues* and Little Brother Montgomery made his *Vicksburg Blues* both had definite, though very different, vocals. Seven years passed between Montgomery's first meeting with Ernest Johnson and Roosevelt Sykes's recording of the tune and it seems unlikely that no words had been given to the blues in that period. But for how long words were associated with the tune must remain conjectural. It is interesting that while Sykes's vocal is on a different tune from the piano theme, Little Brother Montgomery's vocal line is closely related to the melody of the piano theme itself. It is possible therefore, that the piano tune was modelled on a pre-existing vocal tune which survives in *Vicksburg* and that Sykes had not known of the vocal but learned the mature piano version. But it could also have been the natural outcome of trying to fit words to a piano theme already invented and this seems likely, for the piano theme was apparently the extension of a few basic figures.

'These are the first *Vicksburg Blues* I made,' observed Montgomery, recreating the blues he had first recorded thirty years before. As he began, the piano introduction outlined the vocal melody (Example 1):

I got those Vicksburg blues and I sing 'em anywhere I go, (2)
And the reason why I sing 'em, my babe says she didn't want me
   no more.

I got the Vicksburg blues an' I'll sing 'em anywhere I please, (2)
Now the reason why I sing 'em, to give my po' heart some ease.

Now I ain't gonna be your lowdown dog no more.

I don't like this ol' place mama, Lord an' I never will, (2)
'Cause I can sit right here lookin' at Vicksburg on the hill.[2] ©

Instantly recognizable for the sombre, ominous character of its basic tune, *Vicksburg Blues* is marked by its grumbling bass figure which rises like a trombone slide against which the rapid repetition of treble notes in the right hand is placed in contrast. Montgomery's high, taut vocal with its pronounced vibrato and almost whinnying intonation sounds plaintive, even bitter, and the whole of this archetypal performance combines to make one of the most unforgettable of all blues themes. Though the piano tune of *The Forty-Fours*—or *Vicksburg Blues*—is the unifying theme that holds all variants together, it is Little Brother's vocal line which holds the attention first. Even so, it is not easy to

EXAMPLE I

separate it from that of the piano for in this composition the two are complementary. In the vocal line the tune stresses the tonic and dominant notes—in the key of F therefore, F and C. The characteristics by which the tune is most noticeably identifiable are the clear phrases with which it is constructed. The first phrase rises from a dominant C to a long, held note on the tonic F. This held note is on the word 'I' in the first verse:

I got the Vicksburg blues and *I.* . . .

The second phase of the same line commences on a flattened seventh —E♭, which is very characteristic of the tune in all its variants and, answering the first phrase, falls. This might be expressed:

sing 'em-m an-y—— where I go————

EXAMPLE 2

The first two phrases are repeated for the second line of the blues and the third line moves into the final fifth and sixth phrases. The fifth rises as before, but this time from the tonic F to the dominant C which becomes the held note, the final phrase answering, and falling back to the tonic F.

And the reason why *I* . . . sing 'em, my babe says she didn't want me no more.

This is the basic structure of the vocal line which was to be much copied by other singers. The characteristic shape of the bass climbing figure is as follows:

EXAMPLE 3

97

Though especially associated with this tune it was a logical figure, for the most powerful notes are played by the thumb and forefinger, the strongest fingers, of the left hand. As the grace notes lay naturally under the rest of the fingers a lift was imparted to the main note in the playing of the phrase. This bass pattern is combined with the right hand to give a characteristic shape to *The Forty-Fours*. Really a vamping figure, it maintains the beat without appearing to change the harmony, for the bass note (F) is common to the two chords played in the right hand. The first beat of the figure is not played by the right hand and gets greater accentuation by being played alone.

EXAMPLE 4

The repeated quavers in the right hand, familiar in the accompaniment, are played to maintain a regular beat when the long notes are sustained in the vocal line, preventing the arrest of the steady rhythm of the piece.

EXAMPLE 5

These quavers develop into triplets, three notes being played instead of two in the subsequent figure. This figure and that which follows, Example 7, form the elements of the fill-in which is played solo before the next verse is sung.

EXAMPLE 6

In Little Brother Montgomery's recordings the fill-in figure resolves in a final descending sequence, but this is subject to many distinct changes in the variations of the tune played by other blues musicians.

EXAMPLE 7

In the whole piece the relationship of the instrumental to the vocal line is fundamental, imparting the unity and character which makes it one of the most satisfying of blues. It will be noted that the quavers in Example 5 are used to accompany a held note in the vocal, while snatches of the vocal tune are elsewhere being played as they are being sung. In later versions, the instrumental and vocal themes sometimes exchanged, a harmonica player, for instance, playing a close copy of the melody that he had been singing earlier. In Montgomery's performance the fill-in figures that he uses (Examples 6 and 7) are based on the significant notes of the vocal line—F and E♭. From the musical point of view this is important for it means that the elements in the entire composition whether instrumental, interludes between verses, instrumental fill-ins between the lines of the vocal or the vocal melody itself, all spring from two notes which are characteristic of the blues genre. The whole composition is an organic structure developing from the basic sound relationship of these notes, which is quintessential to blues. By the standards of western harmonic principles, the sequence F–E♭ in the key of F would only be used when modulating to another key. Here, in the blues, it is fundamental to the character of the music.

As for the words in Little Brother Montgomery's *Vicksburg Blues*, they are essentially his own, telling a simple story which projects effectively, even poignantly in his first recording when, as a twenty-four year old, he eventually arrived in Chicago after a decade or more of playing in the saw-mill barrelhouses. Perhaps the maverick line:

Now I ain't gonna be your lowdown dog no more,

—which is a one-line verse sung on the last four bars of the instrumental —may refer to an earlier model. It is one which seems to have remained in the recollections of a number of singers who derived their versions from him.

Of the pianists who were working with Montgomery in Vicksburg only Ernest Johnson ever recorded. 'We nicknamed him Ernest Forty-Four or we used to call him Forty-Four Kid, and we called him Flunkey too. He always wanted to work on the railroad; fact he did later on up,' recalled Little Brother.[3] It is possible that Robert Johnson was the pianist who originated *The Forty-Fours* but that it was his younger brother, Ernest Johnson, who was born in 1903 and was three years older than Montgomery, who was the man who developed it. That he was known by the title, Ernest 44, was presumably in acknowledgement of his skill at playing the theme, but it could also be in recognition of his ambitions. Train Number 44 was running on the Illinois Central line whose old Yazoo and Mississippi Valley track from Memphis and Clarksdale ran by the levee at Vicksburg south to Louisiana. In common with many blues the instrumental may have been named after the train although, unlike so many others, it does not imitate the train rhythms to any marked degree. It was as 'Ernest 44' that Ernest Johnson recorded on his only known session in October 1936 as accompanist to the singer, Tommy Griffin. The two-day session on Thursday and Friday, 15 and 16 October 1936, witnessed a remarkable series of recordings by a number of Louisiana and Mississippi singers. In all, some sixty-four titles were cut by Lonnie and Sam Chatman, Bo Carter, Eugene Powell (as Sonny Boy Nelson), his wife Matilda Powell under the name of Mississippi Matilda, Walter Vincson, Little Brother Montgomery and Tommy Griffin. Of the titles only three were unissued, and these it would appear were censored rather than below standard. In his set Little Brother recorded eighteen titles in succession, all of which were issued, a feat without parallel in blues recording to that date. One of them was *Vicksburg Blues—Part 3*. Montgomery took the chair vacated by Ernest 44 at the conclusion of his accompaniments to Tommy Griffin earlier in the long day at New Orleans's St Charles Hotel.

It is possible that Ernest Johnson used *The Forty-Fours* theme in some accompaniment to Griffin but I have been unable to hear all of his recordings. On *Little Tommy Blues*, a very slow number, he played a fairly long solo with many tremolos and later, deep, forward-thrusting phrases which are reminiscent of *The Forty-Fours*. Walter Vincson, the guitarist, accompanied Griffin also and appears to dominate on *Dream Book Blues*, though at the conclusion Johnson played long, crushing phrases. On *Dying Sinner Blues*, a somewhat similar blues, he makes more use of the hammered single notes which correspond to the quavers in Montgomery's *Vicksburg*. This device appears to be the Mississippi blues pianists' equivalent to the ringing treble E on the twelfth fret much favoured by Mississippi guitarists. The result was impressive when Vincson played against them deep, descending riffs and clearly Johnson played well in the company of guitarists. There is more than an echo of the Leroy Carr and Scrapper Blackwell team of piano and guitar which so influenced bluesmen in the mid-'thirties, and Johnson had a mellow, fluent style which linked that of Montgomery's with that of Carr's. Fourteen years had passed since Little Brother had first met Johnson at the Mulberry Street juke and undoubtedly his playing had matured and refined. Though the titles do not suggest it there may be a *Forty-Fours* accompaniment among the other Griffin titles; if not, there exists no evidence of how Johnson earned his name.

Ernest Johnson was not the only pianist to have earned himself the nickname '44'. A Mississippi pianist, Charley Taylor, who recorded with the Jackson singers, Ishman Bracey and Tommy Johnson, was known as '44 Charley'.[4] It is reasonable to assume that this was in acknowledgement of his ability to play the theme; it might even hint that he was an innovator of it. Taylor's records are exceptionally rare and his sides with Tommy Johnson, though listed, remain untraced. A coupling, *Heavy Suitcase Blues* and *Louisiana Bound* made for Paramount about March 1930, featured him as soloist. His low, sad voice was accompanied by strong piano playing which, while it did not employ *The Forty-Fours* theme, was clearly closely associated with it. The bass figures growl and climb, the treble notes are hammered throughout the record with alternating runs. It is not *The Forty-Fours*, but listening to the accompaniment to *Louisiana Bound* is like hearing a pianist who is exploring the piano, feeling his way to the creation of the theme. It is an impressive performance, less polished and formalized than recordings of *The Forty-Four Blues* and *Vicksburg Blues*, more wild and in many ways more exciting. The vocal line does not recall that of either theme and the words show little relation. One verse in *Louisiana Bound* alone anticipates, however, Muddy Waters's *Louisiana Blues* of a score of years later:

I'm going down in Louisiana, baby behind the sun, (2)
And when I get back pretty mama, my work will be done.[5]

Both the manner of his singing and the tune that 44 Charley used were similar to those used by Lee Green. On this evidence a connexion between the pianists seems likely, but little is known of Charley Taylor and no such link can be established at present. He was not one of the pianists mentioned by Little Brother Montgomery as being one of the originators of *The Forty-Fours* and he did not mention him when talking of Lee Green.

'So there was a feller there by the name of Lee Green used to be always hanging' around us tryin' to get in on it,' said Little Brother. 'He was pressin' clothes—he was a clothes presser in Vicksburg. So then I met him again at Sondheimer, Louisiana, and I taught him to play the *44 Blues* then, and later years he taught them to Roosevelt so they beat me to Chicago and put them out.'[6] Lee Green, known as 'Pork Chops' had a reputation as a tough man, in recognition of which he was also called Turpentine Joe. Roosevelt Sykes, who learned the tune from Green, considered him 'a mighty fine feller, he was a stylist, he had his own style and wrote his own tunes, like he was a great pianist'.[7] In common with a number of other Lower Mississippi and Louisiana pianists and singers, Montgomery and Griffin included, Lee Green had a sad, strained voice and strongly emphasized vibrato. But his singing was a little deeper and a little rougher than his fellows on a number of his records. In 1929 he recorded for Vocalion his *Number Forty-Four Blues* which clearly indicated the train connexions of *The Forty-Fours* theme:

Ah I heard my baby cryin' and I heard the 44 whistle when she
    blow, (2)
And I feel mistreated, and your sweet mama is bound to go.

Oh baby when you get loaded and think that you want to go, (2)
You know you ain't no better mama, than the black woman I had
    before.

Some of these mornin's babe and it won't be long, (2)
You gonna look for your daddy, baby and I'm goin' to be gone.

My blues will last me nine months from today,
Baby I got blues, will last me nine months from today,
I'm goin' to get my sweet woman to drive my blues away.[8]

Number Forty-Four Blues shows Green's indebtedness to Montgomery though he used a more melodic bass. Example 4 became quavers instead of crotchets and he used a fill-in form with sixths in quavers. This fill-in figure he appeared to have passed on to Roosevelt Sykes. In its basic form it was as follows:

EXAMPLE 8

The following year, 1930, Lee Green recorded the theme again as *Train Number 44* in similar form but, by 1934 when he made his *44 Blues*, it had undergone some subtle alterations and the vocal had changed. As he sketched in the introduction to the theme he spoke a terse, almost disinterested prologue:

Mmm . . . mm, just as I thought . . . that ole woman o' mine caught that number 44 train this mornin'. Well, all I can say— damn her, and let her go. . . . Ah, she knows she no better than the dame I had befo'. . . .

That lowdown train, train number 44, (2)
Carried away my rider, left me standin' in my back-door.

You talk about trouble, I've had 'em so long, so long,
Bad luck and trouble, I've had 'em so long, so long,
Every time I get a good woman, look like I've somethin' wrong in
   my happy home.

I'm goin' to tell the engineerman, bring my baby right back to
   my door,
Goin' tell the ole engineerman, bring my sweet woman back to my
   door,
If he don't want no trouble—I mean my doggone 44.[9]

In the earlier version he had played a gentle solo, with climbing bass figures, softly hammered notes and many crushed adjacent notes in a slow and pensive blues. His later *44 Blues* was more aggressive and much faster in tempo. The greater speed and the insistent chime-like treble notes set against the rhythm patterns of Examples 4 and 8 combined to give an impressionistic picture of the train. Although nearly all versions of *The Forty-Fours* make some reference to a train, and a number are specifically concerned with one, only Lee Green's *44 Blues* deliberately exploits the train rhythm effects much loved in other piano blues and especially in boogie-woogie. Here Green used thirds as a train rhythm deliberately but it is curious that the obvious relationship between the instrumental and the subject did not occur to more musicians. His vocal had a rise and fall shape similar to that of Little Brother's though he did not employ the E♭ that marked Montgomery's vocal line. In this, too, he had departed from his earlier recording which showed greater affinity to Roosevelt Sykes in the vocal, though the textual reference to the ·44 as a weapon in the 1934 item obviously revealed acquaintance with the Sykes version.

Roosevelt Sykes, whose territory in the late 'twenties was a little farther to the north in Helena, West Helena, Arkansas and up the river, eventually met Lee Green. 'He was the first guy I ever heard play the *"44" Blues*. Several people had been playing it through the country of course—Little Brother Montgomery and several others but nobody had ever recorded it and there was no words to it, no words or lyrics at all. So Lee Green, he took a lot of time out to teach me how to play it, to use my left hand on tenth bass. In music it takes a pretty good stretch to stretch ten keys with your one left hand. But my hands were kind of small. Well I could skip and jump 'em but he showed me how it was done.'[10] It is possible that Green taught him other blues too; at all events four months to the day after Roosevelt Sykes had recorded the coupling *All My Money Gone Blues* and *The Way I feel Blues* at the first session which produced *'44' Blues*, Lee Green followed up with his own recordings of the same two numbers. It is possible that they had already been pressed and issued and that Green had heard Sykes's record but it is more likely that they were both recording an identical repertoire.

'44' Blues was Roosevelt Sykes's first recording and it was to be far more influential than was Green's version. Instrumentally it was clearly the same tune as Little Brother Montgomery's with certain dissimilarities and modifications. The introduction used quavers in the right hand similar to Montgomery's Example 4 and Example 5 but a somewhat different bass figure:

EXAMPLE 9

This figure was in effect Montgomery's Example 3 with diminished time values which made it closer to the more common traditional blues bass patterns. It still retained, however, the 'climb' up to the note which the 'traditional', but probably 'later' bass figures in the blues did not. Rejecting the preliminary, introductory outline of the tune that Montgomery used, Sykes made a new figure of the right-hand fill-in phrases (Examples 6 and 7 above) to become the new figure already seen in Lee Green's version (Example 8 above), played in quavers. The accompaniment to the vocal played around the vocal line with lightly executed arpeggios. It was in the vocal line itself that Sykes's version was markedly different to Little Brother's *Vicksburg Blues*, having none of the latter's rising and falling pattern but instead a succession of falling phrases:

EXAMPLE 10

Lord I walked all night long with my 44 in my hand, (2)
I was lookin' for my woman and I found her with another man.

I wore my 44 so long, Lord it made my shoulders sore, (2)
After I do what I wanta, ain't gonna wear my 44 no more.[11]

'I wrote the words myself, it was my own words, so this is how I done it. This is the way they played the blues in nineteen and twenty-six and twenty-nine,' explained Sykes. His 1929 recording had other verses, however, which played on the differing interpretations of the phrase 'forty-fours'—the train number 44, the ·44 calibre revolver and the 'little cabin' on which was the number 44, presumably a prison cell. Undoubtedly these overlays of meaning greatly appealed to other singers, accounting for the frequent use of Sykes's lyrics. In army and sometimes Negro parlance the term 'forty-fours' also referred to beans, or less frequently to black-eyed peas because of their similarity to bullets. And it is also possible that the term 'forty-four' was in some way connected with that of the 'eighty-eight', or the piano, implying perhaps an ability to play the instrument at least with competence. This, at any rate, might be the implication of the name of the pianist, Forty-Five, according to Big Bill Broonzy, who explained that he 'could go one better than Forty-Four'.

Though the implications of the words in Sykes's version gave it considerable appeal, the tune was less original. It had a similar traditional three-line, twelve-bar structure and the lines were clearly divided in their phrases. The first phrase in the first and second lines fell from the dominant C to the tonic F without the long, held note that imparted special character to Montgomery's tune, while the second phrase of these lines similarly fell from the dominant C to the tonic F with no flattened seventh. The final line was again divided in two phrases, the first staying on dominant C with one rise to the tonic F in the middle phrase and falling back to the dominant, while the second repeated a dominant-tonic pattern. In this extremely simple tune only two notes are prominent and it did not have the 'answering' quality which the rise and fall of *Vicksburg Blues* imparted to the vocal. Both tunes largely lay within the tonic and dominant with breaks in the middle of the lines but the held notes and flattened seventh of Montgomery's made of it a more distinctive tune.

In order of recording Sykes was the first to cut a version of *The Forty-Fours*, his being made on 14 June 1929 in New York. Lee Green followed just over two months later, about 21 August 1929, in Chicago with *Number Forty-Four Blues*. About seven weeks after, James Boodle-It Wiggins on 12 October 1929 made *Forty-Four Blues* for Paramount at Richmond, Indiana. It was the first time that a vocalist accompanied by a pianist had recorded the tune. His version was essentially the same as that of Roosevelt Sykes's vocal line, using the verses quoted above and including, with only fragmentary word changes, the two closing verses of the original recording:

I hate to hear the 44 whistle blow, (2)
It blows just like it ain't gonna blow no more.

I've got a li'l ole cabin and on it the number's 44, (2)
I wake up every mornin', the wolves is standing in my door.[12]

The close relationship of the words suggests that Wiggins had learned it from Sykes's record and perhaps the pianist, Blind Leroy Garnett, had too. If so, Garnett had introduced a novel feature of his own for, while the piano theme was clearly that of *The Forty-Fours*, the right-hand fill-in phrase used by Roosevelt Sykes and Lee Green (Example 8) has been transferred to the bass, substantially altering its character and making it far more melodic. In Garnett's version the thirds appear as triplets and it is possible that the playing of this Louisiana pianist is indicative of an entirely different line of development of the theme. It is not to be found in any other recordings though and may merely be a case of learning imperfectly from the record, with the shift of the right-hand fill-in in the bass, which he repeats many times, as a curious idiosyncrasy.

In July 1930, under his pseudonym of Willie Kelly, Roosevelt Sykes made a second recording of the theme, made in Cincinnati for Victor as *Kelly's 44 Blues*. It was a shrewd move for it established the idea of attaching another name to variants of his own tune, a competitive precedent which inevitably reflected some credit on the original composition. At this time Montgomery had still not recorded his own archetypal tune, but in September that year his *Vicksburg Blues* was made for the Paramount Company, and though the 13000 series, of which it was the sixth, generally had small circulation by this time, a year after the Wall Street crash his record sold extremely well. Within a matter of weeks it was covered by Lee Green's second version of the theme, *Train Number 44* made in November. Soon after, at the end of February 1931, two otherwise 'unknown' musicians, James Parker, a trumpet player, and Charles O'Neill, a pianist, accompanied singer Mae Glover on her record of *Forty-Four Blues*. It was the first—and one of the few—to be recorded by a woman, and it was probably the only version to be related to the recordings by Lee Green. The verses follow in the same order but the first is clearly expressed as a quotation:

Lord, my baby cried, 'Now mama I heard that 44 when she
   blow, (2)
Lord I feel mistreated, your sweet daddy's bound to go.'

the next verse is addressed, as the third, to her man:

Now baby, when you get loaded, think that you want to go,
Oooh, baby, baby, think that you want to go,
You ain't no better than the sweet man I had before.[13]

And the final verse, commencing 'I got blues, will last me nine months
from today' is sung as a soliloquy. Why has she nine-months' blues?
Presumably because she is pregnant as her man leaves her. The blues
makes no particular impact as sung by Lee Green but has immediate
significance when sung by a woman. It suggests that this is in fact, a
woman's blues and that Mae Glover's was the blues in its original form,
transposed with no special regard for the sense by Green. It is certain
that Green's playing had no influence on Charles O'Neill, whose un-
inspired piano accompaniment was in the manner of Fletcher Henderson or any one of a score of studio blues accompanists of several years
before.

   So the main streams of influence began to flow, sometimes to meet
and sometimes to follow separate channels in the ensuing years: *The
Forty-Fours* piano theme as played by Montgomery, Sykes and Green
with its variations in bass patterns and fill-in phrases; the tune of
'*44' Blues* as sung by Sykes; and the tune of *Vicksburg Blues* as Little
Brother sang it. Lee Green's tributary dried up after Mae Glover's
recording, except for his own, previously noted, variant made in 1934.
By that time Roosevelt Sykes, again as Willie Kelly, had made yet
another version himself—*New 44 Blues*, cut in December 1933, while
the year after Green, Little Brother Montgomery made another
Vicksburg Blues in New Orleans in August 1935. Fourteen months later,
at the memorable two-day session already noted, when Ernest 44 accompanied Tommy Griffin, Montgomery made his *Vicksburg Blues—
Part 3*. The previous day, 15 October 1936, at the same sustained
session, Matilda Powell as Mississippi Matilda, made her *Happy Home
Blues*. It was not related to Mae Glover's recording, nor to Lee Green's,
but was sung to the tune of the *Vicksburg Blues* vocal line. The words
were undistinguished and unrelated:

Now let me tell you women how I have done wrong, (2)
I been in love with one man and left my happy home.

I say some day you gonna miss me, be wonderin' where I've gone,
(2)
But it'll be too late to worry, I'll be back in my happy home.[14]

And so on. Its connexion with Montgomery's vocal tune was direct
and Matilda Powell sustained the held notes—on wo*men* in the first
verse—with the same quavering, trembling voice. But the accompaniment by two guitars—probably Eugene Powell and Willie Harris—
revealed no kinship with *The Forty-Fours* theme.

Here it was the tune of Montgomery's recording that had impressed
itself but Johnny Temple's *New Vicksburg Blues*, made in November
1936, used both tune and words. Though he was a guitarist himself,
Temple seldom played on his recordings and it was Charlie McCoy,
a fellow Mississippian, who frequently played on his records. Temple
was accompanied by the Harlem Hamfats the following year, 1937, in
which band Charlie McCoy and the pianist Horace Malcolm both
played. Malcolm and McCoy are presumed to have been on Temple's
New Vicksburg Blues but an insistent guitar phrase, much used by
Big Bill Broonzy throughout his recordings of the late 'thirties, suggests
a different personnel. Neither the guitar nor the piano are related to the
Vicksburg piano line, the pianist playing a dotted, slow boogie bass.
Temple is the only notable performer on the recording. He did not
attempt the high-pitched, almost falsetto singing used by Little
Brother but instead sang in his naturally deep voice with rich timbre
and easy delivery. Just once, at the end of the second line of the pen-
ultimate verse he permitted his voice to drop farther, exploiting his
considerable range. Though he sang the words of Montgomery's
original he completed the one-line verse and added a concluding one
which was perhaps already associated with the song:

Cryin' mama, 'I ain't gonna be your lowdown dog no more, (2)
And I been your dog, baby since I entered your door.'

I don't like this ole place baby, and I never will, (2)
I can stand here and see Vicksburg on the hill.

Vicksburg on a high hill, Louisiana just below, (2)
If you take me back baby, I won't be bad no more.[15]

Big Bill Broonzy, whose guitar accompaniment on Jazz Gillum's
Tell Me Mama made six years later was essentially the same as the
guitar on Temple's recording, does not appear to have used *The Forty-
Fours* theme though he was generally alive to the popular blues vehicles.
He plays guitar in desultory fashion on Jazz Gillum's *5 Feet 4*, which
bears no similiarity to his own recordings under the same title. Jazz
Gillum's song was credited to Broonzy but it would appear to be
Sykes's influence that shaped the tune. Roosevelt Sykes plays the
familiar *Forty-Four Blues* piano theme in the accompaniment but
Gillum unexpectedly sings the blues to the tune of *Vicksburg*, sustaining
the held notes on certain syllables:

Now it was early this mor*nin*', just about the dawn of day, (2)
I was sayin' *bye*-bye baby, I've got to be on my way.

Everybody will be hap*py* when *I* reach my home, (2)
To see my *smi*lin' face baby, because I been gone so long.[16]

Gillum's record was made in the closing months of the Second World
War, in February 1945. The war had, for various reasons, halted the
recording of blues. Roosevelt Sykes had made a Decca recording of
'*44' Blues* in April 1939 but when he resumed making records after a
three-year break he did not return to the theme even though he revived
others like *Anytime Is the Right Time* on Victor, or *West Helena Blues*
made for Regal. Montgomery's break was longer: after his New Orleans
session in 1936 he did not record again for more than a decade, and then
only four titles made with a quintet. Another seven years were to pass
before he was again to record, when in 1954 he made four tunes for a
collector's label, 'Winding Ball'. One of these was *Vicksburg Blues* but it
was not a record to reach the Negro market—he had to wait still another
four years for this. But about 1958, over a score of years after he had
last made a recording intended for the Negro market, he cut four titles
for the old Paramount recording executive, Mayo Williams, on his
Ebony label.

With this hiatus it is only marginally likely that either Roosevelt
Sykes's early recordings or those of Little Brother Montgomery

directly influenced the later singers who used the theme. As veterans, who had survived the fluctuations of taste and who continued to be popular performing artists after many of their generation had been forgotten, they probably had a stronger personal influence. Both men worked in Chicago and both travelled a good deal. Sykes had often returned to Arkansas and Mississippi and had lived, off and on, for a long period in St Louis; Montgomery had returned for a sustained stay in Jackson, Mississippi, and had made frequent trips back to the North.

There would appear to be a number of precedents on record for Big Maceo Merriweather's recording of *Maceo's 32-20* which he made in July 1945, but an examination of the earlier recordings does not substantiate any connexion between them. The earliest instance was, in fact, made by Roosevelt Sykes under his pseudonym of Willie Kelly at the session of four titles which also produced *Kelly's 44 Blues*. It is a curious record; it sounds unusually listless and lacks the organic unity of the traditional theme. The reason lies in Sykes's deliberate intention to produce a variation rather than two recordings of *The Forty-Fours* at the same session. He plays the right-hand tune in customary fashion but does not support it with the characteristic climbing phrases in the bass, creating a surprisingly poorly resolved musical composition. The words are on the pistol theme but are not directly linked with the '44' Blues, except perhaps in the second verse below:

I got a 32-20, shoots just like a 45, (2)
Lord if I happen to go for my woman, I'm gonna bring her dead
    or 'live.

Lord I carried my 32-20 in my right hand, (2)
Lord I'll shoot my woman for wastin' time with a monkey man.

Lord I shoot steel jackets, no lead balls at all, (2)
Lord if I happen to shoot you, Lord you'll soon see St Peter or
    St Paul.[17] ©

The record may have given Skip James the idea for his *22-20 Blues* made the next year, but his words were very different and his wild, erratic and highly individual piano, which had very considerable appeal of its own, was in no way derived from, or related to *The Forty-Fours*.

Skip James knew Little Brother Montgomery, having met him in Yazoo City and travelled with him to Vicksburg. The backing to Montgomery's original record, *No Special Rider*, is the acknowledged source of Skip James's *Special Rider Blues* and one report has it that Montgomery in turn learned *Vicksburg Blues* from him.[18] But if this were so there is no similarity in either musical theme, or text and *Forty-Four Blues/Vicksburg Blues* must be considered as a separate and original composition. Samuel Charters has given an account of the recording of James's *22-20 Blues*, when at the session 'Laiblee mentioned the popularity of the *Forty-Four Blues* and asked Skip, "Could you make a record comparing to that?" They talked about the calibre of the revolver and Skip decided on something smaller, a 22-20.'[19] His record initiated a succession of 'revolver' blues and it may be noted in passing that only the first figure in 32-20 or 22-20 refers to the calibre of the weapon whereas the second figure refers to the percentage of cordite in the explosive charge, a classification system long obsolete but, perhaps for its alliterative appeal, still popular as a phrase among blues singers:

You talk about your 44-40, that it do very well, (2)
But my 22-20 Lord is a burnin' Hell.

I had a 38 Special but it's most too light, (2)
But my 22-20 makes the caps all right.

If she gets unruly and she don't want to, (2)
I'll take my 22-20 and cut her half in two.

Hey hey, and I can't take my rest, (2)
And my 44 right up and down my vest.[20]

Five years later Robert Johnson used Skip James's words for his own *32-20 Blues*, adding a verse or two of his own and giving the song a swinging guitar accompaniment. Any link with *The Forty-Fours* could have been forged then but Johnson's song was still further removed from it. Even remoter was Arthur Big Boy Crudup's *Give Me a 32-20* made six years before his version of *Vicksburg Blues* and three before *Maceo's 32-20*.[21] Big Maceo's record was far closer to Roosevelt Sykes's original '*44' Blues*—and even Willie Kelly's *32-20 Blues*—than any of these. His vocal tune closely followed Sykes's but he used a dotted accompani-

ment with a powerful forward drive. His immensely strong left hand
played the original bass figures with great force but he used fill-in
phrases (Examples 4 and 8) deriving from both Montgomery and Sykes
and probably gained from them personally. His first verse came from
'*44*' *Blues* but others were original, as when he addressed his guitarist,
Tampa Red:

> She started screamin', 'Murder', and I never raised my hand, (2)
> Tampa, she knew I had them covered 'cause I had the pistol right
>   there in my hand.[22]

Maceo's 32–20 was representative of the piano instrumental variations
on *The Forty-Fours* to be encountered in many examples which
frequently depend on Roosevelt Sykes's original. It was an impressive
performance nevertheless, played with great authority. A similar item,
but one which lacked the essential spark of originality, was made by
Memphis Slim many years later and with little variation on subsequent
occasions. His *44 Blues* in a collection entitled 'The Real Boogie-
Woogie' used Sykes's bass (Example 9). The version consists mainly of
Example 5—of thirds in quavers, of phrases being completed by
Example 8 and the basic right-hand configuration (Example 9).
Although a non-vocal performance, there are a few sketchy indications
of Sykes's vocal theme in the playing but, though most of the elements
of the *Vicksburg/Forty-Fours* complex are present, the whole is
mechanical and lifeless.

Of much greater interest is Arthur Big Boy Crudup's late 'forties
recording of *Crudup's Vicksburg Blues*. His high, taut voice was ideally
suited to Little Brother Montgomery's model. The falsetto, 'calling'
vocal is placed against a simple fill-in figure probably developed from
Example 4—but this is played on the guitar:

EXAMPLE II

His vocal line is almost identical to Montgomery's (Example 5);
quavers on guitar are used to accompany the long, held vocal notes
which change on occasion to triplets. A heavily emphasized beat from

the backing drums gives the song a steady, walking feeling, and the words are reshaped to give a new story line while retaining something of Montgomery's and John Temple's blues:

Baby I ain't gonna be your lowdown dog no more, (2)
Well I been your dog, ever since I used your door.

Vicksburg is on a high hill, mama, Louisiana just below, (2)
Now won't you take me back mama, I won't be bad no more.

Down in old Vicksburg, Mississippi, that's where I long to be, (2)
I got a cool, kind, pretty mama, she's waitin' there for me.

Baby if you don't want me, why don't you tell me so, (2)
Lord and you won't be bothered babe, round your house no more.[23]

An extremely influential, though critically underrated singer, Big Boy Crudup showed the way to guitar and rhythm variants of *The Forty-Fours*. It cannot be said with absolute certainty that guitar versions of the theme were not commonly heard. There is some connexion between Charley Patton's *It Won't Be Long* (which was made in Richmond, Indiana, coincidentally on the very same day that Roosevelt Sykes made his first '*44*' *Blues* in New York) and the vocal line of *Vicksburg Blues*. It has a similar rise and fall pattern but lacks the flattened seventh in the second phrase, has no similarity in the guitar accompaniment to either the piano or to other guitar versions, and the words are dissimilar. The link is sufficiently strong to suggest some connexion but insufficient to give any suggestion of the nature of any influence.

Apart from the known Mississippi derivation of *The Forty-Fours* it is significant that nearly all recorded examples are by singers from 'Memphis on down', and generally from Mississippi. The question arises as to whether rural variants of the themes exist and what relation they may bear to the seminal piano themes.

Frederic Ramsey Jr, in a field-recording trip in the 1950s, visited Natchez, where Thurman Monroe, a saxophone player with a local orchestra, led him to Buckner's Alley and Cat-Iron. Cat-Iron was the name by which a heavily built guitarist, who lived in the bottomlands near the town, was known. He had a coarse-grained voice and sang, among a number of spirituals and blues, *Got a Girl in Ferriday, One in Greenwood Town*. This blues had a vocal line which was clearly related to *Vicksburg Blues*, though the words combined apparently original verses with some that derived distantly from Blind Lemon Jefferson:

Got a girl in Ferriday, one in Greenwood town,
Got a woman in Ferriday, one in Greenwood town,
Got a favourite down Natchez on the hill.

I'm gonna tell you women just how to keep your man at home, (2)
You got to eagle rock him whilst he's saddlin' on.

Said I went to the gipsy, had my fortune told, (2)
You got a tailor-made woman, she ain't no hand-me-down.

I don't want no black woman, fryin' no meat for me, (2)
For she studies evil, she's liable to poison me.[24]

Little Brother Montgomery was in Ferriday in the very early 'twenties and it is likely that the theme was already a popular vocal line at this time and that Cat-Iron picked it up at source.[25] His guitar accompaniment, a rhythmic strum, bore no relation, however, to any of the standardized accompaniments associated with any of the variants of the piece. On another occasion, Frederic Ramsey encountered a fisherman and guide, Scott Dunbar, in an extremely rural backwater of Mississippi at Old River Lake, Wilkinson County, not far from Angola Penitentiary with 'Louisiana just below'. His wife, Celeste, and his daughter, Rosa, joined him in a highly rhythmic *Vicksburg and Natchez Blues* with, presumably, Celeste singing the main verse and Rosa joining in with unison humming. The words, though broken, and at times indecipherable, closely followed the *Vicksburg* vocal tune with the held notes strongly emphasized:

You made me love you baby . . . now that's the way you do, (2)
Yes I'm goin' back to Vicksburg. . . .

Yes I love my daddy, tell it everywhere I go, (2)
Yes I'm goin' back to Vicksburg. . . .[26]

Scott Dunbar was taught his songs, wrote Ramsey, by 'outlaws roaming the levee backwaters, by escaped convicts . . . by singers and players and wanderers now long dead. Then Scott remembers old blues, dance tunes and river songs that have come to him from this other time and other world.'[27] It is impossible to determine whether Scott Dunbar obtained his *Vicksburg and Natchez Blues* from such wanderers, whether he learned it as a 'river song' that had come downstream, or from a record. But either way it is evident that in this part of Mississippi and near-by Louisiana it has become assimilated into the folk repertoire. Some thirty-five miles south, in Louisiana, at a cabin on the Old Slaughter Road, Zachary, Chris Strachwitz and I recorded two country musicians, Butch Cage and Willie Thomas. The previous year the same musicians had been recorded by Harry Oster and a comparison of the resultant records is instructive on the folk process. The later, 1960, recording ran:

Well, I walked all night long with my 44 in my hand, (2)
Well, I was looking for my woman, I found her with another man.

Oh, good morning, Mr Pawnshopper, can I walk in your door, (2)
Well I didn't come here for no trouble, but I want my 44.

Well my buddy got a 45, don't you kill dead that love of mine, (2)
I take my little 44, I meet him in the bar-room door.

Well, I got a little cabin, my cabin number is 44, (2)
When I wake up in the morning, the blues is cryin' round my
   door.[28]

After the second verse both the first two verses were repeated; the second after the third quoted verse, and the first again after the fourth. In Dr Oster's recording, the following verses were sandwiched between the first and second verses and following the last, respectively, and the order of the first two was reversed:

And I tote my 44 so long that it made my shoulder sore, (2)
Oh I woke up this mornin' with the blues knockin' on my door.

Well I thought I heard the 44 whistle blow, (2)
Well it blowed just like it ain't gonna blow that whistle no more.[29]

Again, verses were repeated even though the repetitions affected the sense. But it was clear in the performance that this was essentially blues for dancing and the playing of the fiddle by Butch Cage, though it substituted for the hammered repeat notes on the piano, was the music of the reel. Meaning was less important than function and the excitement of the dance tune accelerated as, train-like, the musicians got under way. The words apparently derived in part from Roosevelt Sykes's recording but Cage and Thomas had devised verses of their own including the ballad-like stanza, verse three above, singing them approximately to Sykes's vocal tune. This was an excellent example of absorption and adaptation of more sophisticated, recorded material by members of an essentially folk community.

Similar in instrumentation and character, but based on the alternative *Vicksburg Blues* vocal theme, is a recent recording by Big Joe Williams, singing the vocal and playing guitar on *Ain't Gonna Be Your Lowdown Dog No More*. He is accompanied on this by two fellow Mississippi musicians, Jimmy Brown, who plays fiddle, and Willie Lee Harris on harmonica. Part of an album which 'attempts to recreate the music and atmosphere of a back-country dance or party, it had its inception in Big Joe's long-expressed desire to record a program of "them old-time songs" in company with a number of blues men with whom he had worked over the years.'[30] The song is a slightly altered version of Little Brother Montgomery's vocal tune, using the same long and held note but with much less use of the flattened seventh. The guitar, unlike Willie Thomas's solely rhythmic pounding, carries both melody and rhythm at times, with occasional single-string imitations of the vocal line. Though dominated by Big Joe Williams, both Harris and Brown play their harmonica and fiddle to the vocal tune. The words demonstrate the affinity to the shifting group of verses which are associated with this blues, commencing with the single line in Montgomery's original:

Lord an' I ain't gonna be your . . . lowdown dog no mo', (2)
Well I'm goin' down the road babe where the weather fits my
   clo's.

You know I'm goin' away to leave you woman, hang *crêpe* on yo'
   do', (2)
Lord I won't be dead woman, but I ain't comin' back here no mo'.

Lord I thought I heard that old Southern when she blows,
Lord I thought I heard that old Southern whistle blow,
Lord and it sound just like babe, wouldn't wanna blow no mo'.

I'm gonna cry this time, an I . . . ain't gonna cry no more, (2)
Change your way, live with me and you won't have to cry no
more.[31]

This was a deliberate attempt to recreate a country atmosphere and
the tune may not necessarily have been one which was in general
circulation in Mississippi at the time when Big Joe Williams was living
in the country. It appears to fit into a general pattern, however. Recorded in Chicago by an emigrant singer from Mississippi, *Louisiana
Blues* was one of the earliest and also one of the finest of recordings
by Muddy Waters. Accompanied by the Louisiana-born harmonica
player, Little Walter, and the steady beat of backing drums, it had the
rural character of the 'down-home blues'. Muddy Waters's slide guitar
introduction played the vocal line of *Vicksburg Blues* and both guitar
and harmonica exchanged the vocal and rhythmic patterns with the full
exploitation of 'bent' and shaded notes and an elongated if simplified
form of Example 4. The held note of *Vicksburg Blues* again appears,
the flattened seventh at the beginning of the second phrase is marked
prominently and the ends of the lines drop in emphasized blues notes.
It is essentially a blues in performance, the words being a mere two
verses.

I'm goin' down in Louisiana, baby behind the sun,
I'm goin' down in Louisiana, honey behind the sun,
Well you know I just found out my troubles just begun.

I'm goin' down in New Orleans, mm . . . get me a mojo hand, (2)
I want to show all you good-lookin' women just how to treat your
man.[32] ©

In content *Louisiana Blues* echoed a popular theme in the blues—that of
going to New Orleans to consult the voodoo 'queens'. Specifically, the
first verse echoed that of Charley Taylor's quoted above, while a hint of
the second is lurking perhaps, in Cat-Iron's visit to the 'gipsy'. The
falling notes in the vocal linked it with *Vicksburg Blues* but the rhythmic

emphasis in the instrumental accompaniment clearly associated it with another theme in the complex of related tunes. This was *Roll and Tumble Blues*, a variant which was to become one of the most popular in the 'fifties, even though its history was as long as that of *The Forty-Four Blues*. In fact, the first recording of *Roll and Tumble Blues* anticipated Roosevelt Sykes's '*44*' *Blues* by three months:

An' I rolled an' I tumbled an' I cried the whole night long, (2)
An' I rolled this mornin' and I didn't know right from wrong.

Did you ever wake up and find your dough-roller gone, (2)
And you wring your hands and you cry the whole day long.

An' I told my woman Lord before I left the town,
An' I told my woman just before I left the town,
Don't you let nobody tear her barrelhouse down.

An' I fold my arms Lord an' I walked away,
An' I fold my arms and I slowly walked away,
Says, 'That's all right sweet mama, your troubles gonna come
  some day.'[33]

Hambone Willie Newbern's *Roll and Tumble Blues* has a vocal line similar to *Vicksburg Blues* but it is marked by an exaggerated falling note at the end of the first two lines. Newbern imitated his own vocal on the guitar, using a bottleneck slide to repeat the falling note. The breaks where, in the alternating instrumental verses, the guitar would have been solo, he played in a rhythmic pattern so that the instrumental versions of the verses and the vocals sounded very much alike. But in the vocals he pitched his voice with some strain an octave higher for the third line while the guitar solos had the third line carried on the bass strings. It was a distinctive performance and, it seems, a memorable one. Although he recorded in Atlanta, Willie Newbern was from Ripley, Tennessee. He has been recalled by another singer from Ripley, Sleepy John Estes, who used the tune of *Roll and Tumble Blues*, on his own first record, *The Girl I Love, She Got Long Curly Hair*, made six months later in September 1929:

Now I'm goin' to Brownsville, take that right-hand road, (2)
Lord I ain't gonna stop walkin' till I git in sweet mama's door.

Now the girl I'm lovin' she got the great, long, curly hair, (2)
And her mammy and her papa they sure don't 'llow me there.

Ef you catch my jumper hang it upside your wall, (2)
Now you know by that babe, I need my ashes hauled.

Now what you gonn' do babe, your dough-roller gone, (2)
Go in your kitchen cookin' till he come home.[34]

In Estes's recording the relationship of melodic line and rhythm emphasized by Newbern was retained. He was accompanied by James Rachell who carried the melody on the mandolin and the pianist, Jab Jones, who did little more than vamp an accompaniment. If there was any connexion at this time with the piano accompaniment to *The Forty-Fours* and the Newbern theme, Jab Jones was unaware of, or unequal to it. The words opened with the leaving theme so frequently found in all variants of the blues but only the final verse suggests a direct link with Hambone Willie's lyrics.

Elements of Newbern's rhythmic patterns are to be found in two titles made by Robert Johnson several years later, *Traveling Riverside Blues* and *If I Had Possession over Judgement Day*. The former is slower and more contemplative, allowing Johnson to play his bottleneck style guitar with subtlety and feeling; in contrast *Judgement Day* is fast, the voice near a screech and there is little room for sensitive guitar work. In neither is the vocal carried in imitation on the slide but the rhythm is Newbern's, while the words of *Judgement Day* are directly related:

If I had possession over Judgement Day, (2)
Lord then the women I'm lovin' wouldn't have no right to pray.

And I went to the mountain just as far as my eyes could see, (2)
Some other man got my woman, and these lonesome blues got me.

And I rolled and I tumbled an' I cried the whole night long, (2)
Boy I woke up this mornin', my biscuit-roller gone.

Had to fold my arms and I slowly walked away, (2)
I felt in my mind your trouble goin' come some day.[35]

In *Traveling Riverside Blues* Johnson makes references to Friars Point, Vicksburg and Rosedale which emphasize his Mississippi origins and may suggest a connexion with *Vicksburg Blues* but, though the vocal line is reminiscent of the Mississippi theme, the accompaniment is still Newbern's. Nevertheless, Johnson, greatly admired and widely imitated, may have been the principal cause of the popularization of the theme among guitarists and may have been a major influence on Muddy Waters in this as in other respects. Curiously neither *Traveling Riverside Blues* nor *If I Had Possession over Judgement Day* was issued as a 78 rpm record and, unlike *Cross Road Blues*, *Terraplane Blues* or *Dust My Broom*, *If I Had Possession over Judgement Day* was not widely copied by such singers as Elmore James and Homesick James Williamson, nor did the title persist. *Roll and Tumble Blues* on the other hand has continued as a title suggesting that, in spite of his relative obscurity, it was Hambone Willie Newbern and his record who were the real influences on versions of the post-war generation of singers. Elmore James's own hit record of *Rollin' and Tumblin'* was not made until 1960. Its heavy rhythm was a simplification of the pattern used on earlier records of the 'fifties.

Exceptional among these was a remarkable two-part recording, *Rollin' and Tumblin'*, by Baby Face Leroy Foster on which Muddy Waters and Little Walter joined in the accompaniment and the singing. Taken at a faster pace than *Louisiana Blues* it had unison singing by all three men humming and vocalizing without words on the first side. Muddy Waters's sliding, vibrating bottleneck on the strings gave a chilling, trembling excitement to the piece and Little Walter's harp assumed an eerie vocal quality. On the second side, Leroy Foster took over with a vocal, once again on a railroad theme, and for the first time for many years the instrumental background to the tune was used to convey an impression of a train. As it accelerated, Muddy Waters played the chimes on his guitar and the drummer, who had commenced with a rhythm phrase, was finishing with a rapid, insistent beat:

I rolled and I tumbled baby, cried the whole night long, (2)
Well now I woke up this mornin' baby, all I had is gone.

Yes I know my baby she goin' to jump and shout, (2)
Now when the train rolls up and baby come walkin' out.

Now engineerman blew the whistle, firemen ring the bell, (2)
I didn't have time boys to tell my baby, 'Fare you well'.[36]

That the *Rollin' and Tumblin'* theme had become extremely popular
with this group of singers is underlined by the recent issue of a previously unissued Aristocrat master by Muddy Waters, *Down South
Blues*, which used essentially the same motif. But it became, in the
early 'fifties, the property of a number of Chicago-based, Mississippi-
born musicians. Sunnyland Slim, Walter Horton and the guitarist from
the Muddy Waters band, Jimmy Rodgers, made another version, *Goin'
Back to Memphis*, for Blue Lake in 1954. Though Sunnyland Slim's
stentorian voice was under-recorded, his shouting style of blues singing
could be heard outlining the vocal line with its exaggerated rise. Dis-
daining the *Vicksburg* bass figure, he maintained a steady, vamping
rhythm in the left hand and joined with Rodger's guitar and Horton's
harp to repeat in unison the rhythmic-melodic phrase that typified the
old Newbern blues:

Well, I'm goin' to Memphis, catch that ole mornin' train, (2)
Lord there's somebody down there, just keep on worryin' me.

Well, I'm leavin' your town and I know you don't even care, (2)
'Cause you act just like you never did want me here.

Well, now what you gonna do baby, when your trouble get like
   mine ? (2)
And you cain't do nothin' but jest fold your arms and cry ?[37]

Again the leaving theme with its emphasis on a return to a Southern
location appeared in company with the characteristic melody and the
instruments acting in unison. It appeared in many other instances,
even with all the elements played by one man, Doctor Ross, who played
guitar, harmonica and drums and sang the vocal too on his recording of
Illinois Blues. It establishes the link between *Rollin' and Tumblin'* and
Vicksburg Blues though, as in the other instances, the individual notes
had fractionally longer or shorter values than in the original *Vicksburg*
sufficient to impart a subtly individual character to the song. In his
instrumental solo Doctor Ross played the vocal line on the harmonica
and both vocal and rhythm phrases on guitar, using instrumental fill-ins

similar to those used by Arthur Crudup and Muddy Waters. His blues was essentially *Vicksburg Blues* with the locale transposed:

I've got the blues for Illinois, sing 'em everywhere I go, (2)
Yes, but when I leave this time, won't be back no more.

I say Illinois up the country, Kentucky just below, (2)
Yes, I'm in love with you baby, don't want you no more.

I said if you don't want me, why in the world didn't you let me
    be, (2)
Yes, I believe you doin', tryin' what you do to me.

I said I'm leavin' this mornin', your cryin' won't make me stay, (2)
Yes, the more you cry, further you'll drive me away.[38]

Of other recordings of *The Forty-Fours* played on guitar or harmonica, mention might be made of those by Junior Brooks, Woodrow Adams and Howling Wolf. Junior Brooks's *Lone Town Blues* was recorded in Memphis about 1951, with the artist singing new words to the vocal theme of Roosevelt Sykes's '*44' Blues*. The melody was apparently familiar to the small backing group which supported him, presumably drawn from Drifting Slim's group. A bass rhythm was probably played by Sammy Lawhorn on rhythm guitar while Baby Face Turner, with great dexterity, used quaver thirds (Example 5) and the fill-in phrase (Example 8) very frequently after most vocal phrases and Example 4. Brooks's own vocal line had more bounce than Sykes's slower theme but bore the same tonic-dominant relationship C/F:

Says when I leave this mornin' I believe I'll run around, (2)
Well and I done got tired baby, kneelin' down in your lonesome
    town.

Well, when I get up early darlin' call you on my telephone, (2)
I know you done miss me baby, you know the days that I been
    gone.

Well, there ain't gonna be no lyin' ain't gonna be no cryin' too, (2)
Well, and I ain't got no money baby, I don't have no darlin' too.[39]

Brooks's recording was evidence of the persistence of *The Forty-Fours* theme in the 'fifties; Woodrow Adams's *Wine Head Woman* of the continuing virility of the *Vicksburg* form. An extremely primitive-sounding item it was recorded in Memphis four years later, in 1955, with Adams, a tractor driver, playing harmonica accompanied by a heavily emphasized statement of a bass guitar figure, echoed by the drums, and all but drowning out the scarcely audible piano. The bass line is a variation of the Sykes bass (Example 9) played on the guitar, though not entirely consistently. It is notable for being the only instance where a glissando to the note is played on the guitar as a downward slide to the first beat of the bar, accentuating it in similar fashion to the upward climb on the piano. As the bass notes would be low on the bass strings of the guitar it would not be possible to rise to the note and this solution was both a natural and yet an original one. Adams's vocal followed the *Vicksburg* tune:

I got a wine head woman and she stays drunk all the time, (2)
Well every time I see her she's somewhere drinkin' wine.

I give her all my money and I give her all my time, (2)
And every time she come home, done got high as a Georgia pine.

I give her all my money, I give her all my love, (2)
And every time I see her, she's somewhere totin' a jug.[40]

If Woodrow Adams's recording was primitive it was the essential crudity of a folk band playing in a style probably assimilated from city-made recordings. Howling Wolf's own *Forty-Four*, on the other hand, had a ferocity, a physical violence which was as aggressive as it was deliberate. With his studied attack, Howling Wolf sings with an angry, half-strangled delivery and the song, based on Roosevelt Sykes's '*44*' *Blues* but sung to a tune closer to *Vicksburg Blues*, has generated to two verses. His harsh singing imparts more meaning to the words than to the two verses contained in the text:

I wore my 44 so long, I done made my shoulder so', (2)
Well now I'm gonna find out everybody, where my baby gone.

Well, I'm so mad this mornin', I don't know where in the world
   to go, (2)
Well I'm looking there for somebody 'cause I just must have some
   dough.[41]

Playing the harmonica in his solo, Howling Wolf moves from vocal to
rhythm phrases while behind him two guitars carry the repeat bass
phrase throughout and the treble of the piano is heard at intervals
above the heavy stress of the bass. The Sykes bass (Example 9) is
accompanied by a dotted-quaver rhythm played on the drums:

EXAMPLE 12

This gives a forward thrust, or bounce, to the recording while Example
4 is also used with a heavily accentuated first beat. The three right-hand
chords in Example 4 have a certain lift, with a choppy, forward-moving
buoyancy while the guitar fill-in, though having the chordal implication of Example 4 now takes a more melodic form.

   Much of the character of Howling Wolf's recording comes from the
new emphasis imparted to the beat and the bounce implied in the
phrases both rhythmic and melodic. Part of this is due at any rate, to the
presence of Otis Spann whose own recent (1966) recording of *Vicksburg
Blues* has these essential characteristics. Commencing with a dotted
rhythm on quavers, it has a rocking variation of Example 4 in the right
hand with a heavily accentuated second beat adding to the sense of
buoyance. A dotted version of the Sykes fill-in Example 8 adds to this
impression. In the vocal he shows his indebtedness to Howling Wolf
in the first verse and uses others associated with various versions of
Vicksburg Blues as he progresses:

Well, you know I'm so mad this morning, don't know whichaway
   to go, (2)
Lord I'm gonna find my woman so I can get some dough.

Vicksburg's on a high hill, Jackson just below, (2)
Well, you know the reason why I left there, my woman didn't
   want me no more.

Well, y'know if ever I get lucky with my train fare home, (2)
Lord I'm gonna tell everybody how you treat me wrong.

Well, you know I looked for you woman this mornin' baby, you
know you was nowhere round, (2)
Well, if I can't find you tomorrow baby, I'm gonna have to leave
your town.[42]

The passing of emphasis from the left hand to the right in his juxta-
posed bass and treble figures adds to the movement of this piece
although, in his solo, Spann returns to the more usual form of *The
Forty-Fours*. Here, after many years the piece regains the plaintive,
nostalgic and moving quality that characterized the early versions of
the tune. It seems likely that Otis Spann's instrumental characteristics
derive from the early years of the blues. He has always acknowledged
the profound influence of Friday Ford on his playing and, if Ford
was indeed one of the original creators of *The Forty-Fours*, he may well
have passed on his own, individual way of playing it to Spann.

It was in 1922 that Little Brother Montgomery first met Ernest
Johnson and began to play *The Forty-Fours*. In 1966 he was still
playing it and many other blues pianists included it as an essential
part of their repertoire: *The Forty-Fours* had reached its forty-fourth
year. It has been possible, by means of recordings and the recollections
of one or two musicians, to trace its lineage in some detail and more
could be revealed of the nature of tradition in the blues if other examples
were similarly examined. Few would probably reveal to quite the same
degree the many aspects of blues tradition within a single, basic
composition, though this is only supposition. *The Forty-Fours*, at any
rate, demonstrates the complex family-tree of the blues. Its basic
instrumental theme provides the groundwork for two major vocal tunes
and a number of subsidiary ones; the instrumental theme itself is also
subject to many variations. The blues shows the degree to which
a singer's individual style may influence the way in which a tune is
interpreted by others; it exemplifies the passing on of traditional verses
and lines, the dropping of some and the grafting of others in the process
of evolution. The association of certain verses only hinted at by a line,
or non-existent in the earliest recordings, with a blues suggests the importance of personal transmission; the copying of verses or even the whole
blues likewise emphasizes the importance of transmission by recordings.

But *The Forty-Fours* still raises a number of problems which may remain unanswered. To what extent, for instance, did the three best-known protagonists, Eurreal Montgomery, Roosevelt Sykes and Leothus Green determine the popularity of the blues? For the decade following the first recording of the theme by Roosevelt Sykes they averaged between them a recorded version of the tune a year. It is reasonable to assume that, during this period when they were travelling widely, they also featured the blues, by which they were well known in their recorded versions, wherever they played. But if they founded the general popularity of the piece why did it appear in so many versions after the war, when a period without recording was followed by the eclipse, for the time being at any rate, of these pianists? Was it the arrival of Otis Spann in Chicago as a blues pianist which substantially contributed to its renewed life? To what extent did Big Boy Crudup's version stimulate the transition from piano to guitar which character-ized the post-war popularity of *The Forty-Fours*?

There are other problems: was it oral transmission that brought the tune to the country guitarists and musicians like Scott Dunbar or Cage and Thomas, or was it feed-back from recordings? Was Lee Green's version adapted from a woman's blues or did Mae Glover add to its meaning in implying a dialogue? Why was Lee Green's *Number Forty-Four Blues* the least influential of those by the three originating pianists, even though he was the only one to have issued three record-ings under his own name before the mid-'thirties? These and other questions come to mind and many of them are unlikely to be resolved. They indicate the complexities in the documentation of a living music in a continual process of evolution and change.

4 POLICY BLUES

One of the most marked features of the recent trends in the blues has been the diminution in importance of the lyrics themselves. The mid-'fifties witnessed the last of the blues of topical significance in the catalogues of record companies catering specifically for a Negro market. Such recordings as Brother Will Hairston's *Alabama Bus*, Bobo Jenkins's *Democrat Blues* or J. B. Lenoir's *Eisenhower Blues* are striking and singular examples whose comment on political or racial issues is exceptional. Exceptional perhaps, at any time in the blues, but even more remarkable at a time when the blues, as a reflection of the society which produced it, was already losing its force. Interestingly, these isolated instances were more outspoken than almost any recordings in previous years and the suppression of Lenoir's *Eisenhower Blues* revealed that the blues was not welcome as a vehicle of protest. The release on Testament of a number of blues on the death of President Kennedy showed that there were still reserves of feeling outside the immediate experience of the singer in the blues. But it is revealing that this interesting and important issue was made for a collectors' market and was not in general circulation in Negro communities. Only one gospel recording on the tragic theme appeared in the Negro record lists. Today, a blues record that has in its lyrics any social implications other than personal and sexual ones is a rarity. It was not always so. Such themes have predominated in the blues but recordings that revealed other aspects of the total Negro environment were an important feature of the Race lists until the mid-'forties.

But these were not direct 'protest', and they were not propaganda. The Negro has been resistant to such themes and has derived pleasure, satisfaction and moral support from the recorded evidence of experiences that he had himself shared with the singer. Many such blues have been obscure, referring to unfamiliar ways of life and often in baffling terms for the outsider. They have a notably 'in-group' character and none display this more than the considerable body of 'Policy Blues'. Policy, or The Numbers, involves laying bets on combinations of numbers. It is not essentially the property of the Negro—it is reputedly Cuban in origin—but it appeals to him because the possibilities of a large return for a small stake are relatively far greater than is the likelihood of a win in the English national and legal gamble of the football pools.

Policy boomed in the 'twenties and 'thirties but it has an older history. The sociologists, St Clair Drake and Horace R. Cayton, have traced its origins in Chicago to the opening of a wheel by Policy Sam in 1885 which offered dividends of 180 to 1, but which was too stacked against the player to appeal to the professional gamblers. Policy Sam depended on the bets of the 'poverty-laden workers, housewives, prostitutes and gambling-house flunkies' until he retired from the game in 1905.[1] In that year the state of Illinois passed an anti-policy law which, however, did not deter the big-time Negro gambler and politician, John Mushmouth Johnson, who had joined in partnership with a Chinaman, King Foo, and a white lottery manager, Patsy King, to put policy on a firm footing in Chicago in the 'nineties. Johnson died in 1907 but by this time the racket was well established.

In New York the game appears to have had a similar history and was so popular by the turn of the century that New York City passed an anti-policy law as early as 1901. That it was playing an important part in Negro life was reflected in its inclusion in some aspects of Negro show business. The celebrated team of Bert Williams and George Walker put on a show in New York in 1899 under the title of *4–11–44*—a policy play—which was a shade too obscure for the breadth of audience they hoped to attract. They changed the name to *The Policy Players* but the show was a failure and they turned their attention to the shows *The Sons of Ham* and *In Dahomey* which made their names. Perhaps *The Policy Players* failed because it was a poor show, perhaps because it was a shade premature, but it indicates well enough the trend. Thirty years later, Wallace Thurman and William Jourdan were to stage *Harlem* at the Apollo Theatre with Ernest Whitman playing the part of a 'numbers king' and Billy Andrews as a 'numbers runner' with immense success.[2]

A couple of years earlier the old title of *4–11–44* had been revived for a 'New All-Colored Musical Novelty' at Hurtig's and Season's Theatre on 125th Street which was billed as having 'Eddie Hunter and an All-Star Cast of 75 Artists Including Lieutenant Tim Brymn and His Famous Jazzharmonic Orchestra'. Presumably an entertainment rather than a revival of the Williams and Walker play, it shows that the numbers combination was compelling enough in itself by this date not to require further explanation. The show toured with Tim Moore, Ethel Waters and Louie Metcalf, who was 'hired as the hot man' playing trumpet in Tim Brymn's sixteen-piece pit orchestra and who 'joined the show when it began and . . . stayed with it for its entire life, about seven months'.[3] It appears that the title of *4–11–44* could draw crowds well outside New York and that policy was well established in Negro communities generally, a situation reflected in the blues for, by this time, the policy racket was a popular theme in blues and Race songs.

Four–Eleven–Forty–Four was the title that Papa Charlie Jackson gave to his spirited little song, recorded in May 1926 to his own minstrel-styled banjo accompaniment. The words were gauche but revealing of the anxieties of the small-time player:

I felt so bad the other night,
I had nothin' left but an appetite,
I looked in my purse t' see if I had a little dough,
So I could policy play 4–11–44.
    Policy is all I have all day,
    What good is it if you don't know what to play?
    You think of any numbers to 34,
    Always policy play 4–11–44.
    The other night I thought I'd always be broke,
    4–11–44 kept me out of a joke,
    So always keep playin' 4–11–44.

I went to the wheel they wouldn't let me in,
I stood on the steps right out in the wind.
'Mister man, mister man, please open the door,
I want to play 4–11–44.'
    Policy is all I have all day etc.

So while they pulled the numbers out I went real white,
I felt like things weren't going to work out right,
I felt nervous, started to go,
Then the last three numbers were 4–11–44.
    So policy is all I have all day etc.[4]

A month later, in New York, Elvira Johnson, with a fast-playing jazz band that included Buster Bailey at his best on soprano sax and Clarence Williams on piano, recorded that she had *Numbers on the Brain*. Her song, with its emphasis on the numbers reflects the distinction between the New York and Chicago variants of the racket, for in the 'twenties the gamblers had 'hit upon the idea of taking bets on the probable last three numbers of the daily Federal Reserve Clearing House Report. This variant of "policy"—known as the "numbers game"—was very popular on the Eastern seaboard because it placed the game "on the level". No racketeer could tamper with the Clearing House figures, and anyone could read them in the newspapers.'[5] In New York the game was also known as *bolito*, echoing the reputed Cuban origins of the lottery. A West Indian, Caspar Holstein, has often been reported as having brought the game from the Virgin Islands in the 'twenties; he did not introduce it, but he did put the business on a systematic basis and organized control of its substantial dividends.[6] The gambling fever affected many players like a disease and Elvira Johnson's introduction that she was 'hitched like a horse to a carriage, trying to beat the game' and her refrain that she had 'numbers on the brain, I seen them I dream them, they're drivin' me insane' were an accurate picture of the obsessional gambling mania which afflicted many players. Her verses gave further sidelights which her listeners would have appreciated:

I put my money on 1–22,
Now what in the world am I goin' to do?
I just have numbers on the brain.

I picked those numbers the other day,
The man with the money done gone away,
I just got numbers on the brain.

Nothin' in the ice-box, nothin' in the trunk,
I don't use a needle, and I like junk,
I just have numbers on the brain.

Lost my money playin' *bolita*,
I went home, robbed my gas meter,
I just have numbers on the brain.[7]

Backed with *How Could I Be Blue*, this was Elvira Johnson's only record and it is not without interest that several singers who recorded little included a policy blues of some form in their few items; Albert Clemens or Yodelling Kid Brown, for instance, for their *only* recording. Yodelling Kid Brown made his *Policy Blues* in August 1928 to an excellent but unidentified blues piano accompaniment and his own kazoo playing—oddly enough, he didn't yodel on this sole record.

It was a slight blues but it, too, indicated the popularity of the game, while adding a note of disillusion:

Have you heard the news I'm gonna sing to you, (2)
Everybody's crazy, crazy 'bout the policy blues.

It takes five numbers to make a jack, (2)
And you must be born lucky to get your money back.

See a woman wearing an overshoe, (2)
You can tell by that she has the policy blues.

Well I dreamed last night my gig came out, (2)
Woke up this morning, my flat fell out.[8]

Though there was a note of warning in Yodelling Kid Brown's blues it was more against the chances of a win than against the racketeering of the policy kings. The big returns from running the policy wheels made fortunes for the operators and for few else. The odds were extremely high, stacked heavily against the player, for whom the selections to be made on the policy slips from twelve numbers, twenty-four numbers or 'any numbers to thirty-four', seemed relatively favourable. In fact, the odds against guessing three numbers in twelve which might 'fall' were over 76,000 to 1.[9] Jim Jackson's *Policy Blues* recorded in Memphis, Tennessee, in February 1928 was more of a cautionary tale, which indicated in passing that the game was already established in the South:

Have you ever taken a chance with the policy game? (2)
You have three numbers, see what you can gain.

If you should lose, don't get mad at all, (2)
You cain't win unless your numbers fall.

I got the policy blues, I ain't got the money to play, (2)
I know my numbers will fall today.

I woke up in the mornin' with one thin dime, (2)
The policy man gets there before the clock strikes nine.

Then you go around hungry the rest of the day, (2)
Waitin' for him to come back with your play.

I tell you what all the boys on Beale Street know, (2)
It is the Black Man in the Trey and 4–11–44.

They almost hurt when the drawin's come back, (2)
That policy man sure can shake a wicked stack.[10]

Jim Jackson's blues probably excited more interest than it promoted caution; there was a willing and ready gambling market and with the coming of the Depression the game expanded rapidly. In Harlem Caspar Holstein operated from the Turf Club on 135th and Madison, while Ida Kelly operated from Garfield Avenue in Chicago, both becoming immensely rich on the profits. During the Depression, policy offered the chance of large returns for very small investments and many impoverished Negroes wrote policy in the hopes of winning sufficient to feed their families.[11] Policy kings made occasional magnanimous gestures with large donations to charities or churches and a mystique developed in which they were viewed as benefactors rather than as parasites.

The policy racket had a folk-lore of its own. The winning numbers were selected by the spinning of large, often decorative policy wheels which had romantic and evocative names—the Red Devil, the Interstate, Streamliner, the Big Train, the Green Gable, the Wisconsin and so on. Later, when adding machines were introduced to log the numbers written and passed furtively on paper napkins or inside card books of matches, the winning numbers were calculated by more sophisticated means. The terminology of the race-track was adopted by the numbers game, which was sometimes known as 'playing the races'. Number combinations were generally laid in threes but as many as twenty-five numbers might be played on one bet, to be read in various combinations to increase the chances of winning, the player stipulating whether he wanted 'saddles', 'gigs' or 'horses'. Two numbers could make only a saddle; three numbers could make three saddles or one gig. One horse could be made from four numbers which could also make six saddles or four gigs. But the graphs rose differently: ten numbers would make forty-five saddles, a hundred and twenty gigs or two hundred and ten horses, the bets being correspondingly higher according to the possible number of combinations. Most players were content to play three numbers on a straight gig and leave it at that, but the policy writers and numbers runners who took the bets by a rapid code of signals in the street or at the 'numbers drop' would urge them to play other numbers and at higher stakes. The play was intentionally complicated, and the complexity added mystery while the illegality added piquancy. During the mid and late 'thirties policy boomed.

In *The Mob's Man*, the otherwise anonymous 'Andy' told James D. Horan, 'The reasons why the game is so widely played are the vast odds and the ease with which you can play a number. All you have to do is ring the elevator button; nine times out of ten the elevator operator is your local runner. Buy a pound of butter and play a number. There are few stores in Harlem which do not take numbers. Walk downstairs for a breath of air—the kid on the steps will take your number to the runner who stands on the corner.'[12]

With the considerable returns accruing from operating policy wheels the racket came under the control of syndicates with muscle-men and hired gunmen ensuring that their 'rights' were protected. In Chicago the Jones Boys operated for a number of years until they relinquished their holdings under the pressure of even more powerful racketeers. In Harlem Dutch Schultz ousted Caspar Holstein who eventually died in poverty in 1941. He outlived Schultz however; Arthur Flegenheimer (Schultz) operated from the Palace Chop House in Newark, New Jersey, where he was cut down by one of his own hired gunmen late in 1935. Within a year control of the New York numbers racket passed into the dominion of a mob enforcer, Bumpy (The Lamb) Johnson—till he in turn was sent to Atlanta prison for a long term on a narcotics charge.

For the Negroes who placed their bets and hoped for a five-dollar return on a one-cent play, the warfare between the racketeers hardly affected them. They continued to pass over their plays at the numbers drops, the beauty salons, candy stores and barber shops where the bets were taken. Reflecting the popularity of the numbers game were innumerable policy blues: the Mississippi Sheiks' *Hitting the Numbers* and Peetie Wheatstraw's *Numbers Blues*; Albert Clemens's *Policy Blues* (*You Can't 3–6–9 Me*) and Bo Carter's *Policy Blues*; Kokomo Arnold's *Policy Wheel Blues* and Jimmy Gordon's *Number Runner's Blues*.[13] Apart from the many blues with passing references to the game, the policy blues generally had a story to tell and for this reason were frequently more interesting both in content and in form than the general run of blues. Several had a wry touch of humour, like Bumble Bee Slim's *Policy Dream Blues*:

Policy is a racket and it's awful hard to beat,
I played my last dime and couldn't even eat.
The writer came to my house this mornin' and knocked upon the door,
He said, 'If you want to catch some money play 4-11-44.'
I said, 'Listen here Mister Writer, is you playin' that yourself?'
He said, 'I had a dream last night and I'm playin' somethin' else.'
I said, 'Go on Mister Writer, that gig ain't comin' out.'
He said, 'You better get on it, I know what I'm talkin' about.'
He said, 'It's split out in the Harlem, also the New York and Rome.'
I said, 'But I promised to leave that policy 'lone.
I need some money and it's true enough.'
He said, 'You better get on it and try and catch the stuff.'
He said, 'Play it Mister, you see I'm on the level.'
That gig jumped right out—in the Red Devil.
I played it that evenin', in the Fast Mail,
Woke up the next mornin' in the county jail. . . .
Saying, 'Go on Mister Writer, that gig ain't comin' out.'
He said, 'You better get on it, I know what I'm talkin' about.'
Six months later I got out of the can,
Met that Policy Mister with his drawin's in his hand.
He said, 'Look here buddy, you been gone so long,
If you play the "police roll" you cain't go wrong.'
I said, 'Your policy racket is a cryin' shame!'
He said, 'Just for that Mister, I'm gonna play your name.
The "police roll" is good, buddy, but your name is the best,
It stood up last night in the East 'n West!'
I said, 'Go on Mister Writer, that gig ain't comin' out.'
He said, 'You better get on it, I know what I'm talkin' about.'[14]

Chicago Negroes purchasing this record would have instantly recognized the names of several famous policy wheels, and the techniques of the policy writer to urge the player on. The 'police roll' (patrol) would have raised a knowing smile: the combination to play would have been 1–2–5–31 which was made up of 1—man, 2—scoundrel, 5—traitor and 31—lie; the significance of 'police patrol' is 'beware of false friends'—in this case the policy writer himself. But the policy writer's revenge of playing Bumble Bee Slim's name would also have amused for this implies bad luck for the nominee. That his real name (Amos Easton) came up in the East 'n West had a punning significance which the seasoned player could not miss. The writer would have played 8–24–60, the play for Amos, which among other meanings can be broken down to killing (8), complaint (24) and fortune (60)—propitious for the player and not for Bumble Bee Slim. The numbers books proclaiming the 'Study of Harmony in Numbers' with 'Keys Based on Systems of the Ancients' also give combinations derived from the letters of names, each letter being given a numerical value. Apparently of Rosicrucian and Kabalist origin, such number-evaluations would have given for Bumble Bee Slim—a three-word name very suited to a straight gig—2, 6, 4, 2, 3, 5–2, 5, 5–3, 3, 1, 4—which would total (or in the player's term would be 'reducible to') 22–12–11.

The name of a lover can provide a good play but no player likes to be unsuccessful in a love affair while waiting for the numbers to come up. Adverse circumstances may affect the fortune of the numbers played:

I heard you was a roller and I come to change your wheel, (2)
Now a roller never knows just how a kid man feels.

I got something to tell ya make the hair rise on your head, (2)
Now this mellow meat I got 'd make the springs cry on your bed.

Rosa Lee, Rosa Lee now baby, please don't stall, (2)
I playin' policy in your name and I hope them numbers fall.

The numbers in your name is 7–14–43, (2)
I'm goin' to tell all rounders to please let these numbers be.[15]

The number combinations for names are not wholly standardized—some numbers books give 15–50–51 for Rosa and 18–42–65 for Rosalie. If there is some disagreement among the numbers books on the meaning of some number combinations or the appropriate numbers to play for a given situation, many are to be found which are common to all the books. Those individual numbers or groups of numbers have taken on a code significance in instances where the event or object which they represent is a familiar, recurrent one. Sickness is played as 44–45–39, death as a combination of 9 and 59, mourning as 42–43–22–50. Such numbers are known to most players, who do not need recourse to the numbers book, for the most propitious plays in the event of illness or bereavement. Racial implications are more subtle and less often listed, but every player knows that a white person is played as 10–18–44, and that a white man and a coloured woman are played as 1–5–14–51. Sexual number combinations are especially familiar to players who will play 1–10–11–39–50 for the male genitalia, 4–22–50–44 for copulation in bed, or will combine 1, a male, and 5, a female to make 15 or 51 as numbers to incorporate in a saddle or gig. That brothels and prostitutes are the subject of 'the dirty, wicked fives' in the blues is no accident. Such number plays are recommended in Kokomo Arnold's *Policy Wheel Blues* which mentions two of the best-known Chicago wheels of the mid-'thirties:

Now while you' playin' policy buddy, play 4–11 and 44,
When you git your money then pack your sacks and go,
> Cryin' oh, look what that policy wheel have done to me,
> It done took all my money and still it won't let me be.

When you playin' policy, play 4–18 and 56,
You can pile up your black money 'cause you sure gonna get it fixed,
> Cryin' oh, look what the Greyhound has done to me etc.

When you change your numbers play 13–32 and 51,
But be careful buddy 'cause you might have to run,
> Cryin' oh, look what that policy wheel have done to me etc.

Now while you playin' policy buddy, play 5–9 and 59,
But be careful buddy, 'cause you might lose your mind,
> Cryin' oh, look what the Coalfield have done to me etc.

Now if you feel like gamblin' play 11–7 and 61,
If they don't give you your money go buy you a Gatlin' gun,
> Cryin' oh, look what the Greyhound have done to me etc.

Now if you wake up in the mornin' ain't got nothin' on your mind,

Play that ole country number that you call 3–6 and 9,
    Cryin' oh look what that policy wheel have done to me,
    It done took all my money and still it won't let me be.[16]

Of the number combinations that Kokomo Arnold lists, a few are easily deciphered. 5–9–59 is the most obvious with power (9) placed between woman (5) and virgin (59). 'When you change your numbers' appears to refer to a change of partners also, for 13–32–51 places exchange (32) between the numbers for lover and woman and man. Other numbers in his blues are more obscure, lending themselves to a variety of interpretations which would be dependent in part on the plays popular at the time of recording in the Chicago Black Belt. But their very obscurantism had its value for the Negro who bought the blues records. They helped to give him the security of being part of a tightly knit community and afforded him a sense of racial solidarity. White people may play policy but they would be unlikely to penetrate the protective code of numbers which screened subversive or taboo themes.

In general use the numbers books are consulted for guidance on the appropriate plays to make after any likely event or promising dream. Most confirmed policy players have stories of coincidences, superstitions and events which have led to successful or unsuccessful plays. John Sellers gave me an example:

'I was kind of broke one time in New York, so my grandmother came to me and said, "Play 6–30." I said, "Oh," because I never won anything. So I didn't play 'til the next night, when she said the same thing, "Play 6–30." So I played the number and put 50 cents on it. I never bothered to ask what the number was the next night. Well, three days passed and a friend of mine came down from Harlem. I said, "What was the number?" He said, "6–30". I said, "Aw, you got it wrong," but he said, "That's what I heard." So I rang a friend who knew the number and he said, "It was 6–30." So I got nervous 'cause the man might've run off. I just ran to his house. When I got to the man he said, "Where you been? I had your money." So I had 50 cents on the number which brought me $270! This was on the 16th of May, and my birthday is on the 27th. Before my birthday my grandmother said, "Play 6–30." I said, "Well now, that's just a foolish dream 'cause I just played 6–30; it's impossible for it to come again." So I told the man who takes the numbers and he said, "Well, you ought to try it anyway." I said,

"Aw it's foolish, it'll never come no more, you know how they do—
I ain't no fool." So he said, "Well, I'm gonna try it, John." So on my
birthday the number came up! The man had five dollars on it which
brought him $3,000 and I had nothing!'

Most players would have tried the tip, for every incident, and especially every dream, has its significance for the policy player. In New
Orleans, Willis James explained that lottery was especially popular with
Negroes ' 'cause they dreams so much. You see, lottery is dreamin' and
dreamin' is lottery. That's the truth. . . . We is just natural dreamers
'cause we eats too much. So eatin' is the cause, and the effects is
dreamin' and lottery. Take me. All I got to do to dream is just eat four
or five bananas before I go to bed. That sure do make me dream!
Then next day I makes me a gig and wins nine dollars. That's plenty of
money, specially for a nickel.' Martha White from the same sector of
New Orleans explained, 'When you dreams you see an angel, there's the
Angel Gig, fourteen, sixty-five and nineteen. You can't miss. When you
dreams your nose is leakin', you get a gig on fourteen, one and six.'
And a shoe-shine boy added, 'You gotta play your hunches. You gotta
play what comes to you. Dreams is a good way. Everybody plays their
dreams. Sure I got me a dream book.'[17]
Recording in New Orleans in 1936, Tommy Griffin sang of the
dream book:

I dreamed about my baby every time I go to sleep, (2)
Then the blues come creepin' from my head down to my feet.

I hate to dream things about her, Lord when it is not true, (2)
It keeps me always worried, always feelin' blue.

I'm gonna buy me a dream book, see what my dream means, (2)
I dreamed I was mixin' sweet milk with my baby's cream.

She didn't make no butter, she didn't even make no bread, (2)
But she began talkin' like she was out of her head. . . .[18]

If he had bought his dream book as he proposed in this *Dream Book
Blues*, Tommy Griffin would have been agreeably surprised. Bad dreams
are frequently interpreted as good omens while milk and cream (14)

are good love symbols. His girl's mad talking was favourable too—he would probably have played 5–8–40–55.

The dream book provides an interpretation of dreams and number combinations to fit them. There are many dream books and they vary in details; nevertheless the interpretations and numbers are rather remarkable for their consistency. They claim mystical origins and undoubtedly have been derived from much earlier sources than might be supposed. A South Side Negro might hardly be expected to dream of a harlequin (49–63), of a dromedary (11–14–41), a hussar (26–29–50), Saint Agnes's Eve (9–27–36) or a glove-maker (4–24–67)—but here are the combinations just in case he does. The range of subjects is so wide that one might be justified in feeling that one's own dreams are rather mundane by comparison, but there are combinations for every situation and event, whether dreamed or not. Beat a cat and expect treachery, play 41 in your combination. Shave a young girl—it's a good omen, play 12–40. If a tooth falls from your mouth play 39–51–62—you risk losing a relative though. Someone fishing in your pond? Try 4–7–9–14–71 for, surprisingly, you can expect good fortune. You will be quarrelsome if you have a mole on your anus . . . but you can turn it to good account by playing 4–5–9.

To the blues collector the commonest numbers are 3–6–9 and 4–11–44. Most casual collectors are probably familiar with Cripple Clarence Lofton's *Policy Blues:*

If I don't get policy, buy me a 45,
If I don't catch policy, buy me a hard shootin' 45,
I'm gettin' tired of these policy writers tellin' me plenty lies.
Says, 'Now look here son, you better not be late,
That gig won't come out in the Interstate.
So you better get down and get down right,
That gig gonna fall out tonight.'
If I don't catch policy, kill every writer I see,
I'm gettin' tired of these policy writers 3–6–9in' for me.
Next day she come around I could tell by her looks,
That I had played those numbers in the wrong books.
Now I plays policy both day and night,
But none of those numbers ever comes out right.
If I don't catch policy, kill every writer I see.
I'm gettin' tired of these policy writers 3–6–9in' for me.[19]

Why should 3–6–9, apparently a favourable and frequent number to play, be used here as an unfavourable adjective? The reason is that 3–6–9 is the combination for excreta both animal and human. Many unpleasant associations have highly favourable number combinations and dream interpretations—there are Freudian overtones in many of these which show unusual awareness of dream interpretation in the psychological sense. But the average player needs his numbers book and dream book to find out what they mean. In the perverse application of symbols 3–6–9 is a good luck sign and advantageous to play. But its literal significance is not ignored and is applied here to the assumed vindictiveness of the policy writer. 4–11–44 is similarly sometimes used in a mildly obscene way when it is thought of as a phallic symbol. The picture of Aunt Sally on *Aunt Sally's Policy Players Dream Book* shows her leering and pointing to the combination 4–11–44, the significance of which being only apparent to those who know the meaning of the combination. But 4–11–44 is also the combination for apples, some animals and for policy itself—all potent good luck symbols. It is the combination for the zebra, the symbol of racial and numerical harmony. Known in New Orleans as 'the Washwoman's Gig', the combination 4–11–44 became so popular as a play in December 1936 that when 'the gig came up' one major company was seriously crippled by the heavy payments to lucky players. Within a week the combination came up again in the Pelican, the largest of the Negro-owned lotteries in New Orleans and the company was nearly broken by its heavy losses.[20] Sara Lawson, a New Orleans rag-picker and washwoman, sang to a writer of the Louisiana Writers' Project a lottery song about the Washwoman's Gig which suggests links with *Four Eleven Forty-Four*, quoted above by Papa Charlie Jackson, who was himself from New Orleans. Part of her song ran:

Four, 'leven and forty-four,
Four, 'leven and forty-four,
Soapy water and dirty clo'es.
I'm bustin' these suds,
Up to my elbows!
Four, 'leven and forty-four,
Four, 'leven and forty-four,
Let me hit that gig.
I'm needin' my man so bad,

I'm feelin' freakish;
It's makin' me mean, lowdown and sad![21]

Clarence Lofton's item was a shorter version of a famous extended
blues by Louisiana Johnny which rapidly became a traditional vehicle
for blues on the theme. A number of singers used the framework of
Louisiana Johnny's original, employing some of his verses and adding
ones of their own invention. Lofton had himself almost certainly been
the pianist on Albert Clemens's *Policy Blues*. Clemens, or rather, Adam
Wilcox under a pseudonym, sub-titled his blues *You Can't 3–6–9 Me*.
He commenced with the verses which became the key to all these
versions:

If I don't catch policy, buy me a 45,
If I don't catch policy, buy me a hard-shootin' 45,
I'm gettin' tired of you policy writers tellin' me of plenty lies.

and added a verse of his own:

Now look here policy writer I play both night and day,
You gets my money and then you walk away,
And if I don't catch policy I'm gonna lay you low,
'Cause I'm getting sick and tired of you takin' my dough,
    If I don't catch policy kill every writer I see,
    I'm gettin' tired of you policy writers 3–6–9in' for me.'[22]

Clemens's record was made in April 1935 and a little over three years
later Washboard Sam elaborated on the same theme with his *Policy
Writer's Blues*. It was, as its name implied, directed against the policy
writer. By the 1950s policy had become more respectable and, as E.
Franklin Frazier showed, was played daily by Negro professional men,
and even the wives of professors in Negro colleges worked as part-time
policy writers. But in the mid-'thirties the numbers game was still
considered the province of the Negro lower class by the 'Black Bourgeoisie' who preferred to gamble on horses.[23] Within the lower class
the policy writer was considered a parasite who lived off his fellows.
Under the camouflage of the number combinations, policy blues could
have been easily employed for racial protest; instead, they protested
against the policy writers who lived off the bets of the poor. Washboard
Sam's blues, like several others, followed Louisiana Johnny's example.

Policy Blues

Louisiana Johnny's composition was a two-part blues entitled
Policy Blues on one side and *Three–Six Nine Blues* on the other. It ran:

Now if I don't catch policy, buy me a 45,
If I don't catch policy, buy me a hard-shootin' 45,
I'm gettin' tired of you policy writers tellin' me plenty lies.

Now she told me to play 'clear water' you know that's 1–2–3, (2)
But I'm gettin' tired of these policy writers 3–6–9in' for me.

The very next day, she knocked on my door,
I told her I was gonna play those numbers just once more.
And if I don't catch, I ain't gonna play no more,
She told me to play 40–50 and 74.
    If I don't catch policy—see if I don't—kill every writer I see,
    I'm gettin' tired of these policy writers 3–6–9in' for me.

Now look here policy writer I plays both day and night,
None of my gigs ever comes out right,
I tried to play policy, play what you say,
None of those gigs have come out today.
    If I don't catch policy etc.

Now I had a dream my numbers would fall,
None of those doggone numbers ever come out at all.
Here you come around with that same old jive,
Tellin' me to play 25–50 and 75.
    If I don't catch policy etc.

Everyday, when you look out,
And see that policy writer comin' to your house,
'Look here son, lay your gigs on the line.
Catch that 4–18 and 59.'
    If I don't catch policy etc.

The next day when she come around I could tell by her looks,
I had played those numbers in the wrong doggone books,
I plays policy both day and night,
And none of those numbers ever comes out right.
    If I don't catch policy etc.

'Now look here son, you better not be late,
That gig's gonna come in the Interstate,
So you better get down, and get it down right,
Man it's gonna fall out tonight.'
    If I don't catch policy etc.

I'm tellin' you policy writers you better walk slow,
I'm gettin' tired of you knockin' my back-door,
If I don't catch I ain't gonna play no more,
'Cause I'm gettin' tired of playin' 4–11–44.
    If I don't catch policy, kill every writer I see,
    I'm gettin' tired of you policy writers 3–6–9in' for me.[24]

The Interstate was one of the most lucrative of the policy wheels at that time when there were some 500 'stations'—lucrative, that is, for the owners who were allowed to keep a quarter of the business they wrote. The takings for a week averaged around $6,000.00 on the Interstate at this period with rather more than a third being paid out on hits.[25] The gross takings for the policy writers were considerable. In spite of the admiration of the policy racketeers, which was everywhere evident, many of the players were jealous and angry over the exploitation, as the variants on Louisiana Johnny's blues clearly showed. Probably they took pleasure instead in the overtones of meaning in the plays which he recited and this served as some compensation for their frustration. For the plays he described were all sexual ones, with clear water being in itself a sexual metaphor—1–2–3 being made up of man (1), scoundrel (2) and filth (3). Similarly, 40–50–74 is a female sexual play made up from bull (40) or siege (40), garters (50) and pregnant woman (50), with gold coin (74) and dryness (74). The next play was an alternative to this, with 50 remaining but flanked by rope 25 (i.e. potency) and 75—potatoes (i.e. genitalia). The play takes on a more sinister tone with 4–18–59 (figs, child-bed, dead woman) and Louisiana Johnny concludes with dissatisfaction at playing the no longer potent 4–11–44. To the player armed with *Aunt Della's Dream Book* or *Aunt Sally's Dream Book*, *The Gipsy Witch Dream Book* or *The Three Witches Dream Book*, the interpretation of the numbers and the subtler levels of the blues presented no difficulty.

With such layers of meaning the policy blues had a strong appeal in the 'thirties, fortifying the feeling of being a part of a tightly knit social group. During the war years business trebled and has shown little sign of abating. Policy and the dream books still have a strong hold on the least privileged in Negro society. A reporter for the *World Telegram* in the spring of 1942 counted 142 men and women placing their bets in a numbers drop within the space of three-quarters of an hour; some indication of the extent of play in Harlem during war-time.[26] In the post-war years blues singers have composed fewer blues directly concerned with policy although references appear in many blues; in for instance James Banister's *Gold Digger*:

My baby must be a gold digger, she got all my pockets clean,
Yes, you must be a gold digger woman, you got all my pockets
    clean,
Now since you know I'm down and out darlin' woman, you begin
    to scream.

You plays policy on a Friday, yes and race horses everyday,
You plays policy on a Friday baby, you race horses everyday,
Well you don't try to help me none baby, you throwin' all
    my money away.[27]

These days the blues singer may sing less about policy and Louisiana Johnny's blues may now be forgotten, but the blues singer still plays policy; visit the home of a blues singer and there will be yellow policy slips on the television set. New York, Harlem and Brooklyn are still the centres of the policy racket and the District Attorney in the late 1950s estimated that the policy crime ring was running a business of around a hundred million dollars a year. The syndicate still controls policy in Chicago and, though there have been concerted efforts to break the policy rings and to stamp the racket out, Arbee Stidham sums up the point of view of the South Side Negro who hopes to 'catch' next time round:

Eeeh Mister Commissioner, do you know what you're doin'?
You're breakin' up the numbers racket and drivin' the poor people
    to ruin.
    Don't you know, Mister Commissioner man, don't you know,
    Mister Commissioner man, don't you know,
    You're knockin' the poor people outa whole lotta dough.

You step t' buy the stamp, you wanna stay the race,
But you can't find a stamp before the police raid that place.
    Don't you know, Mister Commissioner man etc.

Some books went down, they just couldn't stand,
But one bunch stood by with a hard-going twenty grand.
    Don't you know, Mister Commissioner man etc.

Now once they went down they knocked up twenty grand,
I wanna tell all you people, people all of it's banned.
    Don't you know, Mister Commissioner man etc.

When they knocked the numbers racket, the world started them on,
Like when President Roosevelt died, they knew somethin' good was
    gone.
    Don't you know, Mister Commissioner man, don't you know,
    Mister Commissioner man, don't you know,
    You're knockin' the poor people outa whole lotta dough.[28]

While there are still the 'poor people' anxious to pay out small sums in the hopes of a hit, policy will continue to flourish and racketeers will make a fortune out of them. Some days after the police received a call to come to the aid of a dying man, Lawrence Wakefield in 1964, they made an investigation into his circumstances. A police officer found in one of his rooms a number of bags which yielded nearly a million dollars in bills when they were finally counted, together with policy equipment. Wakefield's fortune was divided between the county, the state, the federal government and Wakefield's white, common-law wife, Mrs Rose Kennedy, whose share was $431,000.[29] The disclosures revealed the extent of Wakefield's policy operations, concealed until his sudden demise. No doubt his successors will take even more careful precautions to protect their interests and no doubt, too, the blues singers will continue to be numbered among their clients. For, as Lightnin' Hopkins, himself an inveterate gambler, explained in his *Policy Game*:

You heard 'em at home say gamblers just don't loose out ain't cha? We all taken' a chance when we play one of them numbers and it don't come out like we want it—we play 'em anyhow. . . . Keep on bettin' . . . bound to win. That's the way you gonna play policy all over again. . . .

Tell me sweet baby somebody gone win for you,
Tell me sweet baby some Johnny win for you,
I know I got lucky when I played number 42.

I played number 10 but God knows I couldn't win, (2)
I'm gonna keep on bettin' till my bluff comes back again.[30]

Though the blues is a simple form of music which has flexible applications it is still circumscribed in its content. There are clearly functions which the blues could have performed and themes which blues singers were in a position to sing about which are hardly ever recorded in their songs. The blues, for instance, is seldom concerned with narrative events about people other than the singer and his immediate circle; personal contact seems especially important to the blues singer and though there are exceptions, they are relatively isolated. It is the exceptions, in fact, which tend to underline these limitations of the blues. It would seem that the blues did not assume to any great degree the role of the ballad in reciting the details of events that had acquired heroic, significant or symbolic importance in the lives of Negroes. Though there are instances of blues in which an individual is the subject of the song—Tommy Johnson's *Maggie Campbell* or Sleepy John Estes's *Lawyer Clark* for instance—these were persons known to the singers or with whom they had some immediate contact. There are no blues devoted to the achievements of Paul Robeson, George Washington Carver or Ralph Bunche, though these figures in their different fields would probably have been known to the more literate and especially the city-dwelling singers. It seems likely that their culture, their educational opportunities, their success in areas largely dominated by white people, had separated them from the world of the blues singer to the point where they had very little immediate significance to him, as achievement in a white-dominated activity was until very recently beyond the likely horizons of any blues singer.

It would seem, then, that any blues composed about singular figures who could assume heroic stature and whose importance would be that of ballad heroes would have to be of people whose actions affected the blues singer materially, or emotionally, to the point where he felt personally concerned. This would seem to be the case in the few instances of persons who have been the subject of blues by several singers. President Roosevelt's New Deal had a direct effect on the lives of Negroes and was the subject perpetuated in the memories of Negroes in a small number of blues. The death of Leroy Carr, himself a blues singer whose popularity was widespread, produced a number of blues in mourning from singers who had been emotionally moved by the loss of one of the most important singers of his day. But these are rare instances—the one a politician, whose actions had given hope to many Negroes and the other a blues singer, who was the image of themselves. In the 'thirties the Negro needed desperately to associate himself with a new society in which he could play a part, and the loss of an individual who was a spokesman for him was especially painful. In this period the war in Ethiopia was taking its course and Negro feelings were outraged by the bombing of the Ethiopian towns. The war featured prominently in the Negro newspapers and there was a strong feeling of association with Emperor Haile Selassie and his tribesmen which was not, however, to be found reflected in the blues of the period. The events were too far away for a clear conception of them to be in the experience of blues singers but the successes of the Negro sportsmen in the Olympic Games of 1936, which took place before Adolf Hitler in Berlin, would seem to have within them the elements that could have inspired a folk-lore. With a prodigious 6ft $7\frac{15}{16}$ in, Cornelius Johnson took the Running High Jump record while John Woodruff won the 800 metres in 1 minute 52·9 seconds. Ralph Metcalfe and Jesse Owens together made up half of the winning 400 metre relay team while the incredible, incomparable Jesse Owens won the Running Broad Jump with a record leap of 26ft $5\frac{5}{16}$ in, took the 200 metres with a championship 20·7 seconds and won the 100 metres, with the wind, in 10·3 seconds. Joe Louis, who had been greatly disturbed by the fact that the Olympic games were even being held in Germany, was jubilant over the success of the Negro champions.

But though the Negro Press was naturally overjoyed by their performances and reflected the happiness shared by Negroes throughout the United States, not even Jesse Owens was commemorated in a blues, at any rate on record. Perhaps these events also were too remote for most Negroes for whom the events on American soil before the eyes of watching white Americans would have been more immediate. But the achievements of Jesse Owens and the culminating gesture by Hitler who left the arena rather than have to congratulate the winners from a non-Aryan race did not inspire any blues. For the blues singer, Joe Louis was the singular inspiration of a man who had within his achievements all the drama, the appeal and the invincibility of the traditional Negro ballad hero.

For all his extraordinary successes Jesse Owens was a member of a team, a team which was an American one which fought for America first. This was as it should be, but the state of mind of the Negro in America at the time was not one to moralize on such issues; the pains of the Depression, the injustices of job discrimination were too close.

Joe Louis fought as an individual, as an individual Negro and, in winning his way through a succession of bouts in which contender after contender fell before the skilful placing of his rapid left jabs and swift uppercuts, he enacted in real life the struggle that the Negro felt in his heart was his own. With Louis he could identify himself, every Negro boy on a street corner in Harlem could become, and in his own imagination did become, a Joe Louis battling for his right to live and coming out on top. It was this essential loneliness that made some meaning for the blues singer, himself an individual and speaking more for himself than in abstractions for his society. Identification was simpler and could be for the blues singer almost complete.

In his birth and upbringing Joe Louis echoed, too, the lives of countless numbers of his own generation—that he achieved supremacy in the ring from these beginnings made the possibility of a like success more real for every Negro. Joe Louis was born on 13 May 1914, deep in rural Alabama near Lafayette in Chambers County, a dozen miles from the Georgia state boundary. His parents were tenant farmers and Joe Louis Barrow, to give him his full name, was their fifth child. The Depression halted his rudimentary education and he did not advance beyond the lower grades at school. The grandson of a slave, he seemed destined to a life of tenant farming and up to the age of twelve worked in the fields and picked cotton in the summer. But in 1926 his mother took him and his seven brothers and sisters to join their stepfather in Detroit and it was there that he had an opportunity to develop his skill as a fighter. In the ensuing years he proved himself to be a talented amateur, eventually winning the AAU light-heavy-weight championship. He was working for Ford's motor plant in Detroit for five dollars a day, and playing a cheap violin at night to augment his income when he decided to risk turning professional. On 4 July 1934, for a fifty-dollar purse, he fought Jack Kracken in Chicago to win with a knock-out in the first round. Under the managership of John Roxborough and Julian Black and the careful, wily training of the veteran boxer, Jack Blackburn, he was to win every one of his next twenty-six bouts, and all but four of them by a knock-out.

It was Joe Louis's defeat of Primo Carnera which caught the imagination of the singers. Louis had made an astonishing rise through the bouts which he had fought in the couple of years since he had turned professional but it was not until his confrontation with the immense Italian that the full significance of Louis's conquering progression became evident. Then the whole Negro world listened with apprehension to their radios as the fight came on. The immense Italian towered above Louis, himself no mean height at 6ft 1½ in and weighing 260 lb, for Carnera was nearly 4 stone heavier than his opponent. On the sticky June night Louis fought for the honour of the Negro, for the opponents of Italy and her murderous assault on Ethiopia, and for himself. Darting his blows through the defences of the Italian, he attacked him through five rounds until, in the sixth, he laid the giant to the canvas three times. With blood all over his features the gallant but defeated Carnera was unable to rise from the third fall and Joe Louis was declared the winner. The joy of the Negro populace was expressed in a spontaneous outburst of celebration which was recalled by Roi Ottley, a reporter for the *New York Amsterdam Star-News*:

'The expected pandemonium broke loose when the referee lifted the Negro's hand and radio flashed the word around the country. Whether it was the South Side of Chicago, St Antoine Street of Detroit, or the Hill District of Pittsburgh, Negro communities throughout the nation went crazy with joy. Everywhere Negroes marched through the streets, slapping backs, shaking hands, and congratulating each other. There was shouting, clapping, laughing and even crying. Children who should have been long in bed were on the streets pounding ashcans and yelling. Juke boxes blared from every tavern, and young couples broke into the Lindy Hop. Old folks capered happily. Everywhere this hilarity lasted until the early hours of morning.'[1]

The destruction of the mighty Carnera was an achievement which seemed to signify that the Negro was now capable of surmounting his difficulties. His elation was echoed in an outpouring of songs from blues singers, the first being composed by Joe Pullum, a Houston singer who was accompanied on *Joe Louis Is the Man* by Andy Boy's stomping piano. It was an accurate comment on the role of the new boxer in Negro society as a folk hero, even if it was a naïve piece of folk poetry:

Joe Louis is a battlin' man,
The people think his fame will always stand.
He's the brown bomber of this land,
He's supposed to whop 'most any man.
He's got a real good left and a real good right,
When he grapples he's the one that stops the fight.

He's not a bad dressed guy and his hair is curled,
He's the champion now—of the world,
He's bound to be the next champion of the world.
I said Joe is the battlin' man,
Bought his mother a brand new home and some brand new land.
You can gather his intentions must be good,
'Cause he's doing the things for his mother a boy really should.
He's makin' real good money and it doesn't swell his head,
He throws his fist like a 45 throwin' lead.
He throws 'em heavy and he throws them slow,
Then you know it's powerful Joe,
And boy if he hits you, you sure bound to hit the floor.[2]

Shortly before the fight Louis had bought a house for his mother and furnished it. In the matriarchate of Negro society the boxer's support of his mother won Joe Pullum's approval. But though he was making good money and it didn't 'swell his head' there were others who felt he was not using it wisely.

He married his first wife, Marva, that year, a few days before he met Max Baer and was at this time spending freely 'on trinkets, jewels, furs, trips abroad, gambling on the golf course, poor investments, lavish tips and clothes' according to Gay Talese.[3] His golfing enthusiasm, which eventually led him to gamble as much as a thousand dollars on a hole, commenced some two years later. If he was 'not a bad dressed guy' at this time he was soon to remedy this with a passion for new clothes, while his hair being 'curled' gave an effective endorsement to a Negro firm making men's toilet preparations.

Barely a week after Joe Pullum had recorded his song in San Antonio, Texas, for Bluebird, another singer had a similar idea. Memphis Minnie McCoy in Chicago, singing to the accompaniment of her own guitar and the powerful piano of Black Bob, recorded *He's in the Ring* (*Doin' the Same Old Thing*). If the Vocalion company worked hard at the issue they would have just had it released in time for the meeting of Joe Louis with Max Baer which resulted in a knock-out win for Louis in the fourth round:

When your people's goin' out tonight,
Jes' goin' to see Joe Louis fight,
An' if you ain't got no money gotta go tomorrow night,
'Cause he's in the ring doin' the same ol' thing.

Vocalion Records thank "The Race," while Ma Rainey, Blind Lemon Jefferson, Elzadie Robinson and Charlie "Dad" Nelson are among the blues singers included in Paramount's seasonal advertisement, December 1926.

Eddie "Son" House played slide guitar to accompany his *Preachin' the Blues*. Photo: Paul Oliver, 1967

Georgia Tom, piano partner to Tampa Red and joint composer of *Tight Like That,* in 1928. A few years later, under his real name of Thomas A. Dorsey, he began his career as a composer of gospel songs.

Memphis Minnie's *Joe Louis Strut,* backed by *He's In the Ring (Doing the Same Old Thing),* made with "Black Bob" Hudson on piano and Bill Settles on bass, were recorded on 22 August, 1935.

Roosevelt Sykes, age 23, when he arrived in Chicago to make the first recording of *44 Blues*.

Mary Stafford's suggestively titled record was made with an unknown jazz band accompaniment in New York on 30 March, 1926. Numerous singers tried to cash in on the success of Tampa Red and Georgia Tom's *Tight Like That*.

STUDY OF HARMONY IN NUMBERS

The powerful "Numbers" combination of 4-11-44 is knowingly indicated by "Aunt Sally" on the cover of a "Dream Book."

POLICY PLAYERS'
DREAM BOOK

The True Interpretation of Dreams, and also the Numbers of the Lottery to which they Apply.

ABSENCE.—To see absent persons in your dreams is certain sign of their return. 4, 11.

ACORN.—Denotes poverty. 7, 33.

ACQUISITION.—A favorable sign to the dreamer 2, 19, 46.

ACTIVITY.—If you dream that you are very active, it shows you will have great losses through your own negligence. 10, 11, 75.

ACTRESS.—To see one play, misfortune; if you talk with her, you will have success in what you undertake; if you make love to her, your life will be joyful. If you dream that you enjoy her, you will meet great troubles. 14, 36, 52.

ADOPTION.—To dream of adopting children, foreshadows sorrow and trouble. 21.

ADMIRATION.—If you dream that you are admired, it foretells good fortune; but if you admire any one else, it is a very bad sign. 59, 71.

ADULTERY.—If you commit it in your dreams, you must prepare for misfortune and disgrace. 1, 11, 39.

AIR.—If you dream that it is clear, it signifies that you will come into a great fortune; if the air is foggy, you will have sorrows; if it is filled with sweet odors, you will be successful in love. 42.

ALMONDS.—Signify embarrassments, all which you may avoid by care; to eat them, good fortune. 61, 76.

ALTAR.—To dream that you see an altar, betokens your speedy marriage. 36, 51, 57, 62.

ANGEL.—To dream of an angel, brings joyous tidings; if the angel does not approach you, it is a sign that your life is evil, and a warning to reform. 14, 65.

5

Entries in a "Policy Player's Dream Book" give the appropriate and propitious numbers to play following a dream.

Player's number slips for the "Red Devil" policy "Wheel"—with explanatory note by Brother John Sellers. The third figure "drawn" is printed on the back of the slip.

Edith Johnson's *Honey Dripper Blues* was made in October 1929 and advertised in the *Chicago Defender* on 16 November. Also listed is *Screenin' the Blues* by Ike Rodgers, with piano accompaniment by Henry Brown.

Papa Charlie Jackson's version of the old bawdy song *'bout a Spoonful* was recorded around September 1925, but Paramount waited until the festive season before advertising it in the *Chicago Defender* 6 December 1925.

Dallas pianist "Whistling" Alex Moore recorded *Blue Bloomer Blues* in 1937 and made a new version in Stuttgart over thirty years later. Photo: Paul Oliver, 1969

Well he even carries a mean left,
(*Spoken*) Ya know he do.
An' he carry a mean right,
An' if he hits you with either one,
Tha's the charge from a dynamite,
In the ring boys, doin' the same old thing.

Gonna tell all a you prize fighters,
Don't take Joe for no fool,
If he hits you with that left duke,
Tha's a kick from a Texas mule,
In the ring boys, doin' the same old thing.

Joe Louis is a two-fist fighter,
An' he stands six feet tall,
An' the bigger they come, he say,
'The harder they fall.'
In the ring, oh, doin' the same old thing.
(*Spoken*) I chance my money wid 'im.

Boys I only had ten hunnerd dollars,
An' I laid 'em up on my shelf,
I bet everybody passed my house,
In one round Joe would knock him out,
In the ring doin' the same old thing.

I wouldn't even pay my house rent,
I wouldn't buy me nothing to eat,
Joe Louis can take a chance at me,
I will quit ya on your feet,
In the ring. (*Spoken*) He's still fightin',
Doin' the same old thing.[4]

Memphis Minnie backed her item with another paean to Joe Louis
—a *Joe Louis Strut*, mainly spoken comments and exultant cries which
demonstrated as effectively as any recording the mood of happiness and
new confidence that his bouts had inspired. In the words of the Negro
weekly, the *Pittsburgh Courier*, he 'lifted an entire race out of the slough
of inferiority, and gave them a sense of self-importance'.[5] This sense of

assurance was reflected in yet another song made just a few days later than Memphis Minnie's and still before the Baer fight. On 4 September Carl Martin offered his own challenge to other boxers on Joe Louis's behalf:

Now listen all you prize fighters who don't want to be defeat, (2)
Take a tip from me, stay off Joe Louis's beat.

Now he won all his fights, twenty-three or four,
And left twenty of his opponents lying on the floor,
They all bound to win but his left was too hard,
When he laid that hambone up against their bars.
        Listen all you prize fighters don't play him too cheap,
        If he lands with either hand he'll sure put you to sleep.

He's a real fighter—I bet on him!
He knows just what to do. . . .
I'm talking to you. . . .

Now he packs that might in the left, he carries 'em in the right,
Either one will make you rocky or retire from the fight,
He charges in on his opponents from the beginning of the gong,
He fights under supervision then they all sing a song.
        I bet on the Brown Bomber boy he knows his stuff,
        And lays it on his opponents until he gets enough.

Now he's a nachal born fighter who likes to fight 'em all,
'The bigger they come,' he says, 'the harder they fall.'
That terrific left boys is all he needs,
But that fist in his right comes with lightnin' speed.
        Listen all you prize fighters don't play him too cheap,
        Take a tip from me, stay off Joe Louis's beat.[6]

There were other compositions, Ike Smith's *Fighting Joe Louis*, for instance, and *Joe Louis Chant* by George Dewey Washington. A Negro monologuist, Washington dressed in hobo's clothes, told sentimental or patriotic stories and had enjoyed a successful tour in Great Britain some seven years before. Though further from the blues, his monologue had some affinities with the songs of the blues singers—

optimistic, proud, frankly hero-worshipping. One record distributor, W. Boerner of Port Washington, Wisconsin, grouped some of the records together and, under a passable portrait of the boxer in action, presented them as 'four great records dedicated to Joe Louis, the Brown Bomber, still our bet for the championship. Be sure to get these records'.[7]

Still the best bet, for the Brown Bomber was yet to gain the championship, though the nickname which the Press had given him was so widely acknowledged that one enterprising Negro firm named a brand of bread Brown Bomber in his honour. Paulino Uzcudum followed Max Baer to the mat with a knock-out in the fourth round and, early in 1936, Louis demolished Charlie Retzlaff in Chicago with a knock-out in the first. He seemed invincible and a Chicago singer, Lil Johnson, came up with her contribution in the composition *Winner Joe (the Knock-Out King)*.

Now the stage was almost set for his assault on the world championship, but first he had to meet Max Schmeling, a Nazi whose fight had been resisted in Germany on the grounds that he should not have to contest a Negro. The fight was boycotted by the Jews in New York but the crowd of forty thousand still brought in gate receipts in excess of half a million dollars, though this was little more than half the receipts from the fight with Max Baer. A stunned crowd saw Joe Louis knocked out by the German in the twelfth round.

Negroes took the shock of Joe Louis's defeat by Max Schmeling deeply and personally. The bitterness of their disappointment was a reflection of their dependence upon him as a symbol and the Negroes who wept unashamedly in the streets at the news made no attempt to hide their humiliation. In Germany there was rejoicing and Goebbels cabled the official gratitude of the Nazi Party to the man who had saved, in their eyes, the prestige of the Aryan race.

Though the blues frequently expresses anger, frustration and often passive acceptance of adversity, disappointment as an emotional stimulus to the blues is extremely rare. If the blues singer felt disappointment over Joe Louis's defeat he did not show it in his blues or, at least, not on record, for the degree to which the blues on record represents the blues as sung under other circumstances must always remain an open question. There seems little doubt that as a commercial proposition a blues on Joe Louis's defeat would hardly have offered the incentive for purchase that one on his successes would have done, but it is likely that his defeat at the hands of Max Schmeling destroyed for the singer the quality of an invincible folk hero which he had assumed. He could not in this defeat reflect the death of John Henry whose fatal exhaustion, as he attempted to fight the allegedly impossible odds of the machine, had the truly heroic mould. Joe Louis fell under odds that were human and equal.

Louis's comment was laconic. 'Me and Chappie's going back to school,' he said. And back to school Joe Louis went, with a determination to train for a return bout in which he would avenge not only himself but his race. Louis was himself greatly hurt by the defeat and was acutely aware of the racial implications of Schmeling's success. He trained hard and a succession of contests in the rest of the year did much to restore his confidence. Jack Sharkey was the first to fall. Sharkey had fought Schmeling in 1930 and fouled in the fourth round to make Schmeling the world champion. In a return bout two years later he won on a points decision to become himself the world champion, only to fall himself in the sixth round of a subsequent fight to Primo Carnera. But he was an opponent with a formidable record and when Louis stopped him with a knock-out in the third round on 17 August his anxious race began to breathe more easily. For Negroes this was a remarkable year of sporting successes and it must have seemed that Joe Louis's defeat was avenged by the successes of the Olympic team in Berlin that year at the Reichssports Field.

In fights in Philadelphia, New York, Cleveland, Buffalo and Kansas City, Joe Louis defeated Al Ettore, Jorge Bescia, Eddie Simms, Stanley Ketchell, Bob Pastor and Natie Brown, knocking out his opponents in all but one instance and coming face to face with the Irish-born world champion, James J. Braddock, on 22 June 1937. Braddock fell to a knock-out blow in the eighth round and Joe Louis justified Joe Pullum's prediction that he was 'boun' to be the champion of the world'.

The event was celebrated within two days by one Billy Hicks, who with his Sizzling Six had composed and recorded *Joe the Bomber* on Variety 601 with a group which included the New Orleans clarinettist, Edmund Hall. There do not appear to have been any blues composed about the event and blues singers may have reflected a certain unease at Joe Louis's new-won title. Now that he was world champion he may have represented less of the battle and more of the achievement.

The longed-for return bout with Max Schmeling took place exactly a year after Louis's winning the world championship, on 22 June 1938, when he met the Nazi at the Yankee Stadium, before a crowd of seventy thousand which included a thousand Germans who had come from the fatherland to see the Aryan win. They saw him lose in a terrible, annihilating attack. From the moment that the bell rang for the commencement of the fight, Joe Louis threw a punishing succession of blows, his arms working like pistons. Dazed and scarcely able to defend himself, the German fell, rose, fell again. He was able to return only four punches in that single round before he was laid to the canvas with a devastating knock-out punch.

In the recording studio the very next day, Bill Gaither, in a simple blues, summarized the pride that all his race shared. Joe Louis had regained his folk-hero stature; the successful vengeance had the elements of a Western epic; justice had been done, right had triumphed. But the exultant delirium of the glorious days of the boxer's rapid victories on the way to the 'crown' had gone. A sober composition, Gaither's blues concluded with a wry comment on the money he could have made if he had been in a position to back him heavily enough:

I came all the way from Chicago to see Joe Louis and Max
    Schmeling fight, (2)
Schmeling went down like the *Titanic* when Joe gave him just one
    hard right.

Schmeling made a pass at Joe but Joe was just a little too fas', (2)
If Schmeling thought he was carryin' the crown away, that was
    just his yas yas yas.

Well, you've heard of the King of Swing, well Joe is the King
    of Gloves, (2)
Now he's the world's heavy-weight champion, a man that this
    whole world loves.

It was only two minutes and four seconds poor Schmeling was
    down on his knees, (2)
He looked like he was praying to the Good Lord to have 'Mercy
    on me please'.

If I'd had a million dollars I'd've bet every dime on Joe, (2)
I'd've been a rich man this very day and I wouldn't have to worry
    no more.[8]

If Joe Louis's honour was restored with his demolition of Schmeling there were relatively few blues concerning the fight, though one, *Joe Louis*, was recorded by Sampson Pittman for the Library of Congress in Detroit, but this unfortunately remains unissued.

On 25 January 1939, Joe Louis defended his title against another Negro boxer, John Henry Lewis. Lewis was himself a considerable fighter in the light-heavy-weight class having won the world light-heavy-weight championship on points in a fifteen-round contest against Bob Olin in St Louis on 31 March 1935. Subsequently he defended his title successfully against Jock McAvoy, Len Harvey, Bob Olin again, Emilio Martynez and Al Gaines. In his own class, John Henry Lewis remained a fighter of distinction and, when he eventually was forced to retire through failing eyesight, he was undefeated as light-heavy-weight champion. When he was matched against Joe Louis there was speculation on whether he would topple the champion. The fight did not last a round. Sonny Boy Williamson recorded his own interpretation of the brief events of the contest with an acknowledgement of the skilful training which Louis had received. Commencing by explaining that he was in Madison Square Garden watching the big fight, Sonny Boy indicated how Jack Blackburn coached the boxer to the last minute:

> Oh well, Joe's manager pat him on the shoulder, says, 'Joe, don't you use that right so fast.'
> Ooh well, says, 'Let me talk with you, please don't use that right so fast.'
> Ooh well, I say, 'You stop an' let John Henry catch his breath, ooh well, must as long as he can last.'

Thirty years later it is hard to determine whether Williamson had heard Blackburn's advice on the radio, had read it in a newspaper, or whether he had imagined himself hearing it at the scene of the fight. If it were the latter it was an unusual instance of projection in the blues. He appears to have forgotten that he was in the Garden for he proceeded to explain that he was 'whoopin'' with the men and women in Jackson that night; that he had only fifty cents, but won back his 'business' by betting on Joe. Then he described John Henry Lewis's manager addressing the challenger, again imagining himself as witness to the conversation. The specific details of the two spoken reports contrast with the confusion over his own location.

Well, well, and John Henry's manager told him says, 'John Henry
 why don't you use your right?'
Ooh well, says, 'Son, let me talk wit'chu, John Henry why don't
 you use your right?'
Well, well, he says, 'Joe Louis is a blockin' with his left, ooh well man,
 I swear he just keeps me frightened.'[9]* ©

It seems likely that Sonny Boy was most accurate when he described
himself celebrating in his home city of Jackson, Tennessee, though this
too may have been a projection, for by this time he was well established
as a singer in Chicago. It is probable that few, if any, blues singers ever
saw Joe Louis fight in person—seats were expensive and they admired
from afar and by report.

Demolishing Jack Roper in Los Angeles less than three months
later in a contest that lasted only one round, and following up with a
knock-out win in the fourth round late that June in a fight against Tony
Galento in New York, Joe Louis continued to defend his title with un-
diminished vigour. With the purses from his succession of wins he
indulged in his personal luxury—clothes. 'In 1939,' wrote Gay Talese,
'a year in which he had already purchased twenty suits, thirty-six
shirts and two tuxedos, he also hired tailors to create clothing styles of
his own invention, such as two-tone floppy green trousers, suit coats
without lapels and camel hair jackets with leather piping.'[10] A *Joe Louis
Special* recorded by Jack Kelly and his South Memphis Jug Band in
July that year (1939), following the defeats of John Henry Lewis, Jack
Roper and Tony Galento, was unfortunately not issued. Perhaps this
reflected the quality of the music but though three other titles were
also unissued, some six items from the same session were released. It is
more than probable that the commercial potential of a Joe Louis theme
had already diminished.

Perhaps Joe Louis's sartorial interests were distracting his attention
from training for it took him eleven rounds before he knocked out
Bob Pastor in Detroit in a fight on 20 September that year and,
though he had no further bouts for nearly five months, Arturo Godoy
took him the whole distance in a contest in February the following year.
He claimed another fight which took place in June but between the two

---

* Sonny Boy Williamson suffered from a speech impediment which made
many of his blues verses indistinct. The final line of the last verse is garbled
but the sense is as transcribed.

Joe met Johnny Paychek in New York, regaining his old form with a knock-out in the sixth round. When he met Godoy for the second time, he won decisively in the eighth round with a knock-out.

Detroit, curiously, was always a tougher proposition for Joe Louis than other cities and some of his hardest-fought bouts—against Patsy Berroni, Natie Brown, Bob Pastor and Abe Simon were fought there. But the editorial director of the *Detroit Free Press*, Malcolm Bingay, commented on the Friday-night fights in the Detroit Arena: 'There's never been the faintest hint of anything crooked in any of Joe's fights, which is markedly different from almost every other fighter. He has never struck a foul blow, although many have been thrown at him. No other fighter has ever been as decent and sportsman-like as Joe. The lesson hasn't failed to be learned by the kind of fellows who never before have known a Negro except to hate him.'[11] In his sportsmanship under all circumstances Joe Louis acted as an exemplar for his race.

His successes in the ring continued. Following Arturo Godoy's second defeat, Al McCoy, Red Burman, Gus Dorazio, Abe Simon and Tony Musto fell in a chain of knock-out decisions. A first contest against Buddy Baer in May 1941 was won on a disqualification but it was followed by a knock-out defeat of Billy Conn at the Polo Grounds in the thirteenth round in June. The Polo Grounds witnessed another successful bout some fifteen weeks later when, on 29 September 1941, Lou Nova fell to a knock-out blow in the sixth round. Two days later, a two-part blues with the simple title *King Joe* was recorded:

Black-eyed pea said, 'Cornbread, what makes you so strong?' (2)
Cornbread say, 'I come from where Joe Louis was born.'

Lord I know a secret, swore I'd never tell, (2)
I know what makes old Joe hook and punch and roll like hell.

They say Joe don't talk much but he talks all the time, (2)
Now you can look at Joe but you sure can't read his mind.

Rabbit said to the bee, 'What makes you sting so deep?' (2)
Bee say, 'I sting like Joe and rock 'em all to sleep.'

They say old Joe just lays down, sleeps all day long, (2)
What old Joe does at night, Lord, sure ain't done him no wrong.

I've been in Cleveland, St Louis and Chicago too, (2)
But the best is Harlem when a Joe Louis fight is through.

Lord I hate to see old Joe Louis half-down, (2)
But I bet a million dollars no man will wear his crown.

Bull-frog told boll-weevil, 'Joe's done quit the ring.' (2)
Boll-weevil say, 'He ain't gone and he is still the king.'[12] ©

King Joe was in many ways an exceptional recording. It was made by Count Basie and His Orchestra and had the concert singer, Paul Robeson, as vocalist. The words of the blues were composed by the important Negro novelist, the late Richard Wright. But in spite of, or because of, the impressive credits, the record was a failure, for the combination of the talents of the Basie orchestra and Richard Wright's intent to keep within the folk rather than the literary idiom could not be saved from Robeson's wooden and unswinging delivery. The lyrics themselves struck a false note. Richard Wright had recognized Joe Louis's role as a folk hero and had endeavoured to convey this in equivalent terms. His choice of black-eyed pea and cornbread, rabbit and bee, bull-frog and boll-weevil for the participants in the verse dialogues was a deliberate attempt to keep the ballad and folk-tale heroes in mind when telling of Louis's achievements and the reference to the boll-weevil, in particular, was undoubtedly designed to recall in the last stanza the invincible hero-pest of the *Ballit of the Boll-Weevil*. Richard Wright was correct in assuming the parallel but artistically inaccurate in using the blues form as a vehicle. Without the first, fourth and final stanzas, the composition immediately takes on more of the character of the blues but, though the writer had a genuine involvement in the music, he seems to have been frustrated by the blues' indifference to the symbolic character of an old tradition. If the blues singer recognized in Joe Louis a figure of heroic stature, he did not attempt to compare him with the heroes of the ballad tradition. Significantly, the opportunity to make the comparison between Joe Louis and the 'steel-drivin' man' hero of the greatest of Negro ballads, John Henry, did not occur to Sonny Boy Williamson when he sang his *Joe Louis and John Henry*, quoted above, which was prosaically titled from the names of the ring opponents.

Perhaps Richard Wright was conscious of the fact that the dramatic possibilities of such a comparison had slipped away from the blues singer without realizing that the blues man, while still capable of admiration of the Race hero, was essentially forward-looking. The blues had replaced the ballad, and the plantation connotations of rabbit and bee, bull-frog and boll-weevil analogies were 'Uncle Tom' to the blues singer—and, one would have expected, to the author of *Uncle Tom's Children* too. Blues-based as the music of Count Basie's Orchestra was, it could not have performed the blues singers' part in personalizing the event of Louis's success, but it could certainly have expressed the rejoicing of the black masses. Choosing Paul Robeson to sing the lines that should have come from the shouting voice of Jimmy Rushing was a sell-out to the established artists of the concert hall, who had totally assimilated platform performance values. But in some respects there was here a more apt parallelism for, like Robeson, Joe Louis was now totally recognized, wealthy and honoured. He was a director of an insurance company, the bearer of an award from the Southern Negro Congress and he was also the owner of a ranch where he raised horses. Some commentators considered that he invested his money unwisely but he put much of his earnings into improved housing for Negroes in Chicago, made contributions to the Olympic fund and to Army and Navy relief from a boxing fortune that exceeded two and a quarter million dollars. In 1942 he joined the Army at Governor's Island, New York, and served until his discharge in 1945. Seven days later, on 8 October he was given the first award in the Negro Hall of Fame at Philadelphia and, within another week, was signing the agreement to fight Bill Conn is defence of his title.

Still very much the Race hero, still in the forefront of the news when he was to fight, still admired by the younger generation of Negroes, he was a source of pride to those that grew up with him. But it would seem that his contact with the class from which the blues singer springs had gone; he was no longer the boy from the cotton fields and the Ford plant battling his way to the top—the image in which the blues singer could cast himself. He had achieved fame years ago and no other symbol existed with the same direct emotional appeal to take his place. In 1947 the Dixieaires, a gospel group, could still draw a moral with *Joe Louis Is a Fighting Man* (*Sittin' in With 2022*) but for the blues singer the significance of Louis as a folk hero had gone.

Almost exclusively, the blues found in Joe Louis the theme for a ballad role and the blues singer became briefly a ballad-singer. But it is interesting to note that the majority of the songs created by blues singers in praise of Joe Louis were not in fact blues at all. Though they were sung by persons who were habitually blues singers they were not essentially blues, structurally or musically. Carl Martin's composition, commencing with a twelve-bar stanza and half-recited in a style which was used on recordings of *Red Cross Store*, *WPA Blues* and others, was closest to a blues, though its structure was half-song. Those by Joe Pullum and Memphis Minnie were clearly songs; songs written by blues singers, with something of a blues singer's simplicity of comment and clearly not of a form which gave them any popular song potential. They were somewhat naïve though by no means as gauche as Ike Smith's *Fighting Joe Louis* which opened with the words:

Joe Louis, uncrowned pappy,
Over all other chappies,
Oh when he beats you,
I know he sure will feel blue. . . .[13]

These were songs that unashamedly praised the Race hero in contrast with which the laconic verses of Bill Gaither and Sonny Boy Williamson seem reserved. Lacking the ingenuous hero-worship of the songs they also lack their exuberance; instead, their terse commentaries describe the fights with enthusiasm but without excitement. It is in the character of the blues that it is a vehicle for the expression of the individual, while the ballad serves as an expression for the group. Here, in the rare instance of the Joe Louis songs, the blues singer assumes a ballad-singer's role and the theme in its repetition takes on something of a ballad character. But it is significant that the blues singers rejected the traditional blues form to sing their ballad equivalents and the few instances where the twelve-bar blues was employed are closer to the personalized reporting of blues in general. As blues singers of a generation which had dispensed with the ballad they rejected the ballad form in its familiar four-line structures too and settled instead for song forms which hovered uncertainly between blues, ballad, narrative and popular song idioms of the day. Forgetting for a moment his preoccupation with himself, the blues singer spoke briefly for his racial group as a whole, giving voice to its exultation over the hero's winning bouts. In doing so, he created a small body of songs almost without parallel in the songs of the Negro in the 'thirties which, in their very singularity, help to define the limits of the blues as a form of folk expression.

163

6 THE BLUE BLUES

'The words as I took them down were too coarse for publication. I have, however, been able to re-write the first and third lines of every verse without, I think, wholly sacrificing the character of the original song,' wrote Cecil Sharp on the song *Gently Johnny my Jingaloo* which he collected from William Tucker of Ashcott, Somerset, in 1907.[1] He did not expurgate his collected songs without misgivings as he revealed in his observation in *English Folk-Songs, Some Conclusions*: 'There are also a large number of folk-songs, which transgress the accepted conventions of the present age, and which would shock the susceptibilities of those who rank reticence and reserve amongst the noblest of the virtues. These are not, strictly speaking, bad songs; they contain nothing that is really wrong or unwholesome. And they do not violate the communal sense of what is right and proper.'[2] Believing that they 'throw searching light on the character of the peasant', he felt that it was 'obviously the duty of the collector to note them down conscientiously and accurately, and to take care that his transcriptions are placed in libraries in museums, where they may be examined by students and those who will not misunderstand them.' Sharp's honesty in collecting in the face of the existing taboos on publication in his day has enabled the belated publication and analysis of many of the songs he collected. In their unexpurgated form they were published by James Reeves in the past decade.

Perhaps Sharp was an example to the American collectors who were inspired by the success of his folk-song collecting in the Appalachians; he encouraged them to deposit unexpurgated texts in libraries even if they did not publish them.[3] If this is so it does not appear to have applied to the collecting of Negro songs; to date there appear to be no totally unexpurgated collections published based on the collections made by them to correspond with James Reeves's work on Sharp, Kidson and Baring-Gould.[4] Apparently the material was not lacking for as the Texas collector, Gates Thomas, wrote in 1926, 'The real problem of the Negro work-songs is not to find them, but to get them selected, classified and expurgated for publication so that the point and quality of the songs are not impaired.'[5] How this task was to be accomplished he did not say but it appears that he was unequal to it on occasions. All that we know of the original Texas Negro version of the traditional English song, *Little Ball of Yarn*, are his passing references to it and to

Baldy; 'pornography is such an organic part of their structure that it cannot be excised without destroying the point of the songs'.[6] The collectors, Howard Odum and Guy B. Johnson, did not experience difficulty in obtaining examples either, but they wilfully excluded the 'vulgar and indecent' songs which represented a large proportion of their collected material. 'These songs tell of every phase of immorality and vice and filth; they represent the superlative of the repulsive,' they commented, permitting certain songs to be included by the exclusion of offensive stanzas.[7] Some collectors may have experienced diffidence on the part of their informants who may have been unwilling to sing songs which they felt might offend listeners and it is not clear from John and Alan Lomax's transcription of the version of *Stavin' Chain*, published in *Our Singing Country*, whether the expurgation was on their behalf or for their benefit. Probably the latter, for they note that the version was 'sung and censored for us by Tricky Sam of Huntsville, Texas'. Stavin' Chain they noted, was 'purported to be a Virginia rounder . . . a sort of sexy Paul Bunyan. It is worth nothing that we have encountered a number of guitar players named Stavin' Chain . . . none of whom could or would tell us what the nickname meant.'[8] Though it has been recorded in various forms by a number of singers, among them Furry Lewis, Johnny Temple, J. D. Short, Jesse Fuller, Jazz Gillum and Zu Zu Bollin, none of them give any impression of the character of the song which embarrassed Tricky Sam. But an unissued recording of *Stavin' Chain* by Lil Johnson suggests that she was indiscreet enough to record the traditional, unexpurgated words of the original.

These singers were for the most part blues singers, though included in their number were one or two 'songsters' whose repertoires were far wider ranging than those of the majority of blues singers and who were generally of an older generation. There is evidence that many of the younger men, whose careers have developed during the years when the blues was at its peak, nevertheless drew upon older traditions which included many of the songs noted by name but otherwise uncollected because of their allegedly offensive content. From this one can infer not only a vital thread of vigorous sexual song which runs through successive generations of Negroes but also a broader base in song than might be assumed from casual examination of issued recordings among blues singers themselves. It is an aspect that merits examination.

It has been often acknowledged that in the blues the Negro has treated sexual themes with candour, though the evidence used is almost exclusively from recorded examples. Perhaps because of the quantity of recordings, the spontaneity of many blues improvisations and the decline in field notation during the period of developing recording techniques, little direct transcription from the singing of blues singers has been published. It is possible, therefore, that recorded examples do not give an accurate picture of the emphasis on sexual themes or the character of their expression in the blues. They exist in sufficient quantity, however, to merit study in their own right and from them conclusions can be drawn on sexual imagery. The degree to which they indicate the effect of active censorship is not easily ascertained and the lack of written transcriptions, under other conditions than those of recording, seriously handicaps any comparative evaluation.

There are hints that in unrecorded blues sexual themes were unhampered by the censor but details are lacking. Writing in 1936 the Negro Professor of Philosophy at Howard University, Dr Alain Locke, observed, 'There is a vast difference between its first healthy and earthy expression in the original peasant paganism out of which it [jazz] arose and its hectic, artificial and sometimes morally vicious counterpart which was the outcome of artificial and commercialized jazz entertainment. The one is primitively erotic; the other, decadently neurotic. Gradually the Negro singers and musicians succumbed to the vogue of the artificial and decadent variety of song, music, dance which their folkstuff started, and spawned a plague, profitable but profligate, that has done more moral harm than artistic good. The early blues-singers, for instance, were far from elegant, but their deadly effective folk speech was clean and racy by contrast with the mawkish sentimentality and concocted lascivity of the contemporary cabaret songs and dances.'[9] His use of 'healthy' and 'earthy' to identify the sexual content in the folk forms and his moral judgement on the 'decadent' forms was to be echoed countless times by subsequent writers but he added shrewdly that 'to the folky people for whom this racy idiom' was sung by members of the older generation, it was 'more a safety valve of ribald laughter than a neurotic stimulant and breaker of Puritan inhibitions'.[10]

Most writing on the blues appears in books on jazz apart from the few specialized studies of blues that have appeared. Works on Negro life and culture and on the popular Negro art seldom give more than the most superficial attention to blues. Jazz books, almost without exception, acknowledge the formative influence of the blues on jazz music and may make reference to the instrumental qualities which emulated the forthright expression of the blues. Describing the late-hour playing by Buddy Bolden and his band in the New Orleans music of Tin-Type Hall on Liberty early in the century, the editors of *Jazzmen* reported:

'At about twelve o'clock, when the hall was getting right, the more respectable Negroes who did attend went home. Then Bolden played a number called *Don't Go 'Way Nobody* and the dancing got rough. When the orchestra settled down to the slow blues, the music was mean and dirty as Tin-Type roared full blast. The blues were played much slower than today and the orchestra would really "moan it out". Buddy, who liked to hear the shuffling of feet as a background to his music, would yell to his orchestra:

Way down, way down low,
So I can hear those whores,
Drag their feet across the floor.

And with the final exhortation: "Oh you bitches, shake your asses" he cracked down on the blues.'[11]

Buddy Bolden's band included a number of notorious New Orleans characters whose songs and speech shocked the school-teachers, lawyers and other professional Negroes who heard him lead his band at Lincoln Park. His promoter implored him to 'take it easy with the low-down music and the filthy songs'. Grossman and Farrell, writing in *The Heart of Jazz*, pleaded that 'one may be forgiven for asking why some historians dwell more upon the brothels than upon all these other institutions and occasions together—and, indeed, why they devote more attention to them than to the churches, where, according to a man in a position to have firsthand knowledge, Buddy Bolden derived the concept of jazz'.[12] They quote Bud Scott's statement that 'each Sunday, Bolden went to church and that's where he got his idea of jazz music' but omit his added comments that 'Bolden was still a great man for the blues . . . he was a great man for what we call "dirt music" '. If by 'dirt music' Scott meant that Bolden employed 'lowdown, dirty tone' there is no doubt that the term applied in other senses.[13] 'Dusen and Lorenzo Stall sang, and with Buddy's foul song and talk, that trio had the reputation of being the nastiest talking men in the history of New Orleans,' recalled their contemporary, Buddy Bottley.[14] Describing how the crowd would gather close to hear Lorenzo Stall sing at Bolden's prompting, he added that his words and manner 'would make the skin on your flesh twitter'.[15] Bottley quoted a version of *Salty Dog*, a song known to many blues singers and frequently recorded following Papa Charlie Jackson's original *Salty Dog Blues* made in 1924. Jackson was from New Orleans himself and he recorded the song in a slow version with Freddy Keppard's Jazz Cardinals a couple of years later. But few of these versions give more than a hint of the character of the song, which in Lorenzo Stall's version went as follows:

I got a woman who's big and fat,
She would come and get me but she don't know where I'm at,
Doin' the ballin' the jack—doing the ballin' the jack,
I'm so glad she's big and fat,
She's got crabs on her belly doing the ballin' jack.[16]

His song, or the words at any rate, showed obvious affinities with Chris Smith's composition, *Ballin' the Jack*, which was popular in 1913 and described by Sigmund Spaeth as a 'characteristic dance tune' of the period. But Spaeth added, 'Just how the operation described by the title is performed has never been made entirely clear.'[17] The audience who did not 'hold their ears and rush away' as Lorenzo Stall sang would have needed no clarification. When Lorenzo Stall sang, Bottley recalled, Buddy Bolden and Frankie Dusen got a 'great big happy feeling'.[18] Stall could sing *Funky Butt* for as long as he wanted, introducing verses about the pimps and prostitutes and the famous figures in Storyville.

Funky Butt became Bolden's theme-song but, though it was recalled by many musicians, it was generally only one verse that was quoted. The most complete example comes from another veteran of New Orleans jazz, Ferdinand Jelly Roll Morton, who said of Bolden: 'The tune everybody knew him by was one of the earliest variations from the real barrelhouse blues. Some of the old honky-tonk people named it after him and sang a little theme that went like this:

'I thought I heard Buddy Bolden say,
"Dirty, nasty stinky butt, take it away,
Dirty, nasty stinky butt, take it away,
And let Mister Bolden play. . . ."

'This tune was wrote about 1902, but, later on, was, I guess I'll have to say it, stolen by some author and published under the name of *St Louis Tickle*.'[19]

As a sporting-house pianist from the tenderloin of New Orleans,

Morton had an extensive repertoire of songs and blues of pornographic character. He was known as Jelly Roll and the name was a testimony to sexual prowess, but he was also called Winding Boy or, as he claimed later, Wining Boy. Alan Lomax reports in his biography of Morton that Johnny St Cyr 'was more than a shade embarrassed when asked what the nickname meant. He said . . . "Winding Boy is a bit on the vulgar side. Let's see—how could I put it—means a fellow that makes good jazz with the women." '[20] Two verses from Morton's recording for the Library of Congress of *Winin' Boy Blues* are quoted in *Mister Jelly Roll*:

> I'm a wining boy, don't deny my name,
> I'm a wining boy, don't deny my name,
> I'm a wining boy, don't deny my name,
> Pick it up and shake it like Stavin' Chain,
> I'm a wining boy, don't deny my doggone name.
>
> Every month, the changing of the moon,
> Every month, the changing of the moon,
> I say, every month, changing of the moon,
> The blood comes rushing from the bitch's womb,
> I'm a wining boy, don't deny my name. . . .[21]

But his biographer displays more reticence than did Morton, observing that 'other stanzas of this blues would burn the pages they were written on'.[22] Accepting this risk, the following are the verses that Jelly Roll sang, and his comments explained why he sang them. 'That be one of my first tunes, in the blues line down in New Orleans. In the very early days when people first start to playin' piano in that section, when a man played piano the stamp was on him for life—the femininity stamp. I didn't want that on, so of course I start to playin'—the songs were sort of smutty a bit; not *so* smutty but sort of like this:

> I'm the winin' boy, don't deny my name, (3)
> I can pick it up and shake it like Stavin' Chain,
> I'm the winin' boy, don't deny my name.
>
> I had a gal, I had her in the grass,
> I had that bitch, had her in the grass, (2)
> One days she got scared and a snake run up her big ass,
> Yes, I'm the winin' boy, don't deny my name.

I had that bitch, had her on the stump, (3)
I fucked her till her pussy stunk,
I'm the winin' boy, don't deny my name.

Nickle's worth of beefsteak and a dime's worth of lard, (3)
Gonna salivate your pussy till me penis gets hard,
I'm the winin' boy, don't deny my name.

Every time the changin' of the moon, (3)
The blood comes rushin' from the bitch's womb,
I'm the winin' boy, don't deny my fuckin' name.

I want about ten sweet bitches to myself, (3)
The one I like, gonna keep her to myself,
Winin' boy, don't deny my fuckin' name. . . .'[23]

These additional stanzas, unquoted, 'confirm St Cyr's story' wrote
Alan Lomax. 'Also, Stavin' Chain, to whom Morton compared himself,
lived off women. Hero of a long, rambling ballad, known all through the
Southwest, Stavin' Chain's prowess was sexual.'[24] But the printed and
recorded versions of *Stavin' Chain* give no impression of his fabled
capacities and only a fragment of a verse by Mance Lipscomb gives
some meaning to the phrase 'to do like Stavin' Chain':

Stavin' Chain come from the North,
Couldn't get a woman he'd take a hoss. . . .[25]

In his extensive series of interviews and tunes recorded for the
Library of Congress, Morton did not record a version of *Stavin' Chain*.
Though most of these recordings were issued, a significant block of titles
remained unissued. *Make Me a Pallet on the Floor*; *The Dirty Dozens*;
Now Let Me Tell You; *You Got My Man*; *They Brought That Gal to the
Prison Gates*; *Gal, When I'm Through You'll Think I'm a Man*; *Ask My
Sister, Please Don't Be Like Me* and *Good-bye to the World, I Know
I'm Going* were 'rejected'. The inclusion of *Pallet on the Floor* and *The
Dirty Dozens* suggests the reasons for the rejection of the titles.[26]

Tony Jackson was another New Orleans pianist, a contemporary of
Morton's, who played at the Pekin Inn on 28th and State in Chicago
in the 'twenties. Milton (Mezz) Mezzrow recalled 'a favourite piece of

Tony's, a kind of bawdyhouse blues that the crowd could never get enough of, went like this:

Keep a-knockin' but you can't come in,
I heard you knockin' but you can't come in,
I got an all-night trick again,
So keep a-knockin' but you can't come in.

Keep a-knockin' but you can't come in,
I'm busy grindin' so you can't come in,
If you love me you'll come back agin,
Or come back tomorrow at half past ten.'

'Songs like Tony Jackson's,' wrote Mezzrow, 'show the Negro's real artistry with his prose, and the clean way he looks at sex, while all the white songs that ever came out of the whorehouses don't have anything but a vulgar slant and an obscene idiom.'[27] One of the fundamental tunes used by the New Orleans bands, *Keep A-Knockin'*, is a simple eight-bar, four-line blues song. Familiar under this title in recordings by such singers as James Boodle-It Wiggins or Lizzie Miles it was also recorded as a band theme under such titles as *Bucket's Got a Hole in It*, *To Wa-Bac-A-Wa* and *Uptown Bump*.[28] The band versions are evidence of its widespread popularity among musicians from the old New Orleans tenderloin of Storyville but the recorded versions of *Keep A-Knockin'* for the most part were innocuous. Wiggins, for instance, sings a version which differs little from Tony Jackson's and only *Steady Grindin'* by James Stump Johnson and Dorothea Trowbridge gives a hint of the true character of the song. Johnson, who started his career as a pianist in levee brothels in St Louis, sings a version which suggests that Negroes share an 'obscene idiom':

Steady grindin' and you cain't come in, (3)
I got your man and you cain't come in.

You cain't come in and he cain't come out, (3)
Because you really don't know what it's all about.

Raise your left leg, my baby, and give me your tongue, (3)
That's the way to make me do the beedle-e-bum.

Bring me a towel baby and make it wet, (3)
I been grindin' all day and ain't done nothin' yet.

Ain't but the one thing that makes me sore, (3)
When your steady grindin' weren't no good no more.[29]

'Beedle-um-bum,' recalled a veteran blues singer and composer of the
'twenties, Georgia Tom Dorsey, 'was an expression they used in the
dance joints and creepy slip-in places, smutty dives in the red-light
district. The gals would sing those kind of suggestive words while
dancing around with their fellows.'[30] With his companion, Tampa Red,
he made a popular version of one of these brothel songs, thinly disguised
as a song about a 'gal named Simmie who runs an eat-shop on the
block'. When you passed her door you could hear her crying:

Oh my Beedle-um-bum, come and see me if you ain't had none,
Make a dumb man speak, make a lame man run,
Sure miss somethin' if you don't get some
Of my Beedle-um-bum, oh-oh my Beedle-um-bum,
It's the best Beedle-um that's made in Tennessee.

Every day at ten o'clock she goes down to the station,
To the folks who come to town she gives a little invitation.
Every day from noon to night she's always busy sellin',
Beedle-um hot and Beedle-um cold, you can always hear her
    yellin':

Oh my Beedle-um-bum, come and see me if you ain't had none,
It ain't made small and it ain't made wide,
It's just made up in a medium size.
My Beedle-um-bum, oh-oh my Beedle-um-bum,
It's the best Beedle-um that's made in Tennessee.[31]

It may be argued that *Beedle-Um-Bum* is not a blues. But if it is not
strictly speaking a blues, it is certainly sung by blues singers. The
distinction between blues and the songs of tradition is not easy to
draw, and many of the Negro folk-songs collected in the field reveal
common elements with the later, established blues forms, as well as
with other branches of the tradition. The song supplied to Dorothy

Scarborough by Mrs Bartlett of Marlin, Texas, which described 'the woes of unrequited love, which she says was sung by a colored maid she had some years ago' had elements in common with blues and other folk-songs:

> I ain't no doctor,
> Nor no doctor's son,
> But I can cool your fever,
> Till the doctor comes.
> Oh tell me how long,
> I'll have to wait.
> Oh, tell me honey,
> Don't hesitate!
>
> I got a woman,
> She's long and tall,
> Sits in her kitchen,
> With her feet in the hall!
> Oh, tell me how long,
> I'll have to wait etc.[32]

The song relates to many blues and precursors of blues—Jim Jackson's *I'm Wild about My Lovin'* for instance:

> I ain't no iceman, no iceman's son,
> But I can keep you cool till the iceman comes,
>> I'm wild about my lovin' and I like to have my fun,
>> Y'wanna be a girl of mine, baby,
>> Bring it with you when you come.
>
> I ain't no fireman, ain't no fireman's son,
> But I can keep you warm until the fireman comes,
>> I'm wild about my lovin' etc.[33]

Or Bo Carter's *All Around Man*, an uncompromising blues:

> Now I ain't no butcher, no butcher's son,
> I can do your cuttin' until the butcher-man comes,
>> 'Cause I'm an all around man, oh I'm an all around man,
>> I mean I'm a all around man,
>> I can do 'most anything that comes to hand.

Now I ain't no plumber, no plumber's son,
I can do your screwin' till the plumber-man comes,
 'Cause I'm an all around man etc.

Now I ain't no miller, no miller's son,
I can do your grindin' till the miller-man comes.

Now I ain't no milkman, no milkman's son,
I can pull your titties till the milkman comes.

Now I ain't no auger-man, no auger-man's son,
I can blow your hole till the auger-man comes.[34]*

As might be expected the verses have analogues in the songs associated with building construction. Archie Green, the Librarian of the Institute of Labor and Industrial Relations at the University of Illinois, was a shipwright on the San Francisco waterfront and later entered the building trade. 'We'd be working where we could check the scenery on the street. A pretty girl walked by—someone (an older worker) would ask the rhetorical question, "How'd you like to get into that?" And someone would direct this little recitation at the plumber's apprentice to tease him:

'I'm not the plumber,
I'm not the plumber's son,
But I'll plug your hole,
Till the plumber comes.'[35]†

It is evident that the verses were wide in their currency and had been adapted to songs of different character, crossing cultural frontiers. As often is the case in Negro folk-song many images and sometimes whole verses are transposed from one song to another. Mrs Tom Bartlett's song was a version, it appears, of *Hesitating Blues* which seems to have been one of the earliest blues to gain a specific identity. It was copyrighted in an inoffensive version by W. C. Handy in 1915

* Tony Russell points out that the 'auger-man' symbol has been adopted by Lee Brown in *Carpenter Man Blues* (Decca 7504).

† Tony Russell also cites Charlie Poole's *If the River Was Whiskey* as an instance where a white singer has used this form in a song, the occupation being 'doctoring'. Poole, however, drew often from Negro material.

but, as Abbé Niles noted, 'At about the same time as this a *Hesitating Blues* or *Must I Hesitate* was published by Smythe and Middleton of Louisville, who used this same melody in a slightly different arrangement, the words of which may have started the ball rolling.'[36]

Handy obtained this theme from a wandering musician who, Niles suggested, visited Louisville as well. Neither copyright version suggests that the song could have any pornographic content but Mrs Bartlett's song indicates how an inventive singer could elaborate on the initial verses with ever more ribald metaphors. A description by the Negro poet and novelist, Claude McKay, of the Congo cabaret in Harlem at the end of the First World War gives an impression of the original song:

'The Congo was thick, dark-colorful, and fascinating. Drum and saxophone were fighting out the wonderful drag "blues" that was the favorite of all the low-down dance halls. In all the better places it was banned. Rumor said it was a police ban. It was an old tune, as far as popular tunes go. But at the Congo it lived fresh and green as grass. Everybody there was giggling and wriggling to it.

And it is ashes to ashes and dust to dust,
Can you show me a woman that a man can trust?
    Oh baby, how are you?
    Oh, baby what are you?
    Oh can I have you now,
    Or have I got to wait?
    Oh, let me have a date,
    Why do you hesitate?

And there is two things in Harlem I don't understand,
It is a bull-dyking woman and a faggotty man.
    Oh baby, how are you?
    Oh baby, what are you....'[37]

In Negro idiom, a 'bull-dyking woman' is a lesbian, a 'faggotty man' a homosexual and the use of the terms was aggressively direct. It was this directness no doubt that Mezz Mezzrow admired in the singing of Negro artists. 'The way the white singers tried to deliver their message of sex was tough and brutal and called for two bucks on the line. Twinkle didn't come on with that jive. She sang:

Baby, see that spider climbin' on that wall,
Baby, see that spider climbin' on that wall,
He's goin' up there for to get his ashes hauled.'

'How many whites,' asked Mezzrow, 'would ever think of making sex as downright simple and hygienic as getting your ashbin cleaned out ?'[38]

His is a view that has had many supporters. Iain Laing, stating that 'the frankness is important', commended the blues singers for making 'simple and direct statements about love, without leering *double-entendres* and without the defiant exaggerations of the characteristic English bawdy song. It is a very long time since English popular song has been able to make as plain a statement as "Christ, that my love were in my arms, and I in my bed again!" Blues singers still make statements as direct and unselfconscious as that.'[39] His observation was followed by two verses of May Alix's version of *My Daddy Rocks Me:*

My daddy rocks me with one steady roll,
There's no slippin' when he takes hold,
I looked at the clock an' the clock struck two,
It's tight, like that, I'm tellin' you,
An' he kept on rockin' me with that steady roll. . . .[40]

and three verses from Joe Turner's *Cherry Red*. The third of these was quoted by Rex Harris when he declared that 'surely the uneducated blues-singer was putting as much poetry into the only vocabulary he knew when he sang with straightforward frankness:

'You can take me, baby, put me in your big brass bed,
Eagle Rock me, baby, till my face turns cherry red.[41] ©

'It is after all not so far removed from the Elizabethan

'Christ, that my love were in my arms, and I in my bed again.'

'There is a frank and pleasing atmosphere about many of the early blues lyrics,' Harris continued, 'which is as direct and natural as some of the early English folk songs whose original meanings would scandalize many of the fond mothers who repeat them in the form of nursery rhymes to their toddlers.' Harris cautioned that 'too much stress, however, must not be laid on the sexual flavour of the blues'.[42]

In the writings of jazz authorities there is, apart from a surprising agreement on the examples used, a general measure of agreement on the honesty of blues expression on sexual themes. This is frequently equated qualitatively with the authenticity of the blues, with the implication that the degeneration of the blues as an art form can be related to the pornographic elements within the idiom. 'The reference to sex in many good blues is of an unselfconscious naturalness tempered by native Negro humour,' wrote Rudi Blesh, who applauded the 'healthy, frank sexual imagery of *Empty Bed Blues*' as sung by Bessie Smith. In contrast, he deplored those singers 'corrupted by city ways' who 'fell into cheap or sophisticated singing. Their blues, whether vulgarisations by emphasis on pornography or on a slick and trivial sophistication, represent a decadent type of the form' and he concluded that 'slick and shallow singing is the degeneration of the highly expressive blues into mere entertainment'.[43] Whether 'city ways' have corrupted these singers and 'mere entertainment' marks the degeneracy of the blues are points which in themselves merit argument but the qualitative distinctions in the treatment of sexual content are clear. They are discussed in a note by Martin Williams with reference to the work of one singer, Sara Martin, whose '*Mean Tight Mama* is a blues about sex. In a few brief verses, the singer is able to sketch a character and a situation of pathos, earthiness and humorous acceptance of the facts of life. *Kitchen Man*, on the other hand is a piece of cabaret "smut" clever in its verses and implicitly hypocritical in its outlook.'[44] His view was enlarged upon by Samuel Charters who has discussed the differences in quality of the poetry of sexual blues and the images employed in suggestive blues songs: 'The poetic language of the sexual blues uses a rich and often highly imaginative imagery. It has the enduring persistence of a folk idiom, and it is a part of the repertoire of every singer. There is another area of sexual blues, however, which reflects some of the attitudes of the larger society. It has always been evident that sexual blues could be commercially successful, and there have been occasional efforts made by the record companies to exploit this material. Most of the records which were produced with this in mind used the cheapened styles of the party records which have a large illicit sale in the white society. They relied on an uncomfortable suggestiveness, the point being that the entire record which is made as suggestive as possible, is really not about sex, but about something which can be described in terms that can be interpreted as sexual.'[45] He quotes as an example: 'a typical blues was something like Sara Martin's *Kitchen Man*', commenting that 'the attitude it expresses is the self-conscious sense of shame of the white society that is unable to listen to a song which openly enjoys physical love'.

Kitchen Man, which was recorded by both Bessie Smith and Sara Martin, uses images which are familiar in blues and some that are original. Purporting to be the song of a wealthy woman who had 'servants by the score', it appealed to 'Dan, her kitchen man' not to leave her household, and described his merits in the 'kitchen':

His jelly roll sure is nice and hot,
Never fails to touch the spot,
I can't do without my kitchen man.

His fine feathers are rolled so sweet,
How I love his young pig meat,
I can't do without my kitchen man.

Oh how that boy does open clams,
No one else is gwina touch my hams,
I can't do without my kitchen man.

When I eat his doughnuts tall I leave him just the hole,
Any time he wants them he certainly can use my sugar pole.

His boloney's certainly worth a try,
Never fails to satisfy,
I can't do without my kitchen man.[46] ©

Though the words are undistinguished, the song is sung without salaciousness by Sara Martin, but they seem crude and arch by comparison with the verses of *Mean Tight Mama*:

I'm a mean tight mama, I got to sleep and wake up mad, (2)
But the man who knows his business will find out I'm not so bad.

I'm a mean mama but men don't like my kind, (2)
They always want a gal who has a dozen men on her mind.

Now my hair is nappy and I don't wear no clothes of silk, (2)
But the cow that's black and ugly, has often got the sweetest milk.

Now when a man starts jivin' I'm tighter than a pair of shoes, (2)
I'm a mean tight mama, with my mean tight mama blues.[47] ©

Both these songs were issued by the obscure QRS record company on the same record—QRS 7043. Their records were directed at the Race market and were unlikely to have been affected by white 'party' sales. It is possible that they were designed to appeal to different tastes, but it is equally likely that they performed similar functions in that part of the Negro market which purchased them. They were not Sara Martin's blues, but were both compositions by the lyric-writer Andy Razaf, the partner of Thomas Fats Waller and composer of the words to such jazz standards as *Ain't Misbehavin'*, *Honeysuckle Rose* and *Keepin' Out of Mischief Now*. Though on the fringe of the blues Razaf was familiar enough with blues idiom to compose effectively in Sara Martin's latter song, even if his images were sometimes banal in the former. Like his contemporaries, W. C. Handy, Spencer Williams, Richard M. Jones or Clarence Williams, he was sufficiently close to folk usage to employ it convincingly if he wished, even sharing composer credits with Casey Bill Weldon on *I'm Gonna Move to the Outskirts of Town*. The banality of *Kitchen Man* is undeniable but it is arguable whether Bessie Smith's *Empty Bed Blues* is much its superior as a vehicle or whether it uses the 'healthy, frank sexual imagery' to which Rudi Blesh refers; the imagery is in fact, very similar:

I woke up this morning with an awful aching head, (2)
My new man had left me with a room and an empty bed.

Bought me a coffee grinder, got the best one I could find, (2)
So he could grind my coffee, 'cause he has a brand new grind.

He's a deep-sea diver with a stroke that can't go wrong, (2)
He can touch the bottom and his wind holds out so long.

When my bed gets empty makes me feel so mean and blue, (2)
My springs are rusty sleepin' single like I do.

He came home one evenin' with his spirits way up high, (2)
What he had to give me made me wring my hands and cry.[48]

Empty Bed Blues is honest in that it does not attempt to hide its theme, the metaphors following direct statements. So Bessie Smith sings that 'he gave me a lesson that I never had before, when he got through teachin' me from me elbows on down was sore' and follows with 'he boiled my first cabbage and he made it awful hot, then he put in the bacon and it overflowed the pot'. But the culinary metaphors are innumerable in blues and no one is likely to be misled by *Kitchen Man* into believing that it is anything but sexual in content. *Empty Bed Blues* makes its point at length over six minutes; its merits lie more in the performance than in the content. This is also true of the Sara Martin recordings which, besides being her last, were also her best, poor though the material was.

Commenting on the fact that these were her last recordings, Samuel Charters writes that 'Sara was more or less forced to use material of this kind as her career faded'.[49] Rudi Blesh observes similarly that 'in her later years Bessie Smith was the victim of mismanagement and, faced with diminishing returns, succumbed at times to the temptations of commercialization and pornography and even belittled herself and her race singing *coon* songs'.[50] The recording careers of these and other classic blues singers were liberally sprinkled with coon songs. Imitative of Negro song in a genre which owed more to 'Nigger Minstrels' than to a part of the tradition, they were prominent not only at the conclusion but also at the commencement of their careers. The increased proportion of suggestive and pornographic material in their late sessions does lend support to the view that the record companies, confronted with the Depression, attempted to revive flagging sales with records of this character. Few were as blatant as Lizzie Miles's recording of *My Man o' War* in January 1930:

When he advances, can't keep him back,
So systematic is his attack,
All my resistance is bound to crack—for my man o' war.

He never misses when he brings up his big artillery,
Bullets like hisses and hit the mark with such rapidity.

His operations always increase,
It seems his movements will never cease,
At home he always disturbs the peace—he's my man o' war.

He stomps my trench and he's not afraid,
His bayonets make me cry for aid,
And how he handles his hand grenade—he's my man o' war.

If I'm retreating he goes around and gets me in the rear,
He keeps repeating his flank attack till victory is near,
And then he turns his machine-gun loose.
Then I surrender for there's no use,
He makes me throw up my flag of truce—he's my man of war.[51] ©

For such songs to be issued to recoup losses it is necessary for a market to exist. It is possible that this was a white one, but there appears to have been no relaxing of the strict segregation of record catalogues, nor any apparent attempt to secure a white market for Negro records of this character. Pressed by a financial crisis did the record companies experiment with the issue of suggestive material which they had censored in the past? Did they in fact relax the controls they had exerted on songs considered unsuitable or too dangerous to issue? Did they find that within the Negro community there was a ready market for suggestive songs just as they had discovered a decade earlier that there was a market for recordings by Negroes? Were songs of this character always in the repertoire and performances of Sara Martin and Bessie Smith and only missing from their recordings? It is not unlikely.

Against the suggestions that the singers were 'corrupted by city ways' and pressed reluctantly into recording material of this nature by financial necessity, can be placed the statements of Odum and Johnson. Bearing in mind their views on obscenity there is still no reason to doubt the truth of their notes that 'a great mass of material cannot be published because of its vulgar and indecent content'. They observed: 'Ordinarily the imagination can picture conditions worse than they are but in the Negro songs the pictures go far beyond the conception of the real. The prevailing theme is that of sexual relations and there is no restraint in expression.' Feeling unable to quote examples they could only assert helplessly that 'in comparison with the indecency that has come to light in the vulgar songs of other peoples those of the Negro stand out undoubtedly in a class of their own'.[52]

Odum's and Johnson's censorship is representative of a conspiracy of expurgation that has been passionately condemned by Mack

McCormick: 'The deceit is not a small one: there have been over 700 books dealing with folk songs in the English language, and perhaps half that number of documentary LP albums, and hardly one of them without thorough expurgation of indecorous matter.'[53] He instances such songs as *Hog Eye*, *Stavin' Chain*, *The Derby Ram* and the *Strawberry Roan*, the appeal of which latter beasts 'lies to a large degree in the enormity of their sexual organs and the incredible works they undertake'. Other songs popular with Negroes are among those that he lists in which 'the 'the blue pencil has amputated numerous verses which are traditionally sung as part of such popular pieces as *Salty Dog*, *Willie the Weeper*, *Corrine, Corrina* and . . . *Uncle Bud*. Though bits and pieces have appeared on commercial records and are elsewhere hinted at, it is only in the folk community itself that one will hear *The Dirty Dozens*, *'Bout a Spoonful*, or *Big Balls in Town* in their full-blown classic form.'[54]

It is not possible to determine from collections of Negro folk-song the nature or the extent of sexual material because of the censorship of allegedly obscene material by the collectors, and similarly, it may be found that the record companies have exercised a strict censorship which has only been relaxed through economic pressures or the employment of an involved language of metaphor. If this is so, the evidence of recorded material cannot be considered as a true picture of Negro song any more than can the text collections. What means is there of testing the evidence? Unfortunately, this must be limited, for the resources of recorded but unissued material are as few as those of noted but unpublished texts. From the issued material and comparison with a small number of unissued, or limited issue recordings, some conclusions can be drawn.

PROBLEMS OF CLASSIFICATION

A simple examination of the recordings which appeared in the catalogues of the Race record companies rapidly reveals that no one part of the range of Negro music is the special preserve of songs on sexual themes. It is also apparent that a particular form of song—*The Dirty Dozens*, for instance—is not the property of one particular sector but appears in the repertoires of rural singers, city blues singers and classic blues singers alike. Though it is customary to stratify the blues according to types of singers rather than to types of song, it soon becomes evident that most types of Negro song, to a greater or lesser degree, come into the repertoires of singers of widely varying character. Though the vaudeville singers of the 'twenties may have sung a high proportion of popular songs and a relatively small number of twelve-bar blues of traditional form, while the country singers south of Memphis may have specialized mainly in the traditional pattern and sung few items for the record on a popular song pattern, it is clear that the range was within the compass of both extremes. So it was that a Sam Jones (Stovepipe No. 1) would include *A Woman Gets Tired of the Same Man All the Time* in his repertoire, a song made popular by the vaudeville team of George Williams and Bessie Brown; Uncle Skipper (probably Charley Jordan) and Blind Willie McTell would sing *Cuttin' My ABCs* or some other version of Butterbeans's and Susie's *A to Z Blues*; while *Jail House Blues* would be sung by Bessie Smith, Sam Collins, Virginia Liston and Sleepy John Estes in versions which might differ but would have many elements in common. The instances of blues compositions like Richard M. Jones's *Trouble in Mind*, Virginia Liston's *You Don't Know My Mind*, or Leroy Carr's *How Long, How Long*, which have become essential items in the repertoire of singers of widely differing characters, are too well known to need further elaboration. Of course, certain of these items, whether blues or songs, may appeal more to one group than to another but there are many which are fairly common in most of the customary categories.

If the horizontal stratification of the blues is generally made according to styles, it is also possible to make a vertical classification of song or blues forms. Country blues, rural blues, urban blues, city blues, Mississippi blues, Texas blues, Georgia blues, archaic blues, classic blues, post-classic blues, rhythm and blues . . . these are just some of the all too familiar blues strata into which singers are placed. Applied in detail they have all the errors of generalization but in the broadest terms they have some validity. Similarly, vertical classification according to song types can only be considered in general terms, but it does serve to identify the major groups of song which come within the scope of most blues singers.

'Twelve-bar blues' of the familiar three-line structure constitute the major blues classification, though 'eight-bar', two-line forms are related to them. These are simply divisible between those which are the personalized compositions of individual singers and those which have assumed the character of 'traditional blues' through their employment in their entirety by a number of singers. Next in importance are the 'blues songs', frequently of a sixteen-bar form or of a twelve-bar form but with a four-bar couplet and eight-bar refrain. These blues songs have much of the character and the phraseology of the twelve-bar blues but are less frequently improvised. 'Traditional songs' not of a blues pattern but popular among blues singers, often of unknown origin and probably extending back into a pre-blues tradition, constitutes a third group employed by blues singers. Songs of this type are shared by singers of various types but a fourth group, which might be termed 'jazz-blues songs', though sometimes used by the less sophisticated singers, are more generally employed by professional entertainers. Composed rather than extemporized they may be considered as 'jazz songs' with blues colour which lend themselves to jazz performance or cabaret-club presentation. Their jazz association makes them more subject to changes of musical fashion but in the post-war years a comparison may be made with the rhythm and blues 'ballads'. Though different in character the blues and blues songs have remained similar in kind in recent years.

Such a classification is of song character rather than of style, but applied to stylistic stratification it cuts across the horizontal layers to show correspondences between singers of dissimilar types. Folk blues singers, whether of the country or the city, and from all periods, may use the blues almost exclusively in the twelve- and eight-bar forms—singers like Blind Lemon Jefferson, Texas Alexander, Charley Patton, Robert Johnson, Peetie Wheatstraw, Leroy Carr, Jimmy Gordon, Lightnin' Hopkins or John Lee Hooker, for instance. But almost all of these will make some excursions into traditional blues, blues songs and traditional songs in their singing. Singers like Frank Stokes, Gus Cannon, Jim Jackson, Mississippi John Hurt or Mance Lipscomb of an older generation, are more at home with the traditional songs but draw easily on blues songs and traditional blues on the one hand and occasionally jazz-blues on the other. A number of singers—Bo Carter, Tampa Red and Lonnie Johnson among them—moved easily between these groups but Lonnie Johnson was rare in being a folk blues singer who infiltrated the jazz-blues field. This was largely the province of the so-called classic blues singers, mainly women. Bessie Smith, Ma Rainey, Lillian Glinn or Chippie Hill, moved freely between all categories though their main association was with blues-orientated jazz-blues song. Singers like Jimmy Rushing and Joe Turner paralleled them but Viola McCoy, Eva Taylor or Alberta Hunter were happiest in the jazz-blues vein, whilst Butterbeans and Susie or Grant and Wilson worked almost wholly in this area of song. More recently, in their different ways, a Ray Charles or a Bo Diddley have moved between the jazz-blues and traditional blues forms.

The Blue Blues

Writing their preface to *Blues and Gospel Records 1902–1942*, Robert M. W. Dixon and John Godrich answered their rhetorical question, 'What is a "blues" or "gospel" record?' by explaining that they had 'tried to evolve some more or less consistent criterion for inclusion in this volume, based upon the prevailing opinions among folk-musicologists and collectors as to what is genuinely "Negroid", that is, performed in a style particular to Negro performances, and not derivative or a copy of any white style'.[55] They noted that 'the majority of blues and gospel records were issued in special race series, so-called, consecutively numbered, where all but a very few records in each series were genuinely Negroid'. Excluding the gospel items—spirituals, sermons, jubilee and religious recordings of all types—the many thousands of entries covering a period, with only a few exceptions of a little over a score of years, fall into the broad classifications made above. And in spite of stylistic changes no substantial differences in song classification have taken place in the equivalent period since.

It is usual to consider the 'pure' blues of the twelve-bar or related forms when discussing the work of blues singers, but this can be extremely misleading. The singer makes no such distinctions between what is authentic and what is not but selects and sings what seems appropriate to him. Occasionally this may lead him to an error of judgement as, for instance, Leroy Carr's attempt at singing a popular song in his recording of *Think of Me Thinking of You*; at other times it may extend the singer into unfamiliar and not entirely suitable territory still with some success, as Big Bill Broonzy's *That's the Glory of Love* or Leadbelly's *Springtime in the Rockies*. If Daddy Stovepipe singing *The Tennessee Waltz* is a somewhat embarrassing experience it is none the less remarkable that blues singers make so few lapses of judgement in their selection of material they consider suitable. With this in mind it is as well to consider the wider compass of songs which blues singers perform beyond the limitations of the traditional form; it could lead to a reconsideration of the grouping of singers in terms of their selection of material, rather than in terms of their rural or urban origins, their home states or the period in which they recorded.

NEGRO BLUES AND SONG FORMS

A broad swathe could be cut through the entire repertoire of blues singers in whatsoever category to separate those on sexual themes from those that are not. Arbitrary though it may appear, any assessment of the content of Race records soon reveals the preponderance of sexual themes above all other subjects. It might be even argued that they constitute a third, perhaps more, of all Race recordings—a vast body of songs recorded over some forty-five years numbering literally thousands of items which it is hypocritical to ignore. Issued on labels aimed at the Negro market, publicized in catalogues which were strictly segregated, distributed to record shops in Negro areas throughout the country, they clearly found their purchasers and met a considerable and lasting demand. Some of these may be considered as direct expressions of sexual desire while others have tendencies to obscenity. What constitutes pornography in these terms remains debatable, but the complex evasive tactics employed by some singers to elude the censor suggest that either the singer himself or the recording executives had established in their own minds vague standards of what was deemed acceptable for issue.

The frankness of expression of some sexual blues is not an illusion; many are forthright in their statements. Forthright but not callous: courtship and love play can form the basis of a humorous blues which in its realistic detail leaves no doubt as to its fundamental truth, as in the following example by Whistling Alex Moore:

Women winkin' and wigglin' at me, some of them in their teens, (2)
I knelt down beside one and scratched her on her knees.

Whilst standin' at the corner reckon what that woman done? (2)
She hug and kiss me—then bit me on the tongue.

I asked her to give me what mama did when I was three months
  old, (2)
She said, 'I'll make you a sugar-tit daddy—I can't stand that to
  save my soul.'

I said, 'I believe I'll go' and raised up out of my chair, (2)
She pulled down her blue bloomers and said, 'You ain't goin'
  nowhere.'[56]

This blues describes a situation and employs no imagery, but metaphor is commonly employed in the blues and its use is frequently simple and expressive. The sexual demands of his woman and the physical demands of daily labour are paralleled in this blues by Texas Alexander:

> My woman got somethin' just like the risin' sun, (2)
> You cain't never tell when that work is done.
>
> It's no use a-worryin' 'bout your days bein' long, (2)
> Never worry 'bout your rollin' 'cause they sure is goin' on.
>
> She got somethin' round an' it looks just like a bear, (2)
> Sometimes I wonder what in the hell is there.[57]

Here the blues is directed to a natural union between the singer and his subject, the simile being used to illumine the feelings of the singer in poetic imagery. Sometimes the blues singer has some uninhibited observations on areas of sexual experience which have often remained outside the themes of popular arts—homosexuality, lesbianism and sexual aberrations. Kokomo Arnold's *Sissy Man Blues* is uncompromisingly direct:

> I'm goin' to ring up Chinee see 'bout my good gal over there,
> Goin' to ring up Chinee, see if I can find my good gal over there,
> The Good Book tells me I got a good gal in the world somewhere.
>
> Hollerin' church bells on one Sunday mornin', (2)
> Some dirty deacon come and stole my gal and gone.
>
> I woke up this mornin' with my pork-grinder in my hand, (2)
> If you can't send me no woman, please send me a sissy man.[58]

In using 'pork-grinder' as a phallic synonym he employs an idiom which is not a euphemism for it strengthens rather than weakens the impression of sexual urgency. Another phallic image in Robert Johnson's *Stones in My Passway* achieves similar impact by contrast with the more lyrical metaphors that have preceded it:

> I got stones in my passway and my road seems dark as night, (2)
> I have pains in my heart, they have taken my appetite.
>
> I have a bird to whistle and I have a bird to sing, (2)
> I've got a woman that I'm lovin'—boy she don't mean a thing.

Now you'se tryin' to take my life, and all my lovin' too,
You laid a passway for me, now what are you tryin' to do?
I'm cryin' please, please let us be friends,
And when you hear me howlin' in my passway rider, please open
  the door and let me in.

I got three legs truck on boy, please don't block my road, (2)
I been feelin' 'shamed 'bout my rider, babe, I'm booked out and
  bound to go.[59]

Uninhibited the terms might be, but their use was not unnoticed by
other blues singers. 'God, I thought they'd put him inside for that!'
exclaimed Buster Pickens to me, recalling *Sissy Man Blues* twenty-five
years after, and its impact was strong enough for other singers like
George Noble to make their own versions of it. Robert Johnson, if he
was obscure in *Stones in My Passway*, was more obvious in *Phonograph Blues*; the Vocalion company chose to censor it and it was
unissued. The test pressing survives:

Beatrice got a phonograph and it won't say a lonesome word, (2)
What evil have I done, what evil have the poor girl heard?

Beatrice I love my phonograph but you have broke my
  windin' chain, (2)
And you have taken my lovin' and your jelly to your other man.

And we played it on the sofa and we played it 'side the wall, (2)
But boys my needle point got rusty and it will not play at all.

Now Beatrice won't you bring your clothes back home? (2)
I'm gonna wind your little phonograph just to hear your little
  motor moan. (2)[60]

Perhaps it was the specific reference to Beatrice that occasioned the
rejection of the recording for the Vocalion company issued *Terraplane
Blues* which was a best seller.

I said I flashed your lights mama, your horn won't even blow, (2)
There's a short in this connexion, ooh well babe, way down below.

I'm goin' h'ist your hood mama, I'm boun' to check your oil, (2)
I got a woman that I'm lovin' way down in Arkansas.

Now you know the coils ain't even buzzin', your little generator
won't get the spark,
All in bad condition, you gotta have these batteries charged,
I'm cryin' please, please don't do me wrong,
Who's been drivin' my Terraplane now, for you since I been gone?

I'm goin' to get deep down in this connexion, keep on tangling
with your wires, (2)
And when I mash down on your little starter, then your spark
plug will give me fire.[61]

Terraplane Blues is still the best remembered blues that Robert Johnson
sang among other blues singers, even if *Hell-Hound on My Trail* is the
most famous among collectors. Robert Johnson is widely considered as
the composer of *I Believe I'll Dust My Broom* which was later adopted
by Elmore James as his theme. It was, however, already a traditional
blues, having been recorded in previous years by Kokomo Arnold as
Sagefield Woman Blues, by Carl Rafferty as *Mr Carl's Blues* and in
fragments elsewhere. The force of tradition in the blues is strong with
standard verses becoming part of a common resource for singers of
widely different character, itself an aspect which deserves greater study.
Sometimes a blues will be adopted in its entirety and there are several
traditional blues on sexual themes. Probably the best known is *I Think
You Need a Shot* under this title or as *Bad Blood* which has been
recorded by such singers as Walter Davis, Jimmy Gordon, Brownie
McGhee, Champion Jack Dupree and others, but probably deriving
originally from Walter Davis:

You got bad blood baby and I think you need a shot, (2)
Now turn over mama, let me see what else you got.

I doctors on women, I don't fool around with men, (2)
All right take it easy now mama while I stick my needle in.

Oh your ways is lovin' and your skin is nice and soft, (2)
If you keep on rasslin' you gonna make me break my needle off.

Lord my needle's in you baby and you seem to feel all right, (2)
And when your medicine comes down I want you to hug me tight.

Yeah your medicine come now baby, put your leg upside the wall,
    (2)
I don't want you to waste none of it, I want you to have it all.[62]

The appeal of *Bad Blood* is undoubtedly its bawdiness and it is one of a
large number of 'doctor' blues—*Terrible Operation Blues, Root Doctor
Blues, Toothache Blues* and so on. It is somewhat exceptional in being a
traditional blues, for the adoption by many singers of the same sexual
verses is more common among the blues songs. A large proportion of
these follow the form of *Tight Like That* and not infrequently use the
same tune. Sung to a twelve-bar theme they follow a couplet with a
repetitive refrain:

You go out at night and you stays all day,
When you come back you smell in a different way,
    We can smell that thing, (2)
    Well it may be all right,
    But still we can smell that thing.

Wind blow at night, and wind blow in the day,
But its smell when it blow your way,
    We can smell that thing etc.[63]

Dobby Bragg's song has its equivalent in Peetie Wheatstraw's *What's
That ?* which takes an identical theme:

Now it smells like feet, smells like greens,
Sometimes I know it smells like a can of sardines,
    What's that I smell, (2)
    Now everybody screamin', tell me what's that I smell.

Don't come here, callin' me honey,
Something round here you know is smellin' mighty funny,
    What's that I smell etc.[64]

Or Bo Carter's *What Kind Of Scent Is This ?*:

Now she trying' to make like it's somethin' she's been fryin',
She needn't a-come with that line of jive, says she knows she's
   lyin',
      What kind of scent is that, (3)
      That you bringin' here right in my home ?[65]

Bo Carter was a member of the Mississippi Sheiks, a country band
which made frequent use of this form in such recordings as *Drivin' That
Thing* or *Crackin' Them Things*:

Women went to the doctor, doctor said,
'Crackin' them things is gonna kill you dead,'
      Crackin' them things, (3)
      You really break the record when it comes to
      Crackin' them things. [66]

Blues songs of this type on record depend on the participation of the
listener to supply the necessary meaning to 'them things' or the equivalent phrase. The list is almost inexhaustible and can be drawn from
every type of singer—whether it is Tampa Joe and Macon Ed's *Whip-
ping That Thing*, Charlie Burse with the Memphis Jug Band (Jolly
Jug Band) singing *Tappin' That Thing*, Joe McCoy's *Botherin' That
Thing* or Georgia Tom's *Somebody's Been Using That Thing*. Others
supply a single metaphor and exploit its possibilities in a similar song
structure—Sam Hill's *You Got To Keep Things Clean* for instance:

Last night she gave out her oil,
Baby I think you gonna let things spoil,
      You gotta keep things clean, (2)
      If you wanna be respectable,
      You gotta keep things clean. [67]

Nor is the use of this form mainly the province of the singer who has
settled in the city for it is widely employed by country blues singers.
The afore-mentioned Robert Johnson, widely regarded as an archetypal
Mississippi blues singer, uses a limerick structure:

Hot tamales and they're red hot, yes she got 'em for sale, (2)
      She got two for a nickel, got four for a dime,
      I would sell you more but they ain't none o' mine.

Hot tamales and they're red hot, yes she got 'em for sale,
I mean, yes she got 'em for sale.
Hot tamales and they're red hot etc.
    Me and my baby bought a V-8 Ford,
    We bought that thing on the runnin' board,
Hot tamales etc.[68]

To compensate for the borrowing of folk idioms by sophisticated singers there was often a feedback from the cabaret repertoire to the folk idiom as when, for instance, Lightnin' Hopkins recorded *Fan It* some thirty years after Frankie Half-Pint Jaxon first made it popular. But cross-fertilization between the songs tends to stress the relationship between the idioms—one verse of *They're Red Hot* concerning a 'gal, she's long and tall, sleeps in the kitchen with her feet in the hall' is to be found in Mrs Bartlett's collected version of *Hesitating Blues* quoted earlier, while another has a 'monkey and a baboon' verse which hints at the minstrel show and appears in all types of Race songs. In all probability many of these verses are extremely old but the reticence of early collectors and the censorship of recordings makes comparison difficult. Some indication of the persistence of folk idiom and its wide dissemination in the Race fields can be ascertained from examination of some text collections. In 1906 the Texas collector, Gates Thomas, noted a song *I Ain't Bothered* which he observed had a rhythm and melody which 'pretty well represent the insinuatingly amorous gurgle of the rooster in the earlier stages of his gallantry. The song is the most modern in this group and represents the Negro's re-synthesis of a pornographic bar-room ballad that was current (usually on the cards of whiskey-drummers) about the turn of the century.' It commenced:

Said the ole rooster to the hen, 'You ain't laid an aig in God
   knows when.'
Said the ole hen to the rooster, 'You don't call aroun' any more,
   like you use'ter.'
(*Refrain*) But I ain't bothered; no I ain't bothered.[69]

Over twenty years later in New York, Clara Smith was singing her version of *Tight Like That*, which included the verse:

Oh the little red rooster said to the hen,
'You ain't laid an egg an' I can't tell when.'
The little red hen said to the rooster,
'You don't come around as often as you use'ta.'
   'Cause it's tight like that—long delay,
   Makes it tight like that—hear what I say,
   Oh hear me talkin' to you, I mean it's tight like that.[70]

The verse became firmly established in blues songs and its humour was still fresh when, over sixty years after Gates Thomas collected it, Lightnin' Slim was singing his *Rooster Blues:*

Oh well the little red rooster tol' the little red hen,
'I ain't been to see yer in God knows when.'
The little red hen told the little red rooster,
'You don't come aroun' daddy, like you use'ter.'
We got to rock tonight baby, we got to rock tonight baby,
We got to rock tonight baby, yes, we got to rock tonight.[71] ©

Gates Thomas's note suggests that the verse may have had an origin in popular pornographic song that was not necessarily Negro. There is evidence of a mixed ancestry in a number of songs and themes which the Negro adopted, some of them being taken over from the minstrel shows that aped them, and others belonging to still older traditions. A long heritage that goes back two centuries and more lies behind Blind Boy Fuller's *Cat Man Blues*, Coley Jones's *Drunkard's Special* and the late Sonny Boy Williamson's *Wake Up Baby*, for all of these were variants of the old European song known in France as *Marianne* or *Le Jaloux*, in Scotland and England as *Our Gudeman* or *Our Goodman* and throughout the United States as *The Merry Cuckold, Four Night's Drunk* and other titles. The story-ballad of the wily wife who outwits her drunken husband by explaining away the evidence of her lover with witty lies has many bawdy variants but the examples recorded by blues singers are woefully emasculated, Sonny Boy Williamson's even being faded out by a bowdlerizing recording executive before it reaches its point. The blues versions in fact have a politeness that would have shamed the singers of Somerset or Sussex.

In 1902 the Negro song-writing team of Cole and Johnson were at their peak and Bob Cole, under the pseudonym of Will Handy, wrote the song *Oh, Didn't He Ramble*. It became extremely popular and in New Orleans was perpetuated as a march tune by jazz bands returning from funeral rites. It was, however, widely circulated already in folk traditional song and Gates Thomas had collected it in 1888 along the Colorado River in Texas:

> The habits of that ram,
> They hung upon the wall;
> A couple o' gals came into the shop,
> Says, 'We never eats mutton at all.'

> Didn't they ramble, didn't they ramble!
> Oh they rambled down the streets and through the town!

> Of all the animals in this world,
> I'd rather be a bull;
> I'd curl my tail upon my back,
> And graze my belly full.

'Of course,' commented Thomas, 'the Negro does not use these terms, except in the hearing of respectable people, but obscenities.'[72] The presence of respectable people apparently inhibited Oscar Papa Celestin from singing anything more offensive than:

> The ram's horns were so long,
> They nearly touched the sky,
> An eagle went up to build her nest,
> And the young ones they did cry:

> Didn't he ramble, he ramble,
> He rambled all around, in and out o' the town,
> Didn't he ramble, he ramble,
> He rambled till the butchers cut him down.[73] ©

The verse, recorded in 1951, is interesting only because it is one of those collected by Gates Thomas over sixty years before and differing little from the verses of the original song, *The Derby Ram*, which was sung about 'the old tup' at English village purification ceremonies for centuries before. The original song had a rich bawdiness in its pagan

194

descriptions of the 'habits' of the ram which survived in the States. Respectable people no doubt accounted for its emasculation as they made *The Girls Go Crazy 'Bout the Way I Walk* out of Bunk Johnson's *The Whores Go Crazy 'Bout the Way I Ride*. Something of the romping cheerfulness of the song survives in Old Ced Odum's duet with Lil Hardaway, *In Derbytown*, though it has lost the Rabelaisian fantasy of the original:

> In Derbytown there is a man, a nasty little soul,
> Every time he sees a girl he reaches for her —,
> > Maybe you think I'm foolin' you, maybe you think I lie,
> > But if you come to Derbytown you'll see that I don't lie.
> I know a man of ninety-five, he leans upon a stick,
> But when he sees a girl in bathing, up comes his —,
> > Maybe you think etc.[74]

Optimistically, Odum and Diamonds Hardaway also recorded *Fourteen Hundred and Ninety-Two*, a version of the bawdy song known to any American football player as *Christopho Columbo*, and doubtless too, to the Decca executive who censored its release. *In Derbytown* employs what might be termed a tacit censorship by the obliterating of the final word of each verse through the overlap of the chorus. It is a device which achieves a certain surprise effect in not resolving the lines and, lacking the exaggeration of the traditional ballad, leaves no doubt as to the nature of the omitted words. In so doing the singer is clearly acknowledging the conventional language taboos but also succeeds in flouting them. Crude though the device may be it is amusing in the performance and is used in the recordings of a number of traditional Negro bawdy songs, at least in their recorded versions. *Sweet Jelly Rollin'* is one such traditional song which incidentally is not listed in any collection though it has been recorded over the years by such singers as McKenzie and Crump, Jimmy Gordon and Whistling Rufus Bridey:

> Who's gonna do your sweet jelly rollin', sweet jelly rollin' when
> > I'm gone?
> Who's gonna do your old-fashioned lovin', old-fashioned lovin'
> > from now on?
> Listen here mama, don't you be so fast,
> Keep on this bed and give me a piece of your —,
> Who's gonna do your sweet jelly rollin', sweet jelly-rollin',

Who's gonna do your sweet jelly rollin', sweet jelly rollin' when
  I'm gone,
Who's gonna do your old-fashioned lovin', old fashioned lovin'
  from now on.

I like you baby, you short like a duck,
Oh my soul baby, you sure can — who's gonna do your sweet etc.

Uh-uh, mister baby, you just a l'il too fas',
You'll not cram all that meat up my — who's gonna do your
  sweet etc.

I hear it said baby that you're too slick,
You'll not give me all of that great big — who's gonna do your
  sweet etc.

In Dixieland I'll make my stand,
Can't get the woman I want I'm gonna use my — who's gonna do
Your sweet jelly rollin', sweet jelly rollin' when I'm gone.[75]

Rufus Bridey's rough humour gains strength from the ambiguity of the
sex of the participants in the song, with the implications of homosexuality and masturbation following the initial heterosexual verses.

  How old *Sweet Jelly Rollin'* is cannot be easily determined though
its distinctive tune with ragtime flavouring suggests that it is as old
as the century, and could well be much more venerable. Some sexual
traditional songs included in the repertoires of blues singers have a more
firmly established history and *'Bout a Spoonful* in one of its forms has
been coyly mentioned by a number of collectors who have refrained
from quoting any of its words. It appears in the recorded work of
veteran singers of the medicine shows and those whose songs drew from
an older tradition as well as anticipating the new—singers like Papa
Charlie Jackson, Charley Patton and Charley Jordan. Recorded as early
as 1925, Papa Charlie Jackson's *All I Want Is a Spoonful*, has a light
swing to his syncopated banjo accompaniment which expresses his
enjoyment in the song even if his amendment of the words gives scarcely
a hint of its original lustiness:

You can brown your gravy, fry your steak,
Sweet mama, don't make no mistake,
'Cause all I want, honey baby, just a spoonful, spoonful,
Just as sure as the winter follows the fall,
There ain't no one woman got it all,
'Cause all I want, honey baby, just a spoonful, spoonful,
When you've made a woman you cain't understand
If she's lookin' for you or a monkey man,
'Cause all I want, honey baby, just a spoonful, spoonful,
Now t'you kind mama, says you needn't stall,
Throw it out the winder, I'll catch it before it falls,
'Cause all I want, honey baby, is a spoonful, spoonful,
I got the blues so bad I couldn't sleep at night,
My cool kind mama want to fuss and fight,
'Cause all I want, honey baby, is a spoonful, spoonful. . . .[76]

In his dark and guttural voice, Charley Patton sounds more ominous when he sings *A Spoonful Blues*, but he exchanges lines with another singer, Walter Buddy Boy Hawkins perhaps, as he shared the session with Patton, and it is apparently Hawkins who comments that the song is 'all about a spoonful'. Except for the opening line, Patton does not sing the word 'spoonful' but slides the guitar string to form the syllables. Often he growls and the words are indistinct as he sings:

All I want is a spoonful,
Every man goin' crazy everyday in life 'bout a —,
All I want in this creation is a —,
I went home, want to fight 'bout a —,
Goin' to die, way in Hot Springs 'bout a —,
These women goin' crazy every day in their life 'bout a —,
Would you kill a man, yes I will, yes 'bout a —,
Honey I'm a fool about my —,
Don't take me long, to get my —,
Eeh hey, you know I need my —. . . .[77]

Even Patton, it seems, felt the need to modify the song which, from its slightly scrambled lines, seems somewhat imperfectly learned. His recording was made in 1929 and it was more than thirty years after that the Texas singer, Mance Lipscomb, recorded the song as he had learned it when a boy. On it Mack McCormick commented, "*Bout a Spoonful* would elicit denunciation from the United States Post Office if their moral arbiters were better acquainted with the vigorous symbolism of Negro language. This is one of the oldest and most venerated pieces of bawdy lore,' and noted that it was 'mentioned by Gilmore Millen in his novel *Sweet Man* (Viking 1930) in describing early barrelhouse music'.[78] Mance Lipscomb sang to a rocking guitar rhythm and his version employed repeat lines:

Tell me what you gonna do with your brand new daddy,
'Bout a spoonful?
Tell me what you gonna do with your brand new papa,
Oh Lord mama, 'bout a spoonful?
Out late last night, come home from gettin' a spoonful,
It was late last night I came home, from gettin' a spoonful,
Eve an' Adam was the first two people got a spoonful,
Tell me Eve an' Adam, first two people, oh mama got a spoonful.
Late last night when I lay down got a spoonful,
Baby, late last night I lay down, oh mama got a spoonful.[79]

Also of the songster generation of guitarists, the late Mississippi John Hurt had preserved intact over forty years a technique and a repertoire that he had first put on record in the late 'twenties. One of his songs was *Coffee Blues*, another version of *Spoonful*:

Oh the preacher in the pulpit,
Jumpin' up and down,
He laid his Bible down for,
His lovin' —,
(*Spoken*) Ain't Maxwells House all right . . . ?
Well I just got to have my lovin' —.

You can bring me whisky,
You can bring me tea,
Nothin' satisfies me man,
But my lovin' spoonful.
My lovin' —,
Well I just got to have my lovin' —.[80] ©

Some indication of the persistence of the folk tradition, of the obscurity of much of its terminology and the appeal of a vivid image may be gathered from the words of these songs. When Papa Charlie Jackson sang:

> Now t'you kind mama, says you needn't stall,
> Throw it out the winder, I'll catch it before it falls,
> 'Cause all I want, honey baby, is a spoonful, spoonful,[81]

he was already fragmenting a traditional verse which was so familiar to his hearers that a part of it was all that was necessary to convey his meaning. The extract was part of a verse which slid easily from one song to another and whose origin is apparently lost. A startling flight of sexual fantasy, it refers in its full form to sexual intercourse in a standing position but extends to surreal associations which imply the sexual virtuosity of the singer. Charley Patton did not include the verse in his version of *Spoonful* but significantly it formed the basis of the next song he recorded at the same session, *Shake It and Break It (Don't Let It Fall, Mama)*, where the context suggests that it links with the ballad *Stavin' Chain* and Jelly Roll Morton's *Winin' Boy* quoted earlier:

> You can shake it, you can break it, you can hang it on the wall,
> Throw it out the winder, catch it 'fore it falls,
> You can break it, you can hang it on the wall,
> Throw it out the winder, catch it 'fore it falls,
> My jelly, my roll, sweet mama don't you let it fall.
> > Everybody have a jelly roll like mine,
> > I done left this town,
> > I . . . ain't got no brown,
> > I . . . my money's gone,
> > My jelly, my roll, sweet mama don't you let it fall,
> You can snatch it, you can grab it,
> You can whip it, you can break it. . . .[82]

Apparently favoured in Mississippi, the theme was developed by the young Louise Johnson playing her own piano accompaniment to a tune based on Cow Cow Davenport's *Cow Cow Blues*—another link in a complex chain. To its powerful train rhythms she sang in her strident voice of how she was going to instruct the women of Memphis,

Cincinnati and 'Satchitaw'—apparently a spoonerism of Witchita and Saginaw—in love techniques:

> I says you ain't good lookin' and you don't dress fine,
> But that kind treatment make me love you most any time,
> I says you ain't good lookin' and you sure don't dress so fine,
> But that good kind treatment make me love you most any time.

> Well I'm goin' to Memphis drop by Satchitaw,
> Gonna tell you women how to cock it on the wall,
> I'm goin' to Memphis, drop by Satchitaw,
> I'm goin' to show you women honey, how to cock it on the
>   wall.*

> Now you can snatch it, you can break it, you can hang it on the
>   wall,
> Throw it out and see if you can catch it 'fore it falls,
> I mean you can snatch it, you can break it, hang it on the stinkin'
>   wall,
> Throw it out the window women, if you can catch it 'fore it falls.[83]

A few years later the theme was recorded by a Texas pianist, Pinetop Burks, several hundred miles away in San Antonio. He incorporated it into a two-line, eight-bar blues, part of which ran:

> That li'l woman, that li'l woman she done move to a country town,
> She's the sweetest li'l woman that I ever found.

> You can shake it, oh you can break it, oh you can hang it upside
>   the wall,
> You can throw it out the window and I'll be there when it falls.[84]

A more complex song was Eddie Miller's *I'd Rather Drink Muddy Water* made in Chicago the year before, in 1936. This too, was by a pianist whose steady blues had sudden rushing passages against which his soft but somewhat indistinct voice and heavy boogie bass were placed in effective contrast:

* It should be noted that the term 'cock' in Negro usage refers to the female, rather than to the male, pudenda.

I give you my money to buy you shoes and clothes,
If I catch you messin', then out to the county morgue you go,
I'll pay for your coffin, I'll even pay for your shroud,
But when they gonna lay your cold dead body down,
I'd rather drink muddy water, and sleep in a hollow log.

Women, when you get out of bed you may hang it on the wall,
Throw it out the window, run and catch it 'fore it falls,
Lord I had one living, by the name of Sue,
She shimmied so much, great God, myself what on earth to do,
I would rather drink muddy water, sleep right in a hollow log.

Mmmm—fast life is killing me,
Seems as though fast life won't let me be,
Seems like fast life has followed me all my days,
Seems like fast life is goin' to follow me to my grave,
I would rather drink muddy water, sleep right in a hollow log.[85]

In character essentially a blues and with a blues piano accompaniment, the song is none the less structurally comparatively complex in verse form, in spite of its fundamental twelve-bar pattern. It suggests a fairly composed song and one that uses other blues fragments of some familiarity—the refrain line is one, while one verse commences on the theme of 'you don't know my mind'. It is possible that in this form it bore some relation to the version to which James P. Johnson referred when he spoke of Dude Finley—'a pianist who played a rag in D minor that had the same trio that was later used in *Shake It, Break It, Throw It out the Window, Catch It Before It Falls*'.[86]

At one time it was thought that Louise Johnson was accompanied by the Chicago pianist, Cripple Clarence Lofton, on her record of *On the Wall* already quoted. According to Son House, the pianist was Louise Johnson herself, whose playing was similar to Lofton's. Nevertheless, some years later, in 1939, Lofton used the same theme in his rollicking *I Don't Know*, embellished with his humming, finger-snapping and the words:

Shake it and break it so's you can hang it on the wall,
Pitch it out the window, catch it 'fore it fall,
Stop a while and shimmy if it's all night long,
Sometimes that thing got your habits on,

But you shouldn't a' (shouldn't do what darlin' ?)
I don't know, I don't know, (2)
I'm tellin' you lover,
How you been struttin' that thing, night and day.[87]

It was still possible a dozen years after for a young Chicago pianist named Willie Mabon to establish a reputation and the beginnings of a recording career with the same song. Now rationalized and seemingly innocent, the words have been freshened with the suggestion of 'taking in washing', a metaphoric parallel to 'hauling ashes' or 'keeping the kitchen clean':

The woman I love she got dimples in her jaw,
The clothes she's wearin's made out of the best of cloth,
She can take in washin', she can hang it upside the wall,
She can throw 'em out the window, run out and catch 'em a little
    bit before they falls,
Sometimes I think you has your habits on:
I said, 'What should I say to make you mad this time, baby?'
She says, 'Mmmm . . . I don't know, my, oh my, oh my. . . .
I don't know, what my baby's puttin' down.'[88] ©

It was the successful use of traditional and folk idioms that imparted to many of the jazz songs a certain authenticity of character. Occasionally they fed back to the folk musicians directly as has been noted, or through adaptations and parodies. Two Negro song writers, Cecil Mack and Chris Smith—the latter being the composer of the famous *Ballin' the Jack*, a dance song whose popularity lay largely in the insinuating title—composed a comic song in 1908, *You're in the Right Church But the Wrong Pew*. It inspired a number of variants, from Virginia Liston's *You've Got the Right Key But the Wrong Keyhole* of 1924 to the knockabout song of the barrelhouse pianist, Speckled Red, *You've Got the Right String But the Wrong Yo-Yo*. Made in 1930 it had the potential for a minor blues hit for Speckled Red's brother, Piano Red, a score of years after. But though there were a number of exceptions, in general the jazz-blues songs borrowed more from the folk idiom than they fed into it, and the jazz singers or classic blues singers made occasional use of folk material without any sense of incongruity. Ethel Waters was widely celebrated for her singing of *Shake That Thing* which she was featuring in 1921, some four years before both she and Papa Charlie Jackson recorded it. Some songs which might be considered as composed in the jazz-blues vein were based on traditional bawdy material—thus the fate of the obscene song, *The Boy in the Boat*, which refers to the clitoris. It was recorded by George Hannah in a singularly inoffensive version, rather contrary to the character of most of the songs by that uninhibited blues singer. It used to be featured by Charlie Johnson's Paradise Orchestra at Atlantic City with Frankie Half-Pint Jaxon singing the vocals, but Jaxon did not record it and when Johnson made a record of the song it was of the melody only. It did in fact become a standard jazz number but only after a process of bowdlerization. 'One of the most frequently heard songs in the rent-party repertoire was *The Boy in the Boat*,' wrote Fats Waller's biographers, 'a broadly sexual song with many verses composed over the years by many singers. It was to have an important place in the career of Tom Waller, who came to use its melody as a speciality.'[89] He called it *Boston Blues* and used to sing the original words to the theme, later reducing it to a sixteen-bar tune with words that parodied Victor Herbert's *Kiss Me Again*. Finally, after further title changes, it was published as *Squeeze Me* by the Williams Publishing Company. 'Four or five tunes strongly resembling *Squeeze Me* and obviously adapted from its melody line were subsequently released by rival publishers but Clarence took no action against them.'[90] So the tune survived but the words that gave it the bawdy virility of its early life sank with scarcely a trace.

In September 1936, Georgia White recorded *The Boy in the Boat* with the subtitle *BD's Dream*. Alone among seventy-odd successive titles recorded by her this one was unissued. The *BD's Dream* subtitle was an abbreviation of 'Bull-Dyker's Dream', the bull-dyker being, as previously noted, a slang term for a lesbian. In her version of *The Boy in the Boat*, the connexion between these related songs must have been especially marked. The songs were popular among the East Coast rag and 'stride' piano players. One of them, Willie (the Lion) Smith recalled, was John (Jack the Bear) Wilson, the 'well-known dope addict who played piano when he felt like it'. His most famous rendition was a tune called *The Dream* which had actually been written by old man Jess Pickett, another piano-playing gambler who died around 1920. The number was also known as *The Bull Diker's Dream*, it was a tune dedicated to lesbians. He continued, 'It had a tango bass and Wilson would start playing it at a fast tempo and then take it into slow drag style where it got mean and dirty. It was one of those "put out the lights and call the law" things that went over big just before dawn.'[91]

Smith did not quote the song, or record it himself, but it was extremely well known—often titled simply, *The Dream*. 'The number was also called the *Ladies' Dream*, the *Bowdiger's Dream* and the *Digah's Dream*, the latter titles having pornographic reference,' wrote Rudi Blesh, adding that '*The Dream* was never published, but it can be heard in two recorded versions, as an organ solo, *The Digah's Stomp* and a later twelve-inch Asch record by James P. Johnson with a small band'.[92] It was also recorded, in fact, by Fats Waller with Morris's Hot Babies but, needless to add, all these were non-vocal versions, like the band recording of *The Boy in the Boat* made by Charlie Johnson's Paradise Orchestra from Atlantic City. These were jazz-blues and jazz-rag songs which were in popular currency in the sporting-houses of the East. Many had been in circulation for a long time, being modified as the idioms changed. 'One of my favourites was the famous *Don't Hit That Lady Dressed in Green*, man, the lyrics to this song were a sex education, especially for a twelve-year-old boy,' recalled Willie the Lion, 'other lively tunes I learned were such titles as *She's Got Good Booty* and *Baby, Let Your Drawers Hang Low*.'[93] Before 1908, James P. Johnson had learned similar tunes, playing them in Jersey City as a child. 'Like other kids, I used to work around saloons, doing a little buck dance, playing the guitar and singing songs like *Don't Hit That Lady; She Got Good Booty . . . Left Her on the Railroad Track . . . Baby, Let Your Drawers Hang Low*.'[94]

Like the others of the stride piano generation, Johnson adapted such songs for publication, learning the technique from a Negro song writer, Will Farrell. 'With him,' he said, 'I set down my first composition to be published, *Mammas' and Pappas' Blues*. There had been a piece around at the time called *Left Her at the Railroad Track* or, *Baby, Get That Towel Wet*. All the pianists knew it and could play variations on it. It was a sporting-house favourite. I took one opening strain and did a paraphrase from this and used it for *Mammas' and Pappas' Blues*. It was also developed later into *Crazy Blues*, by Perry Bradford.'[95] In his autobiography, Bradford devoted much space to the recording of *Crazy Blues*, but not to the origin of the song, except to note that it was originally entitled *Harlem Blues* by him. It seems likely, however, that the extraordinary success of the song, which according to Bradford sold

800,000 copies of Mamie Smith's original Okeh recording and 600,000 of Mary Stafford's version, was in part due to familiarity with the origins of the tune.[96]

Of the original words of these songs nothing remained in the course of publication; it was not commercial exploitation of the lyrics but rather the total obliteration of them for commercial interests. Many of the famed singers of the early 'twenties—Mattie Hite, Mary Stafford, Edith Wilson, Josephine Beatty, Josie Miles and many others—were noted for their ribald songs, though these were seldom represented on record. Recorded examples made greater use of *double-entendre*, exploiting heavy innuendo to achieve their effects. These were deliberate devices much used by the professional entertainer. Mattie Hite, Willie the Lion recalled, 'had the kind of personality that made them whoop, yell, and scream for more. She was one of those tall brownskin gals, a natural showstopper, who could wreck any joint she worked in. One minute she had everybody laughing at one of her *risqué* jokes and then she'd turn around and sing a sweet or sad ballad that brought tears to a roomful of eyes'—a technique familiar in vaudeville and music hall.[97]

Undoubtedly a large number of jazz-blues and jazz-rag songs were tediously suggestive, but there were others that had the directness of any in the folk tradition. With a fierce line in 'scat' singing which had the 'dirty tone' of a muted trumpet, Mary Dixon sang with no apparent restraint:

I've had men of all sizes, had 'em tall and lean,
Had 'em short, had 'em flabby, had 'em in between.
    I'm an all-round mama, I'm an all-round mama,
    I'm an all-round mama, with an all-round mind.

Had a boy, young and tender, treated me so fine,
Never had nothin' else but that thing on his mind.
Met a man in the gin-mill, we drank gin so fas',
Took me home, I remember, I said, 'Oh my yas!'
    I'm an all-round mama, I'm an all-round mama,
    I'm an all-round mama, with an all-round mind.

I met a man, was a butler, when he spoke I ran,
Was too mannish for a woman, too girlish for a man.

Had a man, good old sweetback, said that I should know,
Said he didn't do no loving' lest he had some dough,
I'm an all-round mama, I'm an all-round mama,
I'm an all-round mama, with an all-round mind.[98]

Other singers made comparatively innocuous words sexually potent
by the manner of their singing. In general this was a field in which
women singers excelled and there were relatively few male jazz-blues
singers. The women dressed exotically and were supported by scantily
clad chorus girls wearing the shimmy dresses of the period. 'Jungle
scenes', with erotic dancing, were by no means solely performed for the
benefit of white audiences as has been frequently suggested. 'Freak
shows' and 'drag shows' were regular features in many Harlem and
Chicago nightspots—evenings set aside for homosexuals and lesbians.
One male entertainer, Frankie Half-Pint Jaxon, made the best of a
high-pitched voice with female impersonations and sexual ambiguities.
His *Fan It*, a libidinous song of markedly genital character, gained
greatly from his miming while he could evoke erotic images with his
humorous comments on such jazz-blues as *She Can Love So Good*:

Sometimes she makes me sneeze, sometimes she makes me cough,
Lawd you ought to see her when she starts me off.
Oh . . . so good. . . .
Oh she loves me so . . . *boogie-woogieshly*,
And everybody wants her, 'cause she loves so . . . *peculiar*. . . .

Against Tampa Red's fierce kazoo blowing he ecstatically gasped, 'Aw,
yes honey . . . I am that—just anything you want to call me. . . . Oh kiss
me now—oh right *there*. . . . Oh Lord . . . what you doin' to me . . . ?
Oh so good . . . so good. . . .'[99]

Singers who were raised in the cities were no strangers to sexual
excesses and aberrations. 'By the time I was seven I knew all about sex
and life in the raw, I could outcurse any stevedore and took a sadistic
pleasure in shocking people,' wrote Ethel Waters, who lived as a child in
the heart of the red-light district of Philadelphia's Bloody Eighth Ward.
'I came to know well the street whores, the ladies in the sporting houses,
their pimps, the pickpockets, shoplifters, and other thieves who lived
all around us.'[100] Her memories were paralleled by those of Billie Holiday
who was raised in near-by Baltimore. 'Alice Dean used to keep a whore-

house on the corner nearest our place, and I used to run errands for her and the girls,' she wrote. 'A whorehouse was about the only place where black and white folks could meet in any natural way. They damn well couldn't rub elbows in the churches. And in Baltimore, places like Alice Dean's were the only joints fancy enough to have a victrola and for real enough to pick up on the best records.'[101] At the age of ten she was raped by a neighbour in a house on Pennsylvania Avenue. The avenue was the subject of a jazz-blues by Bertha Idaho, who still lives in the city:

I want to tell you about a street I know,
In the city of Baltimore,
And every night about half past eight,
The broads that strollin' just won't wait,
You'll find 'em every night on Pennsylvania Avenue.

Let's take a trip down to that cabaret,
Where they turn night into day,
Some freakish sights you'll surely see,
You can't tell the he's from the she's,
You'll find 'em every night on Pennsylvania Avenue.

Now if you want good lovin', and want it cheap,
Just drop around about the middle of the week,
When the broads is broke and can't pay rent,
Get good lovin' boys for fifteen cents,
You can get it every night on Pennsylvania Avenue.[102] ©

IMAGERY AND SYMBOLISM

Though a number of jazz-blues directly described a sexual situation or, as in Bertha Idaho's *Down on Pennsylvania Avenue* or in Lillian Glinn's *Atlanta Blues*, a situation where sexual desires could be gratified, a very large number implied them indirectly through a complex of symbolic images. Drawing an artificial line between such songs which are acceptable and those which are not, those which are 'frank and healthy' and those which are not, a number of critics have defended the attitudes expressed in the folk blues compared with those in the jazz-blues forms. They parallel the views of the authors of *The Heart of Jazz* who, in a defence of New Orleans jazz, arguing from a Christian standpoint, refer to the sexual element in the music as 'direct, earthy, and unsentimental. The atmosphere of the jazz band hardly suggests dalliance in the boudoir. In most New Orleans jazz performances, indeed, the sexual element is indistinguishable from the general vitality of the music'.[103] By these criteria almost all jazz-blues are acceptable for the content is earthy and unsentimental and the sexual terms so familiar as to have created a language of their own. If 'arse' could not be spoken or sung on a record the singer settled for 'yas yas', a childhood equivalent which was understood by every listener in the audience for whom the blues and songs were created. *That's Your Yas Yas* was in a terminological sense more explicit than *That's Your Red Wagon*; *Keep Your Yas Yas Clean* more explicit than *I Keeps My Kitchen Clean*. A child's ritual game rhyme became *The Duck's Yas Yas*; an adult's bawdy humour was expressed in *Hannah Johnson's Big Jackass* or its variant, *Jackass for Sale*. *Yas Yas Yas* was the special blues of Jimmy Strange, whose unmasculine voice suggests that this was a pseudonym in itself, and who sported the sobriquet of 'The Yas Yas Man'. The challenging name was matched by Merline Johnson who, on almost all her records, bore the name of 'The Yas Yas Girl'. The arrogant self-abasement in the chosen nicknames is a form of sexual bragging and is a counterpart of the prowess implied in Ferdinand Morton's nickname of 'Jelly Roll', or the equivalent use in the names of Jelly Roll Anderson, Steady Roll Johnson or Boodle-It Wiggins. It is evident from these names that the singers were employing terms which may at one time have been somewhat obscure to white listeners but which were totally familiar and in general usage among Negroes. The distinction between metaphor, euphemism and sexual terminology is therefore not easily determined. There is never any doubt that 'jelly' means sexual pleasure in Negro parlance and leads, by a complex of sexual associations, to many extensions. 'Jelly bean' becomes a lover, 'jelly roll' coitus or, in some instances, ejaculation, and so 'jelly' becomes the semen, the rhythms of intercourse, the skill itself. In *Jelly, Look What You Done Done*, Clara Smith uses the term rhetorically to an irresponsible Eros,

Jelly, oh jelly look what you done done,
You caused your grandmother to marry her youngest son,

an Eros who has 'sent your poor mother crazy and your poor father go blind' which is a clear reference to venereal disease.[104]

By extension, dough-rolling, biscuit-rolling, bread-baking and other baking terms have stemmed from the 'jelly' image to become in themselves widely understood terms of sexual significance. These have been dealt with at length elsewhere together with the meaning of many other phrases frequently employed. There is in Race music of all forms a seemingly unfathomable reserve of images on which to draw, but to the listener some of these may seem tortuous and contrived. 'Some of the women singers did blues about their "Handy Man" or their "Kitchen Man" usually with a verse that explained that they loved their handy man or their kitchen man for his various skills and they described exactly what he could do. It is the same use of double meaning and the singing usually had a leering style to it that added to the effect of cheap vulgarity.'[105] Aesthetically, this is fair criticism on a song such as Victoria Spivey's *Handy Man*:

He shakes my ashes, freezes my griddle,
Churns my butter, strokes my pillow,
My man is such a handy man.

He threads my needle, gleans my wheat,
Heats my heater, chops my meat,
My man is such a handy man.

He flaps my flapjack, cleans off my table,
Leads the horses in my stable,
My man is such a handy man.

Sometimes he's up before dawn,
Working on my front lawn,
My man is such a handy man.[106] ©

But it is arguable to state that 'usually a handy man was described as being able to "haul ashes", a folk expression for being able to make love, but his other skills usually were only vaguely related to an open expression of sexuality' for the images employed are quite apposite. Intuitively perhaps, Victoria Spivey's chosen symbols are psychologically valid, the reference to bodily warmth (heats my heater), to phallic-weapon symbolism (chops my meat), to oral gratification (flapjacks), to harvest (gleans my wheat), bodily orifice (threads my needle), bodily landscape (my front lawn), totemism (horses in my stable) are immediately identifiable basic sexual symbols. Far from being vague they are particularly apt and in their exteriorization of subconscious symbols are an open expression of sexuality. This is not to gainsay that it is a dull record, but it does raise problems of criteria. As a recording St Louis Bessie's *Meat Cutter Blues* is much its superior artistically; as imagery there is probably little to choose between them:

I want you to cut my liver, chop my veal and cut my steak, (2)
Every time I think about it, it make my poor heart ache.

I had a fire in my range and water in my pot, (2)
You ain't cut my meat yet and my range is still hot.[107]

In *Handy Man*, Victoria Spivey sang, 'When my fire gets hot he turns my damper down', while St Louis Bessie, in *Meat Cutter Blues*, used the lines, 'If you cain't cut my meat I'll get a butcher from down town, 'cause my range is still heated and my damper needs turnin' down'. Both singers were drawing on a phrase that was totally familiar by 1925: 'I'm the baby that turned your damper down,' sang Coot Grant in *Come On Coot and Do That Thing*. It would be hard to determine which singer was more derivative and which more original. Perhaps Victoria Spivey's composition was strained through using too many images, but St Louis Bessie's was as strained in its use of one: the dangers inherent in mixed metaphor on the one hand, and in sustained metaphor on the other.

Though it is by no means certain that Victoria Spivey was the first singer on record to use a herpetological symbol, her first recording, made at the age of sixteen, was to make a strong impression on blues symbolism. Combining the qualities of an exceptional tune with striking imagery, her *Black Snake Blues* was copied by innumerable blues singers and reinterpreted by many others. 'Some black snake been suckin' my rider's tongue,' she sang in her initial verse, employing a dramatic serpent symbol with associations of oral eroticism. The blues developed through a succession of valid images to a urethral, swimming association and the male body-symbol of a submarine: 'I'd rather be a catfish swimmin' in that deep blue —, Lord, beneath a submarine, behind a floatin' boat. . . .'[108]

Within a few months, Blind Lemon Jefferson recorded the first of three versions of *That Black Snake Moan* and a year later made his *Black Snake Dream*. Victoria Spivey herself made other recordings of her original song and *Garter Snake Blues* was another variant. Martha Copeland made versions of both Spivey's and Jefferson's blues, commencing a chain of interpretations which were still being recorded by John Lee Hooker and Texas Red thirty years later. Among the innumerable versions and new blues on the serpent theme, Rosa Henderson's *Black Snake Moan*, Joshua White's *Lazy Black Snake*, Tallahassee Tight's *Black Snake Blues*, Blind Boy Fuller's *Blacksnakin' Jiver*, Roosevelt Sykes's *Jet Black Snake*, John Henry Howard's *Black Snake* and Peggy Walker's *Blacksnake Wiggle* maintained the black-snake theme. Walter Vincson even formed the Mississippi Blacksnakes in recognition of the potent image. And by extension Peg Leg Ben Abney's *I'm a Rattlesnakin' Daddy*, Tony Hollins's *Crawling King Snake* and many others developed the herpetological symbol. In Victoria Spivey's blues other images were similarly used, to be developed later. Such compositions as Tommy McClennan's *Deep Blue Sea Blues*, Robert Petway's *Catfish Blues*, George Davis's *Flesh Crawling Blues* and a score of others, are evidence of the powerful significance in all styles of blues singing and in all forms of Race music of a basic language of symbols.

So universally applied are sexual symbols in all forms of Negro Race music that they virtually defy criticism on aesthetic grounds. Their range is extensive and includes a remarkable variety of oral symbols, familiar equivalents for the act of coitus and, therefore understandably, innumerable food symbols for the pudenda. As these have been the subject of previous studies, it is perhaps superfluous to deal with them in detail here.[109] It is to be expected, however, that imagery on themes such as these is likely to be constant and the degree to which original interpretation is applied, relatively small. Devious sexual innuendo tends to arise when the symbol is a tired one and the singer has strained to invent some new application of it. It would be reasonable to expect that the more original metaphors are drawn from situations in a state of change—from technological advances in the course of the century for instance. This would likewise tend to exhaust themes that had ceased to have any application in the present—there would be little significance in *My Man o' War* today. From Blind Lemon Jefferson's *Oil Well Blues* to Joe Hill Louis's *Hydromatic Woman*, from Washboard Sam's *Let Me Play Your Vendor* to Little Brother Montgomery's *My*

Electronical Invention, there has been a slender line of blues and songs on mechanical and industrial themes. Few have displayed the wit or the bizarre fantasy of Wynonie Harris's early rhythm 'n blues jazz-blues, *Lovin' Machine*:

> You put a nickel in the slot, hear somethin' buzzin',
> Kisses come hot at five cents a dozen,
> > Up to my house, I'll show you what I mean,
> > I just got wise and built me a lovin' machine.
>
> You put a nickel in the slot, things light up,
> Out comes your lovin' in a Dixie Cup,
> > Up to my house I got somethin' you never seen,
> > I got hip to the tip and built me a lovin' machine.
>
> It'll love you all day an' if you feel run down,
> You don't have to worry and run all over town,
> When my machine finished, that ain't all,
> Out comes a bottle of alcohol:
> > Up to my house I'll show you what I mean. . . .[110]

Superficially, the number of such blues employing mechanical themes is small with one or two marked exceptions of subject matter. In general this reflects the experience and the occupations of the singers and their audiences, for the images are most effective when they come within the immediate world of the Negro. Eminently suitable though rockets and space-craft might appear to be for this purpose, they do not figure in modern blues metaphor because they have little impression on the lives of the majority of Negroes. Themes drawn from manual labour in which the singer or his audience may well have been employed have always been favoured in preference to mechanical themes with which the singer is not familiar. Physical effort in the rhythms of manual work has immediate associations with the rhythms of intercourse, while tools have major importance as genital symbols. So Blind Blues Darby would sing:

> I'm a real good spike driver man, let me drive a spike for you,
> Everybody that knows me knows that spike drivin' is all I can do.
>
> Now when I get drivin' piles it sure gets good to me,
> For I'm a real good spike driver and I carry a written guarantee.

I'm a real good spike driver and my spike it never bend,
For I know how to hold my hammer and I drive it in.[111]

'I got a ten-pound hammer and the women love to hear it sound,' sang Mose Andrews, 'they says "Come on Mose, hurry and drive it on down." '[112] But if these blues draw from spike driving in the laying of railroad tracks, the railroad engines do not figure prominently in blues as sexual symbols in spite of their apparent suitability. There are exceptions—the enigmatic traditional verse line, 'I'm long and tall like a cannonball', which sounds totally paradoxical, has rather more meaning when it is known that 'The Cannonball' is the Illinois Central express from Chicago to New Orleans, though 'tall' is more effective as a rhyme than as an adjective. Generally speaking the train plays a smaller part in blues as a sexual symbol than might be supposed but this is partly because it is a very potent symbol of escape. Trains figure prominently in blues both in content and musically, in imitation, reflecting very directly the desire to migrate. When a Negro takes a train, when as a hobo he rides the 'rods' or the 'blinds', he performs a totally passive role; he is not the engineer with the powerful machine in his control; he is not the fireman stoking—in the days of steam—the fires to heat the boilers. Mechanical imagery demands immediate involvement if it is to be relevant and for this reason the major exception is the automobile.

Many years before Dr Ernest Dichter, the President of the Institute of Motivational Research Inc., made his celebrated study for the Chrysler Corporation on the sexual motivations that influence the purchase of automobiles, the blues singer had already illuminated the 'mistress versus wife' principles.[113] Women blues singers had clearly acknowledged their role in automobile terms, as did Bertha Chippie Hill in her 1927 recording of *Sport Model Mama*:

I'm a sports model mama out on the rack for sale, (2)
It's a mighty poor dog won't wag its own tail.

I'm justa plain little sport, have punctures every day, (2)
You may want a limousine but they puncture the same way.

I know you women don't like me because I speak my mind, (2)
I don't like to make speed, I'd rather take my time.

When the men comes to buy me you'll always hear them say, (2)
'Give me a sports model mama because they know the way.'[114]

Though Negroes soon equated a material scale of values in the manu-
facture of automobiles with sexual equivalents, these ingeniously
reflected their acceptance of their position in a social sub-stratum.
'The best cheap car in the market is a Ford,' sang Sloppy Henry. Only
a few years before, the famous Model T Ford had dropped in price till
a new car could be purchased in 1924 for just $290. When Ford changed
his policy in 1927 and commenced making more luxurious models,
second-hand Model Ts came on the market at sensationally low prices
and the vehicle was widely popular among Negroes. Its near-indestructi-
bility, its dependability, its lack of glamour, reflected virtues that the
Negro liked to see in himself. In an outstanding song on this theme
Cleo Gibson, with her aggressive swaggering voice, boasted that she
had 'Ford engine movements in her hips', itself a punning reference to
the movements of the currently famous Elgin watch:

I've got Ford engine movements in my hips,
Ten thousand miles guaranteed.
A Ford is a car everybody likes to ride,
Just as you will see.
You can have your Rolls Royal, [sic]
Your Packard and such,
Takes a Ford engine car to do your stuff,
I've got Ford engine movements in my hips,
Ten thousand miles guaranteed, I say,
Ten thousand miles guaranteed.[115]

One of the most familiar of blues metaphors, the verb 'to ride'
implying sexual intercourse, has become a standard usage among
Negroes as has 'rider' for a lover. It has been in use at least since the
latter part of the nineteenth century when the motions of riding a mule
were compared with those of coitus, and probably has a much older
history. 'Easy rider' for either a male or female lover has been
in common use for as long a period and gained a wider recognition when
W. C. Handy's *Yellow Dog Blues*, with the line 'Dear Sue, your easy
rider struck this burg today', was published in 1914. Telling of 'Miss
Susie Johnson' who had 'lost her Jockey Lee', it also acknowledged the

similar use of the term 'jockey' for a sexual partner.[116] 'Easy' as a term has subtle sexual implications in itself as the phrases 'slow and easy', 'fine and mellow' or 'keen and peachy' all apply with shades of emphasis to both physical attractions and pleasurable intercourse. Though the associations of the 'rider' with the mule—in spite of the sexual implications of the neuter gender—or with the pony, persist even today in many blues, their application to the automobile was natural, giving an added point to the use of the theme.

Natural too was the extension of the automobile metaphor to the tired lover, comparing him or her to the worn-out machine. There had been a precedent for this, too, in the composition of the white entertainer, Ben Harney, whose use of ragtime themes afforded him a special place in popular music and who had undoubted influence on Negroes, as well as adopting much from them. His song *You've Been a Good Old Wagon, But You've Done Broke Down*, composed in 1896, had its parallels in jazz-blues compositions thirty years later when Virginia Liston, for example, sang her *Rolls-Royce Papa*:

> . . . Your carburettor's rusty, this I really mean,
> Your gas tank's empty, you want oil, gasolene,
> Your windshield is broken, it ain't worth a cent,
> Your steering wheel is wobbly, your piston rod is bent.
> Your fender's broken, your wheels ain't tight,
> And I know darned well your spark plugs ain't hittin' right. . . .[117]

Sung in an insipid voice and with little conviction, Virginia Liston's song gave shape to an extended metaphor which blues singers still employ forty years later. Robert Johnson's *Terraplane Blues* is, in fact, just one of a long line of such blues which exploited the many moving parts and varying conditions of the automobile engine. Some, at any rate, of these versions introduced a new idea or two but basically the elements remained similar and it was the new models, from the Model T to the Terraplane and the Cadillac, which provided variations in the use of the metaphors whose specific meaning was never clear in the references to 'your windshield' or 'my carburettor'. The automobile image often applied to men as well as women, for the driver of a car may think of the vehicle as female in sex but it is well known that in the process of driving he considers the automobile as an extension of himself. So Lightnin' Slim could use similar elements and sing in the first person:

My starter won't start this mornin' and I'm about to lose my mind, (2)
I wanta go and see my li'l baby but my machine is all out of time.

I got water in my gas tank and my battery's all run down, (2)
If I can't see my li'l woman I'm gonna leave this lonesome town.

My starter won't start this mornin', no my coil don't even sing,
My starter won't start this mornin', my coil won't do a thing,
Well I must be—got some kind o' bad disconnexion somewhere
    in my piston ring.[118] ©

With its dragging beat, the guttural voice and abject expression convincingly project the singer's frustration while the song is no more explicit than Virginia Liston's in its employment of mechanical images.

It is superfluous to examine in detail the innumerable blues and blues songs which extend the automobile theme further, from the many variants of Sonny Boy Williamson's *My Little Machine*, which has become a traditional blues, to the versions of *Auto-Mechanic Blues*; their existence, the frequency of their use, are evidence of the appeal of a powerful sexual symbol in the blues. The fact that even a 'dynamic' symbol, one that lends itself to new interpretation and change, still has within it stereotypes of expression and idea, must lead one to speculate on the degree to which commercial exploitation may have encouraged blues in sexual metaphors and the degree to which they were suppressed. For if there is an issued *One More Greasin'* by Joe McCoy or a *Valves Need Grinding* by his brother, Charlie McCoy, there were others like Red Nelson's *Car Greasing Blues* or Merline Johnson's *Don't You Want To Ride?* which were not released. There are many reasons why some recordings were unissued but it is not unreasonable to suppose that these particular items were withheld because they offended some arbitrary standard of what was acceptable for release.

THE RECORD COMPANY AS CENSOR

On the evidence of the titles and the anomalies among issued titles, it is difficult to see any evidence of a consistent standard having been applied as grounds for censorship. Thus Columbia were prepared to issue Blind Willie McTell's *Southern Can Is Mine* but not *Real Jazz Mama*; ARC would issue Spark Plug Smith's *Mama's Doughnut* but not *Buy My Cabbage*; Bluebird were willing to release Walter Davis's

Candy Man but not his recording of *Let Me Dig Your Basement*, and to issue his *Let Me in Your Saddle* but not *Let Me Meg Your Water*. Sometimes the record companies regretted their decision to issue, as when the ARC companies withdrew Lil Johnson's *Get 'Em from the Peanut Man*—or *Hot Nuts*—a rollicking, admittedly bawdy, song from their issues on Banner, Romeo and other labels just three days after issue, but felt no such measure necessary on its release on Vocalion.[119] It is true that certain recordings are withheld because of mistakes on the part of the singer, flaws in the recording take itself, and other technical reasons, while the approach of the Depression brought its problems for the companies who had to speculate on the titles which would sell best. An examination of the recordings for various companies of a single singer can reveal the picture more clearly. Bo Carter, for instance, was a singer who recorded steadily from 1928 until 1940, who used predominantly sexual material with humour and often with originality. He made many records with his brothers, the Mississippi Sheiks, and sometimes as an accompanist, but under his own name he made some 118 titles of which only 10 were not issued. *The Yellow Coon Has No Race*, his first title, may have been held on technical or racial grounds, though probably the latter. *The Law Gonna Step On You* and *You Keep My Spending Change* would appear on the evidence of their titles to have been innocuous enough and only *Squeeze Your Lemon*, *Leads Gone Bad*, *Best Piece of Furniture* and *Total Old Shaker* may have been held back as being inadmissible. This did not deter the Okeh and Bluebird companies from issuing *Pin in Your Pincushion*, *Please Warm My Wiener*, *Your Biscuits Are Big Enough For Me*, *Don't Mash My Digger Too Deep*, *It's Too Wet*, *My Pencil Won't Write No More*, *Banana in Your Fruit Basket* or *All Around Man*—all of which could feasibly have been withheld on grounds of obscenity.

There is evidence that the companies were not always rigorous in their censorship: the file card for the Brunswick issue under the non-committal title, *It Ain't No Good*, by Charlie McCoy, bears the comment 'Dirty lyrics'. It was issued. The back of the file card for Mary Butler's coupling of *Mary Blues* and *Bungalow Blues* has the inscription in pencil, 'Typical Negro blues song sung with all the sex appeal possible of imagination', which can only lead to sad reflections on the limited imagination of the author—Mary Butler's voice was flat, her delivery singularly devoid of any of the usual qualities that imply sex appeal and her words inoffensive.[120] Nevertheless, the censorship was sufficiently effective to encourage the singers to devise means of evading it. Said Edith Johnson, 'I was thinking up words and trying to think of titles that no one had used. Well I thought of one . . . but I couldn't use that! So instead of usin' the right words I changed it to *Honey Dripper*. And then I tried to sit down and think of some words that would fit it!'[121] She came up with the verses:

> He treats me so mean, just comes to me sometimes, (2)
> But the way he spreads his honey, he will make me lose my mind.
>
> Just because I'm down he wants to drive me away, (2)
> 'Cause he know's he's a good honey dripper and I need him every day.[122]

Her euphemism was successful enough for her to record three versions of *Honey Dripper Blues* and for a new metaphor to appear in the blues. Her accompanist on the first version, Roosevelt Sykes, was called 'The Honey Dripper' on his Decca recordings and many variations of the theme were made by other singers. Peter Clayton sang *Honey Stealin' Blues* in 1942:

> You've been stealin' my honey, your fingerprints is all over my hive, (2)
> My honey may be sweet to you buddy, but you know you ain't treatin' me right.
>
> You sneak off in a corner, steal my honey right from my home, (2)
> And when I get back in the mornin' there ain't no honey left in the comb.[123]

Clayton was known as 'Doctor' Clayton having taken for himself the 'doctor' theme as his personal sexual blues. Though a dipsomaniac, Clayton was an exceptionally popular singer touring extensively in a bus which bore his bespectacled, grinning features on the side. Club owners were prepared to accept his irresponsibility and occasional insensibility when he arrived for an engagement because he always drew large crowds to hear him. Sunnyland Slim, who was his pianist for some years and who commenced his own recording career in some reflected glory by using the name 'Doctor Clayton's Buddy', explained that the singer's *Doctor Clayton Blues* and *Root Doctor Blues* were always much in demand and were considerably more bawdy in performance than on record.

It is difficult to ascertain to what extent the record companies interfered with the freedom of the singers to put on record the blues verses they wished to sing. No research to date has revealed conclusively whether the companies actively encouraged the issue of bawdy material and invited it from their singers. Generally this has been assumed from the high proportion of blues on sexual themes in the catalogues of the record firms.[124] But it is also possible that it directly reflects a desire on the part of the singers to record blues of this character and a reticence on the part of the companies initially to issue them before testing the market. Because the blues is largely improvised or, in the less spontaneous examples, is the compilation of original and standard verses by the singer, there is no means of determining the nature of the verses which have been rejected. If a blues singer considered that a stanza had to be modified for recording, if an executive on hearing a blues in rehearsal decided against the use of a verse, there is no means of recovery. Rejected masters were usually destroyed, unissued masters were often destroyed too, sooner or later, and this evidence is also probably beyond reclaim.

SWEET PATUNIA

If there were blues in the 'twenties and 'thirties of a character which was too outspoken, too obscene in the view of the record companies to issue, the lack of recordings, the lack of field notes and written transcriptions combined with the puritanism of the collectors to ensure that their words were lost. A measure of the lost material can only be obtained by comparison with a standard which has received similar treatment, if censorship was applied to recordings. Such standards can be found in the recorded versions of traditional blues songs, a number of which, though appearing in no collections of Negro song, conspicuously overlooked by folklorists and anthologists, have been recorded in a sufficient number of variants to indicate their importance in the tradition. Their origins are as clouded as those of *'Bout a Spoonful* or *Sweet Jelly Rollin'* already noted, but their character suggests that they share a similar history.

One of the best known of these traditional songs is undoubtedly *Sweet Patunia*. It has been recorded many times under variations of this title—as *I'm Wild About My Patootie* by Ora Alexander in 1932 or as *Sweet Patuna Stomp* by Monkey Joe Coleman in New Orleans three years later. Ora Alexander's version was recorded in New York while Curley Weaver made one in Atlanta, Georgia—indications of the widespread distribution of the song. Curley Weaver played guitar, Monkey Joe played piano—unlike *'Bout a Spoonful* it appears in the repertoire of both guitarists and pianists as well as of singers like Ora Alexander who, as far as is known, did not play an instrument. A popular song of this title appears to have been in circulation around 1910, perhaps to give rise to the bawdier version or probably stemming from a common origin. Recorded early in 1928, *Sweet Patunia* was Curley Weaver's first issued song. It was a cautious version:

I got a gal, lives down by the jail,
Sign on the door 'Sweet Patuni for Sale',
    I'm wild about my 'tuni, only thing I breathe,
    Lord I'm wild about my 'tuni, only thing I breathe,
    Sweet patuni, gonna carry me to my grave.

I got a gal, she's long and tall,
Every time she do the shimmy, Lord I holler 'hot dog',
    Lord I'm wild about my 'tuni, only thing I grieve, (2)
    Sweet patuni, gonna carry me to my grave.

If I could holler like a mountain jack,
I'd go up on the mountain bring my 'tuni back,
    I'm wild about my 'tuni etc.

Way back yonder in One-O-One,
Eve and Adam doin' it, but they couldn't get none,
    Lord I'm wild about my 'tuni, only thing I breathe, (2)
    Sweet patuni, gonna carry me to my grave.[125]

Willie Baker was another singer who appears to have come from Atlanta. He also shared with Curley Weaver the theme of *No No Blues*, a Georgia favourite which was recorded a couple of times—as *Yo-Yo Blues* by Barbecue Bob. His voice had a gritty quality similar to Weaver's and it is likely that they learned the song from the same source, or that Weaver taught it to Baker. Baker's *Sweet Patunia Blues* was first

recorded for Gennett in January 1929, was re-recorded on 7 February
and yet again on 13 February. Finally, on 11 March 1929, he made a
version which was to be issued. The others were all unissued but their
rejection may have been due to faults in his performance or in the
recording rather than to content, as other titles were also repeated and
unissued. His final version of *Sweet Patunia* was a somewhat lustier
song than was Curley Weaver's:

I got a gal she's got a Rolls-Royce,
She didn't get off by usin' her voice.
>I'm wild about my 'tuni, only thing I crave, (2)
>Well sweet patuni, goin' to carry me to my grave.

Every time my gal walk down the street,
All the boys holler, 'Ain't 'tuni sweet?'
>Now I'm wild about my 'tuni etc.

I got a gal she lives up on a hill,
You cain't get her 'tuni, she got automobile,
>Now I'm wild about my 'tuni etc.

Well I woke up this mornin' 'bout half pas' four,
Long tall gal rappin' at my door.
>She was singin', 'Sweet patuni, only thing I crave, (2)
>Well sweet patuni gonna carry me to my grave.'

If all the 'tunis were brought to a test,
A long tall gal would swing it the best,
>Now I'm wild about my 'tuni etc.

Tellin' all you men I been well blessed,
I get what I want you can have the rest,
>Now I'm wild about my 'tuni etc.[126]

These were guitarists' versions from singers probably of rural origin.
On record a little earlier, and perhaps the first example of the song on
disc, was Lucille Bogan's *Sweet Patunia* made in Chicago in 1927 with
the spare, sombre, but splendidly phrased, piano of Alex Channey in
accompaniment. Though Lucille Bogan recorded many of the least
inhibited of blues and blues songs, this early example was very reserved:

Let me tell you what sweet patuni do,
Take your money and stay all night for you,
    I'm wild about my 'tuni, only thing I crave,
    Wild about my 'tuni, the only thing I crave,
    Sweet patuni's gonna foller me to my grave.

Sweet patuni man I cain't understand,
He got ways like a boy but moves like a full-grown man,
    Wild about my 'tuni etc.[127]

And she too sings the verse, 'If I could holler like a mountain jack' which suggests some relationship to an earlier model, for this verse appears in blues and blues songs of many different types. Though the melody of the refrain is similar in these examples, Lucille Bogan's verse melody is quite different. Recordings tended to fix melodies, for it was possible for a singer to play a record over and over to learn the tune, while songs learned in an oral tradition and transmitted by aural means often underwent melodic changes. Here again the evidence implies a widespread song which had taken a number of forms before recording commenced. In Lucille Bogan's version 'sweet patuni' would appear to be sexual pleasure and the opening line, 'Let me tell you what sweet patuni do' is close to the traditional, 'Let me tell you what careless love will do' of the song *Careless Love*. This is a change of meaning comparable with the changes which have taken place in the term 'jelly roll', but 'sweet patuni' is generally used as a vaginal simile from the form of the patunia flower.

Though guitarists have recorded *Sweet Patunia* it is favoured by pianists, some—Jimmy Yancey and Albert Ammons for instance—having recorded it as a piano solo. Ammons's recording has been unissued by the Library of Congress for whom it was recorded but Yancey's version is so characterized by his personal phrasing and rhythm that the tune is not readily recognizable. Another pianist, who recorded some years before Jimmy Yancey but who played in a style very similar to his, was Little David Alexander who sang a version of the song which gives a better impression of its origin. His recording includes at least one verse which is common in many songs:

Let's go to town boys, truck 'em down . . . yeah. . . .

I know a lady she lives by the jail,
Got a sign on the door says, "Tuni for Sale'.
    Sweet patuni is the only thing she craves, (2)
    I believe to my soul it'll foller her to her grave.

That same li'l woman she's long and tall,
Sleeps in the kitchen with her legs in the hall,
    Sweet patuni is the only thing she craves,
    Sweet patuni, I declare she just won't hay,
    I believe to my soul it'll foller her to her grave.

Now she took off her clothes and put 'em on the wall,
Said she didn't need no clothes at all,
    Sweet patuni etc.

Now there's sweet patuni out there hangin' on the fence,
If you don't go run to get it you ain't got no sense,
    Sweet patuni etc.

Now the rooster crowed in Germany, they got the news in France,
Says what the womens like he's got it in his pants,
    Sweet patuni etc.[128]

Little David's *Original Sweet Patuni* (*Patootie Blues*) which was recorded in August 1936 was made again in a *New Sweet Patuni* just over a month later and both were issued. But another version, made a couple of months before Little David's and also for Decca, was not issued. This was cut by Jesse James, a powerful pianist with a tough voice who was reputedly on parole from prison when he made his four titles. *Long Lonesome Day Blues* is a classic of the period, deeply moving and entirely in character with this report. On the two other titles which followed *Southern Casey Jones* and *Long Lonesome Day Blues*, there are two reports; one that there were technical faults that prevented issue and the other that Jesse James was overcome with emotion, breaking down and unable to complete the session. The unissued master of *Sweet Patuni* eventually turned up on a 'pirate' issue on the Post label under the pseudonym of 'Hooker Joe'; there was no emotional collapse, no technical fault. Jesse James in fact was in lusty good spirits, too lusty it would seem for the Decca company:

Ah, wake up mama, wake up and don't sleep so sound,
Give me what you promised me before you laid down,
 I can get my 'tuni, only thing I love,
 May you weep like a willer, sling slop like a turtle dove.

Now I got a girl and the kid lives out on the hill,
She got good 'tuni and so did the one she made well,
 She got good 'tuni, I'm a fool, about my yam, yam, yam,
 When I got my yam, yam, yam, goin' back down Alabam'.

Now come-a here baby and sit down in my lap,
Sit one side o' me, I forgot t' tell you I had the —,
 Clap your hands together Charlie, where's you been so long,
 'I been down in Tennessee and I couldn't stay there very
  long.'

Now I got a job, was paid to learn how to truck,
The boss tol' me this mornin' I like to busted one of my —,
 Nut-house is for crazy folks, folks got sense don't go there,
 All the friends I had done shook hands and left there.

Now I got a gal and the kid's playin' deaf and dumb,
Her movements in her hip'll make a dead man —,
 Come on out my winder, don't knock on my door,
 Ain't I done tol' you two, three times, don't want you no
  more?

Now run here baby, 'cause I done got kinda sick,
Ain't nothin' ailin' in my stomach, somethin' wrong with my —,
 Dixie Camp was a camp in Georgia, you can't stay there very
  long,
 All the friends I had done shook hands and gone.

Now here's a verse I don't want a soul to miss,
I done take a chance wit' a girl, had to go outside an' —,
 Shut yo' mouth boy, four of us can't talk at once,
 I done tol' you two, three times I don't want no junk.[129]

With his guttural voice, his stomping piano breaking sometimes into boogie bass figures and the rough humour of his verses with their terminal puns, Jesse James pours out a stiff draught of unadulterated, undiluted barrelhouse entertainment.

SHAVE 'EM DRY

Sometimes sung by women, *Sweet Patunia* with its reference to female genitalia, was primarily a man's song. *Shave 'Em Dry*, on the other hand, seems to have been favoured by women though a number of men also sang it on record. As a term 'shave 'em dry' appears to have layers of meaning; at one level it refers to mean and aggressive action but as a sexual theme it refers to intercourse without preliminary love-making. Big Bill Broonzy put it succinctly: 'Shave 'em dry is what you call makin' it with a woman; you ain't doin' nothin', just makin' it.'[130] The implications of 'shavin' 'em dry' were of pubic contact and therefore applicable to either sex. Gertrude Ma Rainey, the singer often termed the 'Mother of the Blues', recorded the first version of the song. Though he made no reference to its meaning or content, Rudi Blesh commented upon its importance as an archaic eight-bar blues which was 'complete, harmonically and poetically'. Considering it as a blues rather than as a traditional blues song he added that 'no matter how late in blues history it was recorded, this record is of great importance, since it indicates a very early stage of development.'[131] It is likely that it not only preceded blues but had an independent life, one of the many songs much liked by blues singers and containing blues sentiments though not strictly blues in itself. Ma Rainey, as a minstrel and tent-show singer, drew from varied sources for her material and *Shave 'Em Dry* was probably in her repertoire since her earliest professional years. With her relaxed, strong voice she sang the words and half-hollered the refrain line:

There's one thing I don't understand,
Why a good-lookin' woman loves a workin' man,
Eeh, hey, daddy won't you shave 'em dry?

Goin' 'way to wear you off my mind,
You keeps me broke and hungry, daddy all the time,
Eeeh, hey, daddy let me shave 'em dry.

Don't see how you hungry women can sleep,
Shimmies all day without a bite to eat,
Eeh, hey, daddy let me shave 'em dry.

Goin' down town to spread the news,
State Street women wearing brogan shoes,
Hey, hey, daddy let me shave 'em dry.

If it wasn't for their powder and sto' bought hair,
State Street gals couldn't go nowhere,
Eeh, hey, daddy let me shave 'em dry.

There's one thing I don't understand,
Some women walkin' State Street like a man,
Eeh, hey, hey, daddy let me shave 'em dry.

Went to the show the other night,
Everybody on State Street tryin' to fight,
Eeh, hey, daddy let me shave 'em dry.

Ain't crazy' bout my yeller, I ain't wild about my brown,
Makes no difference when the sun goes down,
Eeh, hey, daddy won't you shave 'em dry.

When you see two women runnin' hand in han',
You can bet your life they got the other one's man,
Eeh, hey, hey, daddy let me shave 'em dry.

Don't let that man come in my home,
If his wife is here I don't mean no harm,
Eeh, hey, daddy let me shave 'em dry.[132]

Though the accompaniment is given by Blesh as two guitars and elsewhere as by one, the instrument appears to be a banjo which could very
well be played by Papa Charlie Jackson. Jackson's own recording career
under his own name commenced just at this time—his first record,
Airy Man Blues, was issued when Ma Rainey's *Shave 'Em Dry* appeared
—and it is possible that he learned the song from her, or even taught it
to her. His own version was not recorded for another year but, when it

appeared in 1925, it was very similar. Charlie Jackson sang to a fast banjo accompaniment and his verses were in most instances identical with just one or two changes:

Now here's one thing I can't understand,
Why a bow-legged woman likes a knock-kneed man,
Mama can I holler, daddy let me shave 'em dry.

Why don't you run here mama, lay back in my arms,
If your man catches you I don't mean no harm,
Mama let me holler, daddy let me shave 'em dry.[133]

In neither recording is there more than a hint of the bawdy song which was in the folk tradition but the suggestions of lesbianism—'State Street women wearing brogan shoes' and 'some women walkin' State Street like a man' coupled with her final verse—gave a tougher undertone to Ma Rainey's song. Papa Charlie's first verse would have been more pithy if he had kept to the customary form of 'I can't understand why a knock-kneed woman likes a bow-legged man', but it is clear that both songs derive from the same source. A barrelhouse singer from Louisiana, James Boodle-It Wiggins, recorded a different *Gotta Shave 'Em Dry* with longer verses bellowed with little melodic line until the cadence preceding the refrain line. His heavy, megaphonic voice is difficult to understand above the inadequacies of the Paramount recording but the strength of the song projects forcefully, with its boogie accompaniment by the pianist, Charlie Spand:

If you be my sweet woman tell you what I'm gonna do,
Gonna beg, borrow an' steal, bring all my money home to you,
Babe, now do let me when I call yer, I done swear when your
    duty comes,
You know hot spring water gonna help yer, you know when I'm
    gonna run,
Oh now, sweet mama, your daddy gotta shave 'em dry.

Now don't never let nobody tell you what my baby done to me,
She done made me crazy 'bout her, now she done quit poor me,
Sweet woman I ain't gonna stand no quittin', ain't gonna stand no
    jumpin' down,

Before I let you quit me baby I'm gonna burn Chicago down,
Oh now I holler sweet mama, your daddy gotta shave 'em dry.

No use to callin' me baby when I'm way down in France,
When you begin one of these you know I ain't a possible chance,
You get your crowin' from a rooster, get your eggs from a wren,
You get your feathers from a runner, you get your music from a
    wren,
You know I holler sweet mama, your daddy gotta shave 'em dry.

Now mama, li'l mama what's on your runnin' mind?
Every time you sell people tickets you know somebody's ridin'
    your blind,
And it's mmm . . . have mercy, Lord, watch you when you run,
You know if I keep on worryin' 'bout you baby, you know I can't
    last long,
You know I'm gonna holler sweet mama, your daddy's gonna shave
    'em dry.[134]

Some years after, in November 1936, Lil Johnson cut a *New Shave 'Em
Dry* with a small group that included Alfred Bell, known as 'Mister
Sheiks' on trumpet and Black Bob on piano. Her lighter voice and
greater feeling for melody made more of a song of the theme but it is
clear that her *New Shave 'Em Dry* was related to the tune used by
Boodle-It Wiggins:

I want all you pimps and ramblers to gather round,
While I give you the first lowdown,
About a certain woman, I don't 'call her name,
But she's round here 'whoopy-doopin' ' with her mama's man,
Now must I holler? No, I'm gonna shave 'em dry.

She goes to bed every night and sleeps to twelve,
Gets up and goes, takes off to Nell's.
Now what she's doin' I cain't understand,
All the neighbours say she's with her mama's man,
Now must I holler? No, I'm gonna shave 'em dry.

Now she's the kind that don't pick 'em, she'll take 'em any style,
If they don't drum enough to fall for her jive,
A dollar is a dollar and in God we trust,
You all right with her but your dollars come first,
Now must I holler? No, I'm gonna shave 'em dry.

Now if you want somethin' good and want it cheap,
You can go down on Eighteenth Street,
Step right in with your money in your hand,
You can get it any way you want it then,
Now must I holler? No, I'm gonna shave 'em dry.

I'm gonna tell you-all women and to please understand,
Don't start no 3-6-9 with my man,
'Cause if you do it'll surely go wrong,
I got a 44 that'll put your waters on,
Now must I holler? No, I'll shave you dry.[135]

Part of Lil Johnson's song is 'signifying' or making slanderous accusations, generally of a sexual nature. But it changes to a more positive statement about the tenderloin and concludes with an assertive verse in which she proclaims her own 'mean' character. It is of considerable interest that the aggressive strength of Negro women features prominently in the blues and in blues songs. To a certain extent this reflects the dependence of the Negro family on the mother for its cohesion. Negro women are often depicted in the blues with Amazonian toughness and Junoesque build; their virtuosity in sexual practices, their capacity and prowess is extolled repeatedly. But many blues and blues songs which had a brothel circulation project the prostitute's image of herself with arrogant pride. Franklin Frazier quoted a monologue from a woman in Harlem whose narration of her own history and character corresponds with that projected in the blues songs: 'I don't go in for everything like most of these frowsies. I'm a straight broad. If they can't be natural I don't play no tricks. None of that freak stuff for me. I don't play the streets—I mean I don't lay every pair of pants that comes along. I look 'em over first. I'm strictly a Packard broad. I only grab a drunk if he looks like his pockets are loaded with dough. If they get rough my man (pimp) kicks 'em out. When they're drunk they shoot the works. I've gotten over two hundred dollars, so help me, the bastard didn't even touch me. He got happy just looking at me. Boy! This shape of mine gets 'em every time. . . .'[136]

Something of the same spirit was evident in Lucille Bogan's *Shave 'Em Dry* issued under her alternative recording name of Bessie Jackson. Her pianist, Walter Roland, provided a walking bass to her song which commenced with a warning:

All you keg women, you better put on the wall,
'Cause I'm gonna get drunk and do my dirty talk,
The monkey and the baboon playin' in the grass,
Well the monkey got mad and whipped his yas, yas, yas,
    Talkin' 'bout shave 'em, mama's gonna shave 'em dry,
    And if you don't know, mama's gonna learn you how.

You know a elephant he's big and stout,
He would be all right if it weren't for his snout,
    Talkin' 'bout shave 'em, mama's gonna shave 'em dry,
    And if you don't know, mama's gonna learn you how.

I ain't rough, I ain't tough,
I'm just a stomp-down roller and I like to strut my stuff,
    Talkin' 'bout shave 'em etc.

I met a man lived down the way,
He had so much money until I *had* to stay,
    Talkin' 'bout shave 'em etc.

If you meet your man an' he tell you a lie,
Just pull out your razor and shave him dry,
    Talkin' 'bout shave 'em, mama's gonna shave him dry,
    'Cause I don't want no man to tell me no dirty lie.[137]

On commercially issued recordings these are probably the closest one is likely to come to the song of a 'stomp-down roller' and they give only a faint impression of the unbowdlerized *Shave 'Em Dry*. A test pressing of another recording of the song by Lucille Bogan, again with Walter Roland accompanying and calling out words of encouragement, alters the picture considerably. Here is a woman who really does let fly with her 'dirty talk'; who whoops and hollers, brags and swaggers her way through a whore-house song, even expresses her contempt of the recording studio in the process:

I got nipples on my titties big as the end of my thumb,
I got somethin' 'tween my legs 'll make a dead man come,
    Oooh daddy—baby, won't you shave 'em dry, oooh!
    Won't you grind me baby, grind me till I cry.

Say I fucked all night and all the night before, baby,
And I feel just like I want to fuck some more,
    Ooh, babe, goddamn daddy, grind me honey, shave 'em dry,
    And when you hear me yowl baby, want you to shave 'em dry.

I got nipples on my titties big as the end of my thumb,
And daddy you can have 'em any time you want and you can make
  'em come.
    Oooh daddy, shave 'em dry,
    And I can give you some baby, swear it'll make you cry.

I will turn back my mattress and let you oil my springs,
I want you to grind me daddy till the bells do ring,
    Ooh daddy, want you to shave 'em dry.
    Oh pray God daddy, shave 'em baby, won't you try?

Now fuckin's one thing that'll take me to Hell,
I'll be fuckin' in the studio just to fuck that to leather,
    Oooh, daddy, daddy shave 'em dry,
    I would fuck you baby, honey I would make you cry.

Now your nuts hangs down like a damn bell-clapper,
And your stick stands up like a steeple,
Your goddamn arse-hole's open like a church door,
And the crabs walks in like the people,
    Oooh baby, won't you shave 'em dry. . . .

A big sow gets fat from eatin' corn,
And the pig gets fat from suckin',
Reason this whore got like I am,
Great God I got fat from fuckin',
    Whee . . . tell 'em about me! Fuck it!

My back is made of whalebone and my cock is made of brass,
And my fuckin's made for workin' men, two dollars round to fit
my arse,
    Oooh daddy, shave 'em dry.[138]

DIRTY MOTHER FUYER

Not surprisingly the American Record Company did not issue Lucille Bogan's uncompromising recording and settled instead for a *Shave 'Em Dry* which bore the same title but only a faint reflection of its content. By the standards of the day, and probably by those of most periods, the song would have been considered totally offensive and the terms it employed, Anglo-Saxon in origin or not, obscene. Whether, in fact, either singers or record companies had any moral scruples over the songs as issued is conjectural. Many blues records in the 'twenties and 'thirties were obtainable by mail order before specialized record shops became widespread and it is possible that fear of federal action, prompted by the dispatch of obscene matter in the US mail, made the record companies doubly cautious. Clearly, however, there was a demand for records of traditional blues songs of this character even if they appeared in diluted form. Offensive terms were thinly veiled and doubtless amused the readers of record catalogues as they saw listed *Dirty Mother For You* by Shufflin' Sam and His Rhythm. 'Dirty Mother For You' was a laboured way of writing a phrase which, when spoken rapidly, sounded more like 'Dirty Mother Fuyer'. In turn this was a euphemistic elision of the palatal 'ck' in the expletive 'mother fucker'. This term, almost unknown in England, is common in the United States and particularly so among Negroes who again indicate their acknowledgement of the matriachate by its use. As no documentation exists of its origins in song form one is again obliged to seek the slender evidence offered by the recorded versions. In January 1935, the singer and guitar-player, Memphis Minnie McCoy, recorded *Dirty Mother For You* accompanied by Charlie Segar:

I ain't no doctor but I'm a doctor's wife,
You better come to see me if you want me to save your life,
    He's a dirty mother fuyer, he don't mean me no good,
    He got drunk this mornin', woke up the neighbourhood.

I want you to come here baby, come here quick,
You done give me somethin' 'bout to make me sick,
    Oh, dirty mother fuyer, he don't mean me no good,
    He got drunk this mornin', woke up the neighbourhood.

I went down to the station, talk to the judge,
'Please don't believe none of that doggone stuff you heard.'
    Oh dirty mother fuyer etc.

Now look here baby, what you done done,
Now you done squeeze my lemon, now you done broke and run,
    Now youse a dirty mother fuyer etc.[139]

Memphis Minnie's song is to the tune used by Huddie Ledbetter—Leadbelly—for his blues *Noted Rider*, a very fine one though little recorded. When Memphis Minnie made her *Dirty Mother For You* Leadbelly had yet to record commercially; his first session was in fact just two weeks later and a thousand miles away in New York. He did not record *Noted Rider* at this time but did include it in a session for the Library of Congress in 1938 and again at a later date. Although its content is innocuous a comparison of the words with those of Memphis Minnie's *Dirty Mother For You* suggests that they shared a common source. Sang Leadbelly:

Took me to her house, she called me honey,
She said she loved me but she just wanted my li'l money,
    She is a noted rider, she ain't a bit of good,
    She got drunk this mornin', woke up the neighbourhood.

She was a good-lookin' woman, she had great big legs,
She walkin' like she's walkin' on soft-boiled eggs,
    She was a noted rider, she ain't a bit of good,
    She got drunk this mornin', woke up the neighbourhood.[140] ©

If Leadbelly adapted *Noted Rider* from *Dirty Mother Fucker* it is not surprising that, smarting under the insults of Jim Crow prejudice, he used the tune for the next recording at the Library of Congress session, when he sang *The Bourgeois Blues*. 'Anything you want to know about Wash. D.C. please talk to me about it. We rode all around there in the rain; no coloured people would let me in because I was with a white man and that's a bourgeois place, 'cause they scared to let in coloured people if they with white people,' he said.[141] He probably enjoyed a certain grim satisfaction in fitting the tune to the song but if he did, he said nothing about it. Leadbelly was, for a man of his avowed sexual prowess and fearsome reputation, extremely cautious in the songs he sang for whites and the comments he made on them. 'Really, I mean tell us confidentially what they mean by "Tight Like That",' asked Alan Lomax, but Leadbelly answered, ' "Tight Like That", it means when you got your partner, grab her and hug her tight, keep her goin',' explaining only that it was a reference to dancing.[142]

Although the first recording of *Dirty Mother For You* was made as late as 1935, the fact that the tunes of the earliest versions were so markedly different implies that they had undergone change through previous oral transmission. The song could well have evolved over a considerable period of time and the tune shared by Leadbelly and Memphis Minnie may have been the oldest. Just a year after Memphis Minnie, the pianist, Roosevelt Sykes, made a version to another tune. It proved to be so successful that he recorded it again only three months later.

Mama, I got a hot dog and it ain't cold,
It's just right for to fit your roll,
It's a fittin' mother fuyer don't you know,
I'm a hungry mother fuyer don't you know,
I'm a dirty mother fuyer and I won't tell you no lie.

There's a blind man by the name of Dell,
He couldn't see but he really could smell,
The fishman passed the house the other day,
He thought it was a girl, hollered, 'I'm goin' away.'
He's a smellin' mother fuyer don't you know etc.

When a man gets hairy he needs a shave,
When he gets musty he needs a bathe,
He's a stinkin' mother fuyer don't you know etc.[143] ©

A veteran of joints from Gulfport to Chicago, Roosevelt Sykes roared into the song with gusto.

Some months later, in September 1936, another recording of *Dirty Mother For You* was made, this time by the singer generally known as

Washboard Sam. That his recording was made under the name of 'Shufflin' Sam' was more to conceal his violation of a Bluebird recording contract by making the title for Vocalion than any effort to disassociate himself with the song. His gravelly voice and the powerful piano of his accompanist, Black Bob, made this one of the best versions musically, but the words were similar to those used by Roosevelt Sykes with the addition of one innocuous verse.[144] Even this was sometimes employed by Sykes in live performances. Unrestricted by the limitations of the three-minute recording, he adds a number of unrecorded verses when playing to an audience, mildly suggestive or ribald, according to the company. Certain of these verses may be his own invention but others seem to derive from the common pool of traditional lyrics. The fourth verse quoted above, for example, appeared in Texas Alexander's *Ninety-Eight Degree Blues* recorded in 1929. It was Roosevelt Sykes's record, however, which 'fixed' the form of the song for the singers who recorded it later.

Though the words of the Sykes–Shufflin' Sam song were quite different, the tune was close to that of an engaging version by Shorty Bob Parker. Retaining the consonant and substituting a sibilant for a labiodental consonant, Parker camouflaged the title as *Ridin' Dirty Motorsickle* [sic] and developed it as a metaphor:

Well you ride a motor-cycle, you gotta ride it fast,
Buy some oil, you gotta buy some gas,
    Well it's a dirty motor-cycle, (3)
    Stole my gal and gone.

Now here's one thing babe, you can't do,
You can't ride me and your motor-cycle too,
    He's a dirty motor-cycle etc.

Taken my motor-cycle 'cause its nice and brown,
Taken my gal all over town,
    He's a dirty motor-cycle etc.[145]

THE DIRTY DOZENS

The tune of both Parker's and Sykes's versions of *Dirty Mother Fucker* is closely linked with that of *The Dirty Dozens* but is it difficult to determine whether an earlier tune for the song, such as that used by Memphis Minnie and Leadbelly, has been substituted by this one or whether *The Dirty Dozens* has in fact borrowed an earlier tune. The 'dozens' is a folk game and as such has received careful, though recent, attention. Mack McCormick has indicated that 'the direct basis for "The Dirty Dozens" was a nineteenth-century religious teaching device: a canto of twelve verses setting forth essential Biblical facts which children were made to memorize. It typically began:

'Book of Genesis got the first truth,
God Almighty took a ball of mud to make this earth.'

He explains that 'in a community where there is little literacy such mnemonics play an important role in teaching children and of course, youngsters drilled in this fashion will instantly produce a burlesque. Thus "The Dirty Dozens" was born, a vehicle for tirade and insult dwelling at first on the physical charms of others: "When the Lord gave you shape he musta been thinking of an ape; your mother knows and your father knows too, it hurts my eyes to look at you." '146 A close relation to such religious parodies was sung by Sam Chatman, once a member of the Mississippi Sheiks and brother to Bo Carter (Bo Chatman). He introduced his song with a fragment of vocal exchange:

Say boy, where you from? You nach'l-born is the ugliest man
ever I seen. I wish I played the dozens, but I didn't learn to
count to twelve. Else I'll play the dozens with you.
    I don't play no dozens 'cause I didn't learn to count to twelve,
    They tell me God don't like ugly, so boy your home's in Hell.
Your mammy got scared she started in a show,
Couldn't get scared o' nothin' but the elephant upped and go,
    I don't play no dozens 'cause I didn't learn to count to twelve,
    They tell me God don't like ugly, so boy your home's in Hell.
You standin' round here like bein' big and stout,
All you like bein' a elephant you ain't got a tail and a snout,
    I don't play etc.
Adam named everything, I believe he sent you,
Look like you oughta be up a tree hollerin' boo-boo-boo,
    I don't play etc.
God took a ball of mud, when he got ready to make man,
When he got to make uglies' part 's you, I b'lieve it slipped outa
his hand.
    I don't play etc.

236

Adam named everything they put in the zoo,
I'd like Adam to be here, see what the hell he'd name you,
   I don't play no dozens 'cause I didn't learn to count to
   twelve.[147]

Dr Roger Abrahams has written at length of the insult exchanges of
Negro children playing the dozens, substantially extending John
Dollard's study of the subject. He quotes some thirty dozens rhymes
collected from Negro youths in a single locality in South Philadelphia
over a two-year period and both he and McCormick describe the process
of verbal contest in which the opponent's mother is abused. This would
seem to be the most active and widespread form of the dozens and it
may well be of greater importance than the songs. Nevertheless, the
songs have been known for many years and, as only fragments of dozens
exchanges have been noted in early collections, it is probable that the
songs have a history that is as long. McCormick notes an interview with
the singer Gilda Gray, which appeared in *Current Opinion*, in which
she referred to 'The Dirty Dozen' saying that it had 'a wayward
sound. I don't suppose there'd be room to give all twelve verses. The
chorus runs like this:

'Oh the old dirty dozen,
The old dirty dozen,
Brothers and cousins,
Livin' like a hive of bees,
They keep a buzzin', fussin' and mussin',
There wasn't a good one in the bunch.'[148]

It seems likely that Gilda Gray cleaned up the song for the interview
and perhaps in performance, but it would appear to be related to the
later recorded versions. A few years after, in 1924, Chris Smith, whose
You're in the Right Church But the Wrong Pew has already been mentioned and who was the author of *Ballin' the Jack* which described a
dance but evidently had a double significance, recorded a song *Don't
Slip Me in the Dozen*. It was not a version of the dozens but did describe
the effect of playing the game:

Jones slipped Brownie in the dozen last night,
And Brownie didn't think that was exactly right,

Because slippin' in the dozens means to talk about your family
    folks,
And talkin' about one's family isn't jokes.
Brownie said to Jonesy, 'Really I'm surprised
If you was a man you would apologize. . . .
Makes no difference who you are,
Please don't talk about my ma and pa,
Talk about my sister, my brother or my cousin,
But please don't slip me in the dozen.'[149]

In a more emphatic tone Smith indicated some of the other usages at the time: 'Don't slip me in the dozens, 'cause I can't stand it. It's my cup, it's my bucket, it's my little red wagon. . . .' But this gives no impression of the pungency of the exchanges described by Abrahams: 'Constance's son has to reply in kind, "I heard Virginia (the other's mother) lost her titty in a poker game." "Least my mother ain't no cake; everybody gets a piece." The other might reply:

'I hate to talk about your mother,
She's got a good old soul.
She's got a ten-ton pussy,
And a rubber ass-hole.
She got hair on her pussy,
That sweep the floor,
She got knobs on her titties,
That open the door.'[150]

Such exchanges continued until honour was satisfied or the opponent retired but the game itself, with no conspicuous winner, undoubtedly had a cathartic effect. Frankie Dusen, Buddy Bolden and Lorenzo Stall, Buddy Bottley remembered, were adepts in the art. 'When they arrived on the bandstand they greeted each other with such nasty talk as, "Is your mother still in the district catchin' tricks?" "They say your sister had a baby for a dog." "Don't worry about the rent—I saw your mother under the shack with the landlord." These three men could go on insulting you for hours if you played "the dozens".'[151]

That was in the first years of the century—Bolden was committed to the East Louisiana State Hostpial as insane in June 1907. Sixty years after, when Paul Chevigny, a white blues enthusiast, visited the singer, Will Shade, in Memphis he recounted Shade's reaction to the advances on Paul's behalf by a young Negro named TJ.[152] He had begun 'to explain again painstakingly, what we had been sent for, but Will interrupted. "You talk too much. Back in my day, when people talked too much to the musicians, we used to play them the dozens. Y'all know the dozens." ' Describing it as 'an ancient insulting blues in which each of the victim's relatives is assigned a disease or perversion'. Chevigny went on, 'Will's version is probably unprintable even under the present permissive standards of the Supreme Court, but a snatch of the chorus will give the idea:

'Your sister and your cousin,
Your pappy makes a dozen,
Send your mammy to the Lordy Lord.

TJ turned his face away from Will and hid it, trying to laugh at the song. When it was over, Will leaned out of his chair and peered wickedly up into his face. As Will began another song TJ turned to me and began his story again. Will stopped playing. "Damn it boy, I said quit talking. I never see a nigger bring two white men to see another nigger, and talk his ass off." '[153]

Will Shade's 'day' may be considered as the late 'twenties and early 'thirties when he was a major recording artist. He did not record *The Dozens* as a song though, by this time, versions of the song form were widely circulated, even if on record they are emasculated. *The Dirty Dozen* was first recorded by Rufus Perryman—Speckled Red—in 1929. He explained over thirty years later: 'They asked me could I make it pretty decent. . . . I had to clean it up a bit for the record; it all meaned the same thing and the same words but it was a different attitude. . . . But you see when you were makin' records back in them days you could say some of them smelly words and don't think nothin' of it, but it's a whole lots different now.'[154] In fact he was obliged to expurgate it extensively but, when the song was published in book form in 1963, there was no hint that further bowdlerization had taken place.[155]

An unexpurgated version made by Speckled Red for Bob Koester recreated the song as it was performed in the 'turpentine jukes where it didn't matter'. It revealed how much he 'had to clean it up' and the rough, exuberant, boogie-based piano accompaniment captured the uncouth vigour of the barrelhouse song:

Now your mammy got the blue-ball, you sister got the pox,
Grandma got a dirty rag tied right round her cock,
Born in the cane-brake, you was suckled by a bear,
Jumped through you mammy's cock and you never touched a hair,
  Now you's a jumpin' motherfucker, cheap cocksucker,
  Goin' out in the alley doin' this, that an' the other,
  Just keep on goin', shave your black ass dry.

Now yonder come your mama goin' out across the field,
Her big cock snappin' like an automobile,
Fucked your mama standin' right in the middle of the gate,
She had crabs around her cock like a Cadillac Eight,
  Now she's a runnin' motherfucker, cheap cocksucker etc.

Now I had your mammy, she wouldn't turn no tricks,
Hit her right 'cross the head with a big hickory stick,
The clock on the shelf goin' tick, tick, tick,
Your mam' she's out on the street catchin' dick, dick, dick.
Fucked your mammy, fucked your sister too,
Would've fucked your daddy but the sonofabitch flew,
Your pa wants a wash, you mother turns tricks,
Your sister loves to fuck and your brother sucks dick,
  He's a suckin' motherfucker, cocksucker etc.[156] ©

Speckled Red's original recording was so successful that he remade it
less than seven months later in April 1930. It was rapidly taken up by
Leroy Carr in December 1929, by Tampa Red in June 1930, by Ben
Curry the following year, and continued to be recorded by numerous
singers for many years under this and other titles. Victoria Spivey's
From One to Twelve, Kokomo Arnold's *The Twelves* and the oddly
titled *Dozing Blues* by George Noble, were among the recordings of
The Dozens, most of which were identical to Speckled Red's original
recording.

One version of *The Dozens* which departed from slavish copying of
Speckled Red's song was *New Dirty Dozen* which Memphis Minnie
made less than a year after his. It used the same tune as *The Dozens* but
comparison of one stanza with Roosevelt Sykes's *Dirty Mother For You*
shows a textual link, while the opening:

Come all you folks and start to walk,
I'm thinkin' to start my dozens talk. . . .

hints at a connexion with *Shave 'Em Dry* as sung by Lucille Bogan.

Now some of you womens ought to be hand-in-hand,
Out on the corner stoppin' every man,
Hollerin', 'Soap is a nickel and the towel is free,
I'm pigmeat happy, now who wants me?'
 Now youse all mistreaters, robber and a cheater,
 Slip you in the dozens, your poppa and your cousin,
 Your mama do the—Lawdy, Lawd.

Now funniest thing I ever seen,
Tom cat jumpin' on a sewin' machine,
Sewin' machine, run so fast,
Took ninety-nine stitches in his yas yas yas,
 Now youse a purrin' mistreater etc.

Now I'm gonna tell you all 'bout ole man Dell,
He can't see but he sure can smell,
Fishman passed here the other day,
Hollerin', 'Hey pretty mama, I'm goin' your way,
 I know all about your pappy and your mammy,
 Your big fat sister and your little brother Sammy,
 Your auntie and your uncle and your ma and pa,
 They all got drunk and showed their Santy Claus.'
 Now they're all drunken mistreaters, robbers and cheaters
  etc.[157]

Dirty Mother Fucker still showed its close relationship with *The Dozens* after the Second World War when Nelson Wilborn's record *Mother Fuyer*, with a less compromising title than earlier issues, appeared. Wilborn, who was once called Red Nelson in view of the colour of his skin, became popular in Chicago clubs, including Smitty's Corner, where Muddy Waters played. For his innumerable verses of the song they called him Dirty Red. *Mother Fuyer* sung to the tune of *The Dirty Dozens* shared verses with Roosevelt Sykes's song and included others:

I don't love my woman, tell you the reason why,
Feel my pants full of Red Devil Lye,
    Want a woman mother fuyer don't you know,
    Burnin' mother fuyer don't you know,
    Smokin' mother fuyer an I ain't gonna tell you no lie.

My grandpa tol' grandma last year,
Got too old for to shift your gear,
    You's stiff mother fuyer don't you know,
    Beat out, mother fuyer don't you know,
    You's a rotten mother fuyer and I ain't gonna tell you no lie.[158]

The vigour of the songs is evident from their continued appearance under many guises after three decades. Under the unlikely title of *Sweet Little Woman*, Little Johnny Jones sang an amalgam of both songs using largely familiar verses including the 'man gets hairy' and 'put my mule' stanzas from the one and the concluding verse of Speckled Red's *Dirty Dozen No. 2* as well. In view of the history of the song, *Teenage Love* is an even less probable title for *The Dirty Dozens* but it was sung as this by Oscar Brown Jr in a suitably modernized version, which added a disclaimer that 'I hate to talk about your mama this way, the dozens is a game I don't usually play'. These were heavily expurgated but in the folk tradition the song survived with less whitewashing. Eddie Jones, a street musician who played a one-string guitar with a bottleneck which earned him the name of 'One String Sam', recorded *The Dirty Dozens* with something of the forcefulness that accounts for its longevity. His stanzas were close to those of Speckled Red's but did not depend on his euphemisms. The 'elephant' stanza which has a curiously wide popularity concluded:

. . . He made his eyes just to look on the grass,
Wasn't satisfied till he made him a big fat ass,
Made him an ass, that ass made him sick,
Wasn't satisfied till he made him an nine-inch stick,
He made him a dick and the dick made him sick,
Then the stick made him well,
You know by that the elephant caught him Hell,
He's a fuckin' —.

I want all you women to fall in line,
Shake your li'l hind-pot like I'm shakin' mine,
You'll be a shakin' —.[159]

Newman White quoted an expurgated version of the 'elephant' stanzas
which had been collected in Florida by H. C. Abbot in 1915. It suggests
that Eddie Jones's and Speckled Red's song relate to one with an
older history and identical words. None of these recorded examples
show a clear relationship between the verbal exchanges played as a
game and the songs themselves and it is possible that the two have
developed side by side. If so, the verse exchanges have shown more
variety and possibly more scope for invention and evolution, the songs
having been largely trapped in a form established nearly four decades
ago. One recording alone gives a real impression of the viciousness of
the dozens when played with malicious intent and this, recorded for
Mack McCormick by Lightnin' Hopkins, relates *The Dirty Dozens*,
Dirty Mother Fucker and *Don't Ease Me In* as one shifting song evolving
out of the spoken abuse. A long spoken introduction concludes Hopkins's re-creation of a part in an exchange:

. . . You know your gran'ma got the hoopin' cough,
Your mama got the measles,
Your sister died with a rag in 'er ass,
Now the poor soul's gone home to Jesus,
(*Spoken*) Now what do you think about your father, your dirty
black mother fucker? Oh, I'm talkin' 'bout you, les' you keep
on, but I don't play the dozens, don't ease me in, you'se a dirty
mother fucker, you goin' see it again. Did you hear me? Is
that clear—you ole whore you? You couldn' be a whore though
'cause you ain't got nothin' to whore with.
You know what? Your goddamn feet,
They ain't meat,
You got a crooked ass-hole, nigger,
An' you can't shit straight.
(*Spoken*) You black fucker you—is that clear? Goddamn, I'm tired
of talkin' to you—go ahead, go on.
A white man was born with a veil over his face,
He sees dirty things, or anything, before it takes place,
You old black southern bitch, you was born with a rag in your arse,

243

And you never did see it until it done past.
You know your sister had the blueballs,
And your poppa had the pox,
And your mamma had the shingles,
All round her bloody cock.
(*Spoken*) You big black bastard you, so now get on outa here. . . .

(*Sings*) You dirty mother fucker, you gonna see it again,
You gonna do like — don't you ease me in.
I don't play the dozens, don't you ease me in,
You'se a dirty mother fucker, you gonna see it again.

You know the red rooster told the little barren hen,
You keep on fuckin' you gonna see it again,
You gonna see it again. (3)
(*Spoken*) Get your black arse out o' my face. . . .[160] ©

The merciless stream of abuse spoken and sung without humour might help an adolescent prepare himself for maturity but in the mouths of adults must inevitably lead to conflict. Howard Odum's recreation of a Negro's experiences in the First World War is given more point with this in mind, though the only reference to the song is a brief stanza fragment which shows that Lightnin' Hopkins's verse dates from at least that period. Odum's 'Black Ulysses at the wars' relates:

'Boys mighty ruffish in war camp, same as wus in road gangs an' construction camps. One night in camp in France boys got to playin' dozen. Jes *would* play dozen 'scusin' captains an' lieutenants not bein' round, 'cause been told not to do it. Mighty ruffish game, boys talkin' 'bout other boys' folks. So one big boy tells 'nother big boy no use worryin' 'bout his lovin' wife back home, 'cause somebody else shovelin' coal in his furnace. Told him she jes' like street-car anyhow, plenty folks payin' fare an' she ain't gonna starve. So this boy gets so mad he jumps up an' takes shoe-heel an' kills him dead. After that captain tells boys he's jes' natchelly gonna shoot next man goes to playin' dozen.' The warning was apparently not effective against the emotional release that the dozens provided for ' 'nother time I seen boys playin' dozen one boy took razor and cut fellow up till he nearly dies. Cut his head near 'bout off.

Lawd, I don't play the dozen,
An' don't you ease me in.'[161]

If violence is the outcome of the ritual of the dozens it would seem on first impression to be curiously placed in a military context where the aggressive instincts would be better and more logically employed against the enemy than against the members of the players' group. John Dollard's contention that Negro youths find in playing the dozens a release mechanism for their fears makes the game viable in a military situation, though Abrahams disagrees with him in his interpretation of the dozens as misplaced aggression against the players' own Negro group. Under military conditions it would seem more likely that it constitutes misplaced aggression against the enemy; misplaced because it is more real, and in the end, probably safer. Such reactions are by no means unfamiliar in time of war if a ritual game is not necessarily the outlet.

But *The Dirty Dozens* as sung on record presents a somewhat different problem, for here the singer, adult, and sometimes female, uses the device in a singularly one-sided contest. If the dozens is provocative as a game, and if *The Dirty Dozens* is equally provocative as a song, there is no question of the singer's being able to provoke the listener. And even if he did there is no possibility of a return in the bout on the part of the listener against the singer. Obviously too, *The Dirty Dozens* as recorded by Lightnin' Hopkins has no parallel in the versions which are available on commercial record. In view of the popularity of the song and its persistence in one form or another over a long period it must perform a different role. The Negro purchaser of *The Dirty Dozens* or *Dirty Mother For You* may hope for a more outspoken example of dozens exchange than he might reasonably expect, he may enjoy the joke of the camouflaged title, he may take pleasure in interpreting terms which may have slipped through the company's censorship. These might possibly be reason enough for purchasing the record, even reason enough for making it but the psycho-social implication is a more important reason: that the purchaser is not challenged by a one-sided game because he feels a bond with the player-singer. Blues singer and listener are bound, through the medium of the record, whose mild terms they can interpret in a shared tradition of a more abusive nature, against a common opponent.

Now you think you are smart,
But you really ain't worth a —,
 Oh the buzzards oughta laid you,
 Man you know the sun gonna hatch you,
 Oh you dirty no-gooder, you don't mean me no good.

When I first met you I thought I fell in good luck,
Now I know you ain't worth a —,
 Oh the buzzards oughta laid you etc.[162]

In Negro parlance 'double dozens', like 'double trouble' is twice as bad as the singular form, but Sweet Pease Spivey's *Double Dozens* on record is relatively inoffensive: the 'double dozens' is implicit rather than stated.

Dr Abrahams makes acknowledgement of the dozens as played by young Negroes in the Army but had not himself noted much use of the insult game among females or adults generally. He emphasized that playing is important in adolescent growth within the Negro community arguing that the Negro youth must rid himself of his oedipal fixations engendered by the dominance of the mother in the family. In order to attain his manhood he must assert his masculinity and reject the influence of the mother which threatens it. The game permits him to abuse someone else's mother in the knowledge that there will be an attack on his own. By so participating in a rejection of the matriarchy he prepares himself for acceptance within the adolescent gang.[163]

There seems little cause to doubt the validity of Dr Abrahams's argument as applied to the playing of the game among adolescent youths, to whom he mainly confines his discussion. He criticizes Dollard's 'failure to differentiate between the Dozens as played by youths and adults' noting that 'when used by older males in verbal battle, in such places as a bar or poolroom, it also ends in a battle. As such, the institution functions quite differently among men than among adolescents'.[164] It is evident, however, that the game is, or was, extensively played by adults and not infrequently by women too, and that a song form evolved which gained rapid and widespread circulation. It raises the problem whether, in the special incidence of *The Dozens* on record, with its adult play, its song form on a blues structure, its essentially non-reciprocal one-sidedness, it performs any other function.

Before discussing the implications of recorded examples, it is important to bear in mind that *The Dirty Dozens*, or other songs within its complex, form only a fraction of the great body of blues and songs of a sexual nature. The other songs whose variants have been examined above, *Sweet Patunia*, *Shave 'Em Dry* and, under its recorded title, *Dirty Mother For You*, define three major lines of approach along which this corpus is directed: *Sweet Patunia* is a bawdy song, *Shave 'Em Dry* a sexually boastful song, and *Dirty Mother For You* or *The Dirty Dozens* a pornographic one. Such distinctions are of emphasis rather than kind for to a certain extent these descriptions apply to them all. In that they do identify certain positions on a broad sexual front they can be useful in grouping the many different songs which appear in the repertoires of blues singers—*Salty Dog, Dirty No-Gooder, The Ma Grinder, You Got Good Business, Stavin' Chain, Winding Ball, Don't Ease Me In, 'Bout a Spoonful, Don't Sell It, Don't Give It Away, Rank Stud, Keep A-Knockin', Squat Low Mama, Dirty Ground Hog, That's Your Red Wagon, Steady Grindin', Sweet Jelly Rollin', I'll Keep Sittin' on It* and a great many others, a few of which have been mentioned here, and most of which in a mild form have appeared on commercial record.

Only extensive research, objective collecting and recording can reveal now the extent of this song tradition or the degree to which the songs have been doctored for issue on record, but the examples quoted in the three main trends are evidence enough of the disparity between the songs as sung within the tradition and the songs as they have appeared on disc. No distinction has been attempted here between those songs which may be said to have an honest declaration of sexual content and those which display a prurient interest in sexual themes. Nor has more than a passing reference been made to obscenity or pornography in Negro song in the sense that some are repulsive, offensive to taste or display an interest in sex apart from that which is related to love. To a large extent these distinctions reflect the mores of the society and the standards which it imposes; what is obscene to one group and at one period in time appears very differently to another; what is socially acceptable in one context is socially inadmissible in another. In considering Negro sexual songs and blues without making such a differentiation one can still accept that some statements of sexual desire may have integrity even if they may offend, while others may be deliberately repellent: to the companies which issued the blues and Race records they were all subject to an uncertainly applied but undeniable censorship.

Censorship of traditional songs and blues songs by the recording companies is a fact; censorship of blues can be deduced from discographical study and is lent support by the interchangeable elements of stanza and symbol which pass from songs to blues. It is possible that less offensive elements appeared in the blues of blues singers than in the songs of blues singers, but the evidence of numerous recordings indicates that the terminology, the idioms and the sentiments they expressed were common to most categories of Negro secular song. Blues, traditional blues, blues songs, traditional blues songs, jazz-blues songs—all shared, as has been shown, images, phrases, even whole verses, which communicated effectively through many different social contexts within the Negro community. If this is so on record in the censored and partially-censored forms it is reasonable to assume that it was also applicable in these blues and song forms when censorship was not exerted under non-recording conditions, whether in Mississippi jukejoint or Harlem cabaret. Extensive, and at this stage in its history, extremely difficult research into early as well as recent blues forms might show this conclusively. It is possible that the blues on record give an accurate picture of the blues off record, while the songs on record give only a faint hint of their nature off record. Possible, but unlikely. In either case the songs are those sung by blues singers and, as has been shown, within the country idioms are many elements that probably originated and certainly flourished in highly urbanized idioms, while conversely, the urban songs have assimilated forms and content from unsophisticated origins.

Were the singers forced into singing material with which they had no sympathy? While this may possibly be true of commercial entertainers it seems less likely in the instances of rural singers recording for the first time and only a marginal possibility when they had been recording for a long period. Again, this is a theme for inquiry, but the variety of versions of, for instance, *Shave 'Em Dry*, suggests either a very rich source of material from which to draw, or a highly fertile inventiveness on the part of the singers if pressed to record the song against their wishes. The imputation that the singers were pressured by the record companies which is frequently made, though probably having some measure of truth, is probably much overstated.

Yet the fact remains that the quantity of sexual songs ranging from the direct to the sly, the outrageous to as near obscene as could be permitted, is extraordinarily high in the output of blues singers of all descriptions. From this one can deduce that the singers were quite prepared to record them and that there was a ready market for them. If the companies did in fact persuade the singers to record this material it would have been purely for commercial reasons; if they did not, it was clearly still commercially a good proposition to do so. It is safe to assume that if the songs had been unacceptable to a Negro market to whom they were specifically directed they would have been withdrawn and no further issues of this character made. For it cannot be argued that record companies recorded Negro singers for philanthropic reasons but, in accordance with the American way of life, for the purpose of making a profit. The history of commercial recording of Negro singers from Mamie Smith on has undoubtedly been shaped by this and, if the singers seemed totally 'uncommercial' by standards of white entertainment business, they could still be a profitable investment to the company which knew and exploited its rural market. Again, it has been suggested that Negro sexual songs were recorded for a white 'party' market but the use of segregated catalogues with issues for Negroes separately listed as Race Records and often published separately makes this less likely. It would have been perfectly possible to list records which might have 'party' appeal in catalogues of white recordings, perhaps under pseudonyms. There are several instances of Negro singers and instrumentalists whose work appeared in the hill-billy catalogues but their inclusion was on general appeal or stylistic and repertoire similarity.

In order to meet the demands of the market the record companies appear to have evolved a double standard in which they accepted, and may have invited, sexually suggestive material but suppressed direct speech which might be interpreted as obscene. Their success in applying this compromising standard was variable, with the total expurgation of songs at one extreme and the admission of moderately bawdy items at the other. As the market was tested and the laws of obscenity tested too, some of the prohibitions were relaxed. Innumerable federal laws against obscenity, which were not codified into one chapter of the Statute of Federal Crimes and Criminal Procedure until 1948, made the distribution of unacceptable matter a difficult problem.[165] Generally the laws referred to 'every obscene, lewd, lascivious or filthy book, pamphlet, picture, paper, writing, print or other publication of an indecent character' or words to similar effect, while State laws were also enacted which added further complications for the distributor. The New York Penal Law makes specific provision against any 'indecent or disgusting book, magazine, pamphlet, newspaper, phonograph record, picture, drawing, photograph, motion-picture film, image or figure', and other states had similar reservations which covered recordings.[166]

If censorship of Negro recordings was intended to suppress sexual themes, it failed. But the intention appears to have been to limit the degree of offensive matter while meeting the requirements of the market, at least to some extent. Curtailing the range of expression may have reduced unacceptable, direct statements but inevitably it provoked the use of *double-entendre* phrases. In a very large proportion of blues, even on non-sexual themes, a layer of innuendo renders them capable of pornographic interpretation and the game played out with the censor may even have promoted it. It cannot be denied that large numbers of sexual blues are ineffably boring and, during the 'twenties and 'thirties, they were issued in hundreds. The countless versions of *Tight Like That* which appeared in one form or another using its all-too familiar tune can wilt the enthusiasm of the most ardent lover of the blues. If in fact, they were equally boring to Negro ears, if they appear repetitious to those for whom they were made, the problem of their volume becomes perplexing. Endless restatement of the same ideas must ultimately become monotonous and monotony in any art that is linked with commercial interests must mean its end. The end, that is, if it does not serve a deeper purpose. And the longevity of the sexual blues idioms suggests that they may have a special function within the community. At all events, the sheer quantity of the recordings, whether frankly sexual or obscurely symbolic, suggestive or pornographic, demands attention.

Of course the functions that Negro sexual songs perform are those that, in the first place, such songs perform in American society as a whole. At one level their unembellished expressions of sexual desire, their unashamed statements, which in Sharp's phrase 'transgress the accepted conventions of the present age', link them with other folk-songs. But, as has been seen, horizontal categorization by style, with the implicit laws of what is acceptable within the style, has obscured the fact that similar devices of innuendo and suggestiveness exist in all forms of blues. These have the titillating effect that partial screening of the content generally exploits. In fact, the slow process of minute relaxations in the lyric censorship has permitted marginally more daring implications in recorded blues and has doubtless contributed to their success. As the strip-tease artist compares with the artist's model, so the seductive effects of slow unveiling are more stimulating erotically than the starkly naked. Perhaps the singer had no wish to win the battle with the censor.

Though listening to records is not as active a form of participation as singing songs with a group, it does demand participation of a kind. It may be passive, but the process of ordering, purchasing and playing, let alone replaying, all involves some active move on the part of the listener and in erotic songs is part of the means whereby he gains the stimulus he desires. In this way the purchase and the playing of sexually pornographic records corresponds with the group singing of obscene songs which is familiar in college fraternities, sports teams, gatherings of servicemen and so on. That these are often by groups of a single sex or, less frequently, by mixed groups in which social taboos still apply is not without significance. Such songs play a masturbatory role, providing sexual release in a deeply symbolic way by substituting for the sexual act itself. It is a familiar process, accompanied by the laughter that goes with the release of tensions, and is a common, probably necessary phenomenon. Bawdy song is humorous, it acknowledges the comic aspects of sex; it titillates too, and bawdy blues play this part.

Nevertheless, the group singing of bawdy songs is primarily an adolescent activity, or a process whereby older men act out their adolescence when their own maturity has been frustrated. It is a means whereby the youth asserts his manhood. Though no adequate study of Negro consumer tastes in the blues has ever been made, the audiences for blues singers are not only young ones: Negroes of all ages attend the blues clubs and have blues records stacked on the floor or beside the phonograph. Just as the blues singers have often sung essentially the same type of material over the passing of decades, with veteran singers like Roosevelt Sykes or Victoria Spivey, Lonnie Johnson or Big Joe Williams performing pornographic songs throughout their careers with the evident enjoyment of both themselves and their hearers, so the audiences have grown up with their music and continue to listen to it. A shifting audience of adolescents of a limited age-group may obviate the problem of monotony as successive generations pass rapidly through a period when the songs have a particular significance for them. As the player bids farewell to his football or the soldier his webbing and settles down, he may leave behind him a large body of bawdy song which he may only occasionally recall with nostalgia for a spent youth. But this is not the case, at least on present evidence, in Negro communities where, outside the Church, pornographic blues and blues songs are popular. It is therefore incumbent upon the blues singer to invest his songs with some element of originality within the limitations imposed by censorship.

To a certain extent censorship has been of some value; it may have enriched Race music rather than impoverished it. By circumscribing the degree of freedom with which the singers could express themselves, it stimulated them to new imagery and the reinterpretation of accepted symbolism. Metaphors and symbols in Race music are nowhere as richly applied as they are in the sexual blues where, in evading the use of obscenities and direct statement, they have sought new ways of communicating a familiar theme. The repetition of direct statements in song form could well have become tiresome and to implied censorship some of the credit for the variety of imagery in the blues must go. Not that sexual blues are free from repetitive ideas; the singer continually seeking new yet interpretable images evidently finds his inventiveness flagging if the evidence of say, Walter Davis, Bo Carter or Jazz Gillum is any indication. None of the foregoing has been concerned with the aesthetic merits of these blues which often lies in the performance rather than the content, but in small numbers some of these sexual blues have realized a poetic potential.

Examination of the metaphors employed by blues singers reveals that certain themes are persistent. If the sexual blues have any function outside the obvious ones of titillation, the use of metaphor may have additional layers of meaning or significance. Earlier the basic image of the automobile was instanced as an example of a persistent metaphor and it would be right to question whether it has any special value to the Negro beyond its usefulness in providing a variety of sexual applications. It is, in all respects, an excellent example of a symbol employed in virtually all types of Negro blues and Race music. Furthermore, it is what might be termed a 'dynamic' symbol, being one which is in a state of change because the referent, the automobile, is also in a state of change. This tends to revitalize the theme, for the 'static' symbols—those in which the referents undergo no change—can become stale; themes drawn from popular fads such as the yo-yo, or from fixed mechanisms, such as the telephone, are examples.

Its changing state is one clue to the popularity of the automobile theme, a classic example of the material theme in the psychological sense. But there are other reasons which lie in the importance of the automobile to the Negro in the truly material sense. As the price of automobiles came within his horizons, the Negro coveted them as he did few other material possessions. The value of the automobile as a possession was again largely symbolic, for it was an object which could be seen by his neighbours, on which he could lavish care and attention, which could be the expression of his personality or of how he pictured his personality. In city streets where hot-bed apartments and kitchenettes were the only dwelling units available to Negroes, where there was little or nothing that they could call their own, the automobile parked in the street became the front parlour—a home more real than the one shared with three other families. Groups of Negroes would club together to purchase a vehicle, or at least, to lay down the initial instalment. And the wealthier Negro, who had succeeded in some activity, whether it was in sport, in the church, in the funeral business or in blues singing, bought first an automobile as an outward sign of his achievement. So Sugar Ray Robinson's 'Caddy' was recognized immediately by its tartan-plaid painted roof, Bishop Grace was chauffeured in an enormous Packard and blues singers from Walter Davis to Muddy Waters and Little Walter sported distinctive colours on their 'l-o-n-g Cadillacs'.

So the automobile became for the Negro a special status symbol, one of quality, glamour and luxury with which it was easy to identify his woman. But behind the wheel he could feel the sense of power that he could not feel in other circumstances; could display his driving skill, feel the response of the engine to his own manipulation of the gears. The primitive appeal of driving is well known and the means whereby the driver considers the vehicle an extension of himself, but associates himself with the machine, a familiar one. Driving provides an outlet for sexual-aggressive instincts and though the safety factors in many vehicles are criminally low, as has been effectively proven recently, the appeal of the car is not one where consideration of its safety plays a significant part. In this the Negro is fellow to every car driver in societies where the automobile is widely used. The special significance for him is that the car often provides him with the only opportunity to physically taste the pleasures of power. A large proportion of Negroes are not vehicle owners but the appeal of the automobile remains. Through the blues the Negro gives ample voice to its fascination, the vehicle becoming an object of his fantasies while still beyond the reach of his pocket and the subject of his aspirations when he can ride in it. The transference to the sexual metaphor is a simple one. In the blues it becomes a potent image, powerfully charged with the Negro's bitter awareness of his place in American society.

At first glance it may be less easy to draw conclusions from the use of other persistent images, but the very fact of their longevity as symbols suggests that they have layers of importance. The 'baker' theme which appears in its endless 'jelly roll' and 'stove' applications, as previously noted, has numerous side allusions. *Hot Jelly Roll Blues, I Got the Best Jelly Roll in Town, You'll Never Miss Your Jelly Roll Till Your Jelly Roller's Gone, My Stove's in Good Condition, This Is Not the Stove To Brown Your Bread, No More Biscuit Rollin' Here,* and countless others, have domestic associations, fire symbolism, as well as oral-anal implications. Anal-monetary symbolism also lies in the use of the word 'bread' which has punning links with 'daily bread' and means both sexual intercourse and money. These songs and blues too, run the gamut of bawdry, sexual aggressiveness and implied obscenity. It is in fact the images which allow for numerous interpretations at many levels both conscious and subconscious which persist in the blues. Through them the listener can indulge in sexual and aggressive fantasies and in these songs, as often in real life for the Negro, sex and violence are closely linked.

In his songs the Negro may unconsciously accord with the white segregationist's stereotypes; his 'animal virility' remains unproven but he may well be flattered by the superiority in one sense with which it credits him. In the sexual blues he assumes the attributes that were once those he invested in his folk heroes; he has the invincibility of the boll-weevil, the superhuman strength of a John Henry who succumbed but only against impossible odds, so he 'rolls all night long'; he has 'a stinger as long as my arm'; his 'stick of candy is nine-inch long'. And he has cunning, he is 'the spider in your dumpling'; he is prepared, for he is 'gonna keep my skillet good and greasy', and he threatens 'don't mess with me, baby', 'don't spin your web around my bed'. He accepts his position in the social sub-stratum on, as George Schyler termed it, 'the mud-sill of America' in numerous self-abasing metaphors and then rejoices in them: 'I'm ragged but right'; 'it's dirty but good', 'I'm blue, black and evil and I did not make myself'.

This projection of the self-image in the blues is sexual fantasy which has its parallels in pornographic invention. In blues songs the dream

world of sexual mastery is realized and the realities of racial oppression
are side-stepped. The power-seeking manifestations of masculinity in
an Adlerian sense are denied most Negroes and are expressed instead
through aggressive sexual fantasies. Sometimes these take direct forms
in the many blues devoted to weapons, to *Long Razor Blues*, *Johnson
Machine Gun* or *Pocket Knife Blues* wherein violence is the theme—
though the subjects themselves are potent sexual symbols. Sometimes
these are extended into fantasies of unrestricted sexual aggressive
viciousness, running literally through the alphabet of brutality:

> I'm gonna cut RST on your abdomen and secret place,
> When I get down there that's what runnin's goin' take place,
> I'm gonna cut UVW on your sides, legs and feet,
> So you can't even walk up and down the street,
> > Now I done got tired o' the way my baby's treatin' me,
> > When I get through with my left-hand razor,
> > I swear she'll stop messin' with me.[167]

Such expressions of unreasoning violence are sung as humorous songs,
but the humour is chillingly grim; as double-edged as recordings of
The Dirty Dozens but less circumscribed by censorship, at least when
apparently directed against the Negro group. *Cutting My ABCs* casts
a thin veil of humour over a brutal theme; *The Dozens* obscures in the
recordings a fathomless well of bitterness, humiliation and anger, which
the uncensored version by Lightnin' Hopkins openly reveals. The anal-
eroticism of the song may be exemplary of arrested adolescence, but
it is the stunted development of a racial minority which has not been
permitted its full maturity.

In his essay Dr Roger Abrahams criticizes Dollard for seeing 'the
game as a displaced aggression against the Negro's own group instead
of against the real enemy, the white, a reading which [he finds] untenable
not because it is wholly wrong, but because it is too easy.'[168] He quotes
Samuel J. Sperling's similar view to Dollard's that 'frustrated outgroup
aggression is safely channelled into the ingroup. In this way the formalized game of *The Dozens* has social value to a group subjected to suppression, discrimination and humiliation.'[169] Abrahams disagrees with
this, as has been noted, concentrating on the game as played by youths
and as a means of ritualizing the opposition to the authority of the
mother in the matriarchate. But this does not take into consideration

the importance of the dozens in adult circles, nor the prevalence of the song form. It is difficult not to concur with both Dollard and Sperling in their view of aggression displaced against the group instead of against the whites, and Paul Chevigny's account of the encounter with Will Shade, quoted above, is a significant instance of it. Though Dr Abrahams considers it facile to view the playing of the dozens as aggression redirected against the Negro rather than the white person and that rejection of the matriarchy is its true function, his opinion still begs the fundamental question: why is it that *Negro* children find the need for this particular outlet? Negro families are not the only ones dominated by the mother, but if they were, the continuation of the dozens into manhood suggests another psychological target.

Undoubtedly the sexual blues and blues songs offer a release mechanism for the frustrations of the Negro living under stress conditions. Denied for long years full citizenship, equal rights, parity of status and esteem, he has been prevented from maturing as a member of society. Traditionally the white man in the South has had an avuncular relationship with the Negro and if, in growing from youth to manhood, he has had to shake off the rule of the mother, he has been unable to reject the father-figure of the white boss. If Negro songs display an adolescent absorption with pornography they afford some outlet for repressed aggression canalizing, at least, the frustrations of stunted growth. Recently the blues singer has been lionized in some small sections of the white community, and not every singer can adjust himself to the situation. It is a tribute to their personal qualities that most do, but the rare displays of exhibitionism reveal the emotional turmoil that they hide. 'I spent a whole week watching Howling Wolf. He did a savage show—putting the hand microphone between his legs while making masturbating motions; rolling on the floor screaming; playing two harps at the same time, one with his nose, and sweating profusely,' wrote Mike Desilets of one singer who was then performing at a white club in Cambridge, Massachusetts, but who a few years ago made no secret of his dislike of white people.[170]

'The hostility of the Negro must be expressed through various intricate procedures which do not always dramatize the situation. The conflict in its indirect action is intense, often because of emotionally charged considerations of status,' concluded Charles S. Johnson, in summarizing covert hostility and deflected aggression among lower-class Negroes.[171] It seems inescapable that much of the importance of pornographic Race songs and blues lies in their effectiveness as catalysts of these suppressed emotions. This is not to contend that they do not perform the customary roles of titillation, sublimated sexual gratification and the satisfaction of prurient interest; undoubtedly they do. But their inability to fulfil these adequately through the medium of the phonograph record under censorship emphasizes their other function.

In the blues and its related forms there are few examples which even hint at racial intolerance, of white oppression, of segregation or violence as a result of prejudice. Once more, the lack of published studies of work in this field, with the rare exception of that by Lawrence Gellert, make conclusions difficult but it would seem that, though there are a small number of 'protest' songs in the tradition, there are few in the blues.[172] Probably there are many more than have been noted but they are conspicuously absent from recordings. Indeed, this could well be the result of censorship and there is some evidence that this is so in the oblique references in an isolated song by a Frank Stokes or a Julius Daniels. But if it is the result of censorship one would expect to find it sublimated in some other form.

Singing as he does of personal affairs, the blues singer is likely to sing of such pressures only if he himself has experienced them—but for fear of recriminations even less likely to record such a blues if he had. As a member of a victimized minority rather than as an individual victim of prejudice, he shares with other Negroes the common frustration that a repressive social system has provoked. Through the blues songs and the traditional songs, through the ebullient reiterations of time-worn themes, he bolsters his ego with sexual fantasies and shares them with the listeners for whom he sings and whose repressions are his own. Through them he asserts his masculinity, and achieves the power that the system denies him; through them he, or she, brags of his prowess, asserts his superiority and challenges all comers. Listening to the records and purchasing more, the Negro joins the singer in a shared experience, feels with him a sense of racial solidarity. The symbolic language of the songs and their evasion of the censor are themselves both a code by which identity is established and a device by which both singer and listener play a game of cunning. *Dirty Mother For You* is a joke at Mister Charlie's expense; *The Dirty Dozens* can be sung on record because both the singer and his listener can join forces against the opponent in a racial battle—without, it must be fairly admitted, suffering the consequences, but enjoying the vicarious thrill.

Against the vast quantity of the exuberant blues songs, traditional songs and jazz-blues songs and the occasional blues and traditional blues which share this quality, must be placed the category of sexual blues which reflect the Negro's insecurity and sense of failure. At the surface level they tell of broken love affairs, of unfaithfulness, of family disintegration. On a deeper plane they are indicative of the unrest and uncertainty, the fear and humiliation of the group. In them the blues singer has found, consciously or subconsciously, a vehicle for protest; they are the reverse of the same coin. For every 'king bee' there is a 'honey-stealer' in the hive; for every 'black mare' there is 'another mule kickin' in the stall'. The 'rattlesnakin' daddy' who boasts that he 'wants to rattle all the time' is endangered by the 'mean black snake crawlin' in my room'. The 'creeping man' and the 'monkey man' are objects of contempt in the blues, but they are the lovers who succeed where the singer fails. They 'play in his orchard', they 'steal his peaches', they 'feed in his pasture' and 'dig his potatoes'. In blues, significantly, the singer is often deceived, often frustrated in his love affairs. And his opponent is surprisingly successful, 'slippin' out the back-door' as the singer comes in at the front. Significantly, in the blues again and again, the singer is cheated; cheated by an enemy whom he may despise but who seems to have luck on his side. It is as though the odds are stacked against him; cuckolded whilst he is at work by one who does not have to work.

Neither the blues singer nor his listener is likely to be aware of the function of the songs as a sublimation of frustrated desires; they are ready to take the themes at their face value. But they provide the same catalyst; they sublimate hostility and canalize aggressive instincts against a mythical common enemy, the 'cheater'. In buying them, listening to them, hearing them again and again, the Negro listener feels a bond of sympathy with the blues singer in a shared predicament. That this is sometimes quite literal—anger at the unfaithfulness of a lover—does not alter the fact that the high proportion of these blues strongly indicates that they do perform an important function in giving some release from repression. But they do not offer much hope; the singer seldom succeeds in having his revenge against his woman's lover. He threatens, he sings of his violent intentions, but he sings out the action. In the blues he states the hopelessness he feels, and often the assumed disinterest. His response to the situation is frequently apathetic.

To a great extent these blues bolstered a sense of racial solidarity but they also diverted repressed hostilities which may otherwise have found more immediate expression. These dispirited blues in which the singer was sexually 'mistreated' are typical of the 'thirties when the effects of the Depression hit the Negro hardest and civil rights was a meaningless phrase. But the recent developments in the blues parallel a change of attitude. 'In the ebb and flow of racial change,' wrote Joseph Himes in 1956, 'the spirit of compromise and accommodation is being curtailed and the orientation towards militancy is being accentuated and glorified.'[173] And while he wrote, a blues singer in Chicago, with his clothes soaked in sweat, with his face contorted and with staring eye, was singing in front of a clamorous, deafening band. 'I'm a *man* . . . spelt M . . . A . . . N. . . .' shouted Muddy Waters. Since the early 1950s the blues has undergone marked changes, the older singers who are still the leaders in the urban blues of Chicago augmenting and sometimes replacing the sexual content of their blues with aggressive delivery and the younger ones of a new generation undulating in libidinous movements. Their guitars and electric basses are slung at hip level in phallic gestures and the combined volume of amplified instruments played at their maximum output have the thunder of battle. It may not be coincidental that the marked changes in Negro music took place in the period that led to the desegregation decision of 1954. Like the 'New Negro', the blues singer has become more militant; in a harsh, strained voice of unprecedented ferocity, the massive singer, Howling Wolf, roared one of the oldest of blues songs in an idiom essentially of 1960:

Cut me a spoonful of diamonds, cut me a spoonful of gold,
Cut me a spoonful of your precious love,
To satisfy my soul.
Men lies about that . . . some of them cries about that. . . .
Some of them dies about that. . . .
Everybody fightin' 'bout that spoonful.[174] ©

'It has become painfully evident in the past few years that, unless the nation begins to take longer strides on the first mile of the long road to equality and integration, the Negro revolt will change from a nonviolent to a violent one,' wrote the authors of *Racial Crisis in America* in 1964.[175] It was the year before the tragedy of Watts; the riots of

Chicago's West Side followed in the summer of 1966. To this the blues has offered, in the changing nature of its sexual expression, a warning signal. It may yet continue to do so.

In *The Mark of Oppression*, Doctors Kardiner and Ovesey observed that the spirituals and the folk-lore elements surviving in the Br'er Rabbit and Uncle Remus stories contained expressions of the Negro personality through fantasy creations in the slavery period. In their view, and in direct contrast to that expressed by Miles Mark Fisher in *Negro Slave Songs of the United States*, the spirituals were without hatred or protest but were representative of an accommodative attitude to slavery. Their value in providing an emotional release they accepted, but found the protest theme in the folk tales. 'It is always the clever rabbit who outwits the strong and wily fox. This was a vehicle for expressing hatred to the white, the wish to torture, outwit, ridicule and destroy him. This hatred is clearly envisaged, but kept under suppressive control . . . these tales must have had a good deal of release value.'[176] The authors were aware that the spirituals and the folk tales were not part of contemporary Negro culture but were at a loss to know where to look for an equivalent expression of the Negro personality in the present day. They sought an answer in the areas of Negro literature, in the Church and other aspects of Negro society but did not find in the community as a whole 'the vicarious aggression in the folk tales' which they identified as one of the four types of adaptation used by the Negro slave.

It was the lower-class Negro who carried the heaviest adaptational load and who had inherited 'the greatest amount of self-preservation anxiety in our culture' Kardiner and Ovesey commented. Earlier the authors noted that 'for true expressions of personality structure we must look . . . in traditional and living folklore and social ideologies or movements. Living folklore was once a spontaneous manifestation, at least until the early 'twenties. Since then, it has been subject to a kind of benevolent censure, so that more recently the imagination of creative writers has had the short tether of censorship attached to it. All this occurs before the public gets its chance to approve or disapprove by patronage.'[177]

From their observations on Negro music it is evident that Kardiner and Ovesey did not look further in that direction. In gospel song and in some aspects of blues they might have found an accommodative trend such as they had noted in the spirituals. The toasts, the urban and rural 'lies' and stories, the game of the dirty dozens, they might have found to be the counterparts of the folk tales, offering the same outlets for emotional release. And they could have discovered that a rich storehouse of the fantasy productions of the twentieth century Negro are to be found in profusion in the vast corpus of sexual blues and songs. Both the recorded examples and the live performances unfettered by censorship are the folk expressions of the Negro personality and within them emotional release and vicarious aggression find their outlet. Cecil Sharp's admonition to the collector to conduct his work 'conscientiously and accurately' stands as an indictment of past field work and as a directive for the future. Perhaps it is not too late to discover from this extensive tradition what it may reveal of the Negro personality in this century's period of racial change. And it could yet offer a gauge for the crisis years ahead.

NOTES

SCREENING THE BLUES: AN INTRODUCTION

1. Henry Edward Krehbiel, entry in Rupert Hughes (ed.), *The Musical Guide*, McClure Phillips & Co. *c.* 1903. Quoted in Henry Edward Krehbiel, *Afro-American Folksongs, A Study in Racial and National Music*, G. Shirmer, New York 1914, p. 2.
2. Charles S. Johnson, *Shadow of the Plantation*, University of Chicago Press 1934, pp. xi–xii.
3. Charles Keil, *Urban Blues*, University of Chicago Press 1966, p. 71 et seq. Keil applies Robert F. Bales's *Interaction Process Analysis: A Method for the Study of Small Groups* to the blues singer and his audience.
4. Len Kunstadt, 'Mamie Smith—The First Lady of the Blues', *Record Research*, no. 57, p. 3.
5. These stockists were listed in the General Phonograph Corporation's fly-sheets for November 1922.
6. Listed in Paramount Record Company fly-sheets for November 1928.
7. Charles S. Johnson, op. cit., pp. 184–5.
8. Howard W. Odum and Guy B. Johnson, *Negro Workaday Songs*, University of North Carolina Press 1926, p. 27.
9. Muriel Davis Longini, 'Folk Songs of Chicago Negroes' in *Journal of American Folk Lore*, vol. 52 1939, p. 106.
10. Ibid., p. 96.
11. Odum and Johnson, op. cit., pp. 33–4.
12. Dan Mahony, *The Columbia 13/14000–D Series: A Numerical Listing*, Walter C. Allen, Stanhope NJ 1961, p. 12 et seq.
13. Computed by Robert M. W. Dixon on statistical sampling of entries in Robert M. W. Dixon and John Godrich, *Blues and Gospel Records 1902–1942*, Brian Rust 1963.
14. A complete discography of blues records since 1942 is being completed by Mike Leadbitter for publication in 1968/9.
15. Robert Redfield, *Tepoztlán, A Mexican Village*, University of Chicago Press 1930, p. 1. See also Charles S. Johnson, op. cit., p. xi.
16. Milton Metfessel, *Phonophotography in Folk Music*, University of North Carolina Press, Chapel Hill 1928, remains the outstanding example in the study of Negro song by this method.
17. Comparative figures may be obtained from discographies, notably Dixon and Godrich, op. cit.
18. Paul Oliver, *Blues Fell This Morning*, Cassell 1960.
19. Paul Oliver, *Conversation with the Blues*, Cassell 1965.
20. Ibid., p. 25.
21. Pete Welding, 'The Art of the Folk Blues Guitar' in *Downbeat*, 1 July 1965; Charles Keil, op. cit., pp. 50–68 and 217–21; and Samuel B. Charters, *The Bluesmen*, Oak Publications 1967, have identified broad categories. In *Blues Unlimited*, issue 42, pp. 7–8 and issue 43, pp. 8–9, Gayle Dean Wardlow and David Evans have discussed Clarksdale and other local styles.

22. Blind Lemon Jefferson, *Match-box Blues*, March and April 1927, Okeh 8455 and Paramount 12474.
23. Leroy Carr, *Blues Before Sunrise*, 21 February 1934, Vocalion 02657.
24. Ma Rainey, *Lost Wandering Blues*, February 1924, Paramount 12098.
25. Elements of these verses are to be found in *Dink's Blues* noted by John A. Lomax from the singing of 'Dink' in the Brazos bottoms, *c.* 1908. See John A. Lomax and Alan Lomax, *American Ballads and Folk Songs*, Macmillan 1934, pp. 193–4.
26. Tommy Johnson, *Maggie Campbell*, 4 February 1928, Victor 21409, Origin OJL 1.
27. Oliver, *Blues Fell This Morning*, pp. 64–75.
28. Oliver, *Conversation with the Blues*, pp. 165–70.

THE SANTY CLAUS CRAVE

1. Examples from magazine advertisements of the 'forties and 'fifties.
2. Leadbelly, *On a Christmas Day*, 4 October 1944, Capitol H369.
3. William Bollaert, diary entry for 31 December 1843. *William Bollaert's Texas*, University of Oklahoma Press 1956, p. 299.
4. Cato in B. A. Botkin (ed.), *Lay My Burden Down*, University of Chicago Press 1945, p. 86.
5. Bessie Smith, *At the Christmas Ball*, 18 November 1925, Columbia 35842, CBS BPG 62380.
6. Jenny Proctor in Botkin, op. cit., p. 92.
7. Booker T. Washington, *Up from Slavery*, Doubleday 1900, Bantam reprint 1959, pp. 94–5.
8. Ibid., p. 96.
9. Julia Peterkin, *Roll, Jordan Roll*, Robert O. Ballou, New York 1933, p. 244.
10. Blind Lemon Jefferson, *Christmas Eve Blues*, *c.* August 1928, Paramount 12692.
11. Reverend J. M. Gates, *Death Might Be Your Santa Claus*, 3 November 1926, Okeh 8413.
12. Victoria Spivey, *Christmas Mornin' Blues*, 28 October 1927, Okeh 8517.
13. Blind Blake, *Lonesome Christmas Blues*, *c.* September 1929, Paramount 12869.
14. Elzadie Robinson, *The Santy Claus Crave*, *c.* November 1927, Paramount 12573.
15. Jack Ranger, *Thieving Blues*, 28 June 1927, Okeh 8795.
16. King Solomon Hill, *Down on My Bended Knee*, *c.* January 1932, Paramount 13116, Origin OJL 10. If King Solomon sings 'Allah' and not 'At last' the words are even more apt.
17. Black Ace, *Christmas Times Blues*, 15 February 1937, Decca 7387.

18. Mary Harris, *No Christmas Blues*, 31 October 1935, Decca 7804.
19. Peetie Wheatstraw, *Santa Claus Blues*, 31 October 1935, Decca 7129.
20. Champion Jack Dupree, *Santa Claus Blues*, c. 1946, Joe Davis 5107.
21. Butterbeans and Susie, *Papa Ain't No Santa Claus (Mama Ain't No Christmas Tree)*, 13 August 1930, Okeh 8950, CBS (M) 63288.
22. Lil McClintock, *Don't Think I'm Santa Claus*, 4 December 1930, Columbia 14575.
23. Bo Carter, *Santa Claus*, 22 October 1938, Bluebird B–8147.
24. Lonnie Johnson, *Happy New Year, Darling*, c. November 1947, King 4251.
25. Robert Nighthawk, *Merry Christmas*, c. 1965, Decca LK 4748.
26. Sonny Boy Williamson No. 2, *Sonny Boy's Christmas Blues*, c. 1951, Trumpet 145, Blues Classics BC 9.
27. Louis (Jelly Belly) Hayes, *Christmas Time Blues*, c. 1948, Arhoolie R 2005.
28. Jimmy McCracklin, *Christmas Time*, parts 1 and 2, c. 1959, Art-Tone 826, Outa-Site 45–501.

PREACHING THE BLUES

1. Richard Wright, *Twelve Million Black Voices*, Lindsay Drummond 1947, pp. 130–1.
2. Ibid., p. 134.
3. Paul Oliver, *Conversation with the Blues*, Cassell 1965. Interviews pp. 165–70.
4. Texas Alexander, *Justice Blues*, 29 September 1934, Vocalion 02856.
5. Son House, *Preachin' the Blues*, part 1, July 1930, Paramount 13013, Origin OJL 5.
6. Son House interviewed by Julius Lester, 'Preachin' the Blues' notes in *Sing Out!* vol. 15, no. 3, p. 46.
7. Al Wilson, *Son House*, 1966, Collectors Classics 14, p. 3 and p. 5.
8. Son House, *Preachin' the Blues*, part 2, Paramount 13013 as above.
9. Hi-Henry Brown, *Preacher Blues*, 14 March 1932, Vocalion 1728, Origin OJL 11.
10. Coley Jones, *The Elders He's My Man*, 6 December 1929, Columbia 14489D.
11. Mississippi Sheiks, *He Calls That Religion*, July 1932, Paramount 13142.
12. Arnold Rose, *The Negro in America*, Beacon 1956, p. 280, condensed from Gunner Myrdal, *An American Dilemma*.
13. Rob Robinson and Meade Lux Lewis, *The Preacher Must Get Some Sometime*, c. November 1930, Paramount 13028.
14. E. Franklin Frazier, *The Negro in the United States*, Macmillan 1949, p. 354.

15. Hambone Willie Newbern, *Nobody Knows What the Good Deacon Does*, 13 March 1929, Okeh 8679, CBS (M) 63288.
16. Louis E. Lomax, *The Negro Revolt*, Hamish Hamilton 1963, p. 87.
17. Benjamin E. Mays and Joseph W. Nicholson, *The Negro's Church*, Institute of Social and Religious Research, New York 1933.
18. George Noble, *Sissy Man Blues*, 5 March 1935, Vocalion 02923, CBS (M) 63288.
19. Luke Jordan, *Church Bells Blues*, 16 August 1927, Victor 21079.
20. St Clair Drake and Horace R. Cayton, *Black Metropolis*, Harcourt, Brace and Co. 1945, pp. 418–19.
21. For extensive analyses of such traditional 'parson' and 'preacher' stories see Antti Arne and Stith Thompson, *The Types of Folktale*, Helsinki 1928, and Stith Thompson, *Motif-Index of Literature*, Bloomington, Indiana 1958. Examples from Negro folk-lore are to be found in many works including Richard M. Dorson, *Negro Folktales in Michigan*, Cambridge, Mass 1956, and Roger D. Abrahams, *Deep Down in the Jungle*, Folklore Associates 1964.
22. William Francis Allen, Charles Pickard Ware and Lucy McKim Garrison, *Slave Songs of the United States*, Simpson, New York 1867, p. 89, Oak reprint, p. 144. Miles Mark Fisher in *Negro Slave Songs in the United States*, Cornell UP, New York 1953, p. 82, suggests that this is derived from the *ante-bellum* religious song *Run, Mary Run*.
23. Lafcadio Hearn, 'Levee Life' in *Cincinnati Commercial*, 17 March 1876.
24. Sigmund Spaeth, *Read 'Em and Weep*, Doubleday, Page and Co. 1927, pp. 125–7.
25. Howard W. Odum, 'Folk-Song and Folk-Poetry as Found in the Secular Songs of the Southern Negroes' in *Journal of American Folk Lore*, vol. 24, no. 94, 1911, p. 370.
26. Roark Bradford, *Kingdom Coming*, Harper and Brothers, New York 1933, p. 160.
27. Dorothy Scarborough, *On the Trail of Negro Folk Songs*, Harvard UP 1925, Folklore Associates, 1963, pp. 165 *et seq.*
28. Newman I. White, *American Negro Folk Songs*, Harvard UP 1928, Folklore Associates 1965, pp. 134 *et seq.* and pp. 370–2.
29. Frank Stokes, *You Shall*, August 1927, Paramount 12518.
30. Howard W. Odum, op. cit.
31. Red Hot Shakin' Davis, *Too Black Bad*, October 1928, Paramount 12703.
32. Kansas Joe and Memphis Minnie, *Preachers Blues*, 31 January 1931, Vocalion 1643, Blues Classics BC 13.
33. Frank Stokes, op. cit.
34. Reverend George Jones (John Byrd) and His Congregation, *That White Mule of Sin*, 29 July 1929, Gennett 6979.
35. Texas Alexander, op. cit.

36. Fats Heyden, *Voodoo Blues*, 26 May 1939, Decca 7614. Text in Oliver, *Blues Fell This Morning*, p. 145.
37. Washington Phillips, *Denomination Blues*, 5 December 1927, Columbia 14333D, CBS (M) 63288.
38. Stith Thompson, op. cit., K 1961. 1, 2. See also Dorson, op. cit., Abrahams, op. cit.
39. Butterbeans and Grasshopper, *Deacon Bite-'Em-in-the-Back*, 24 March 1926, Okeh 8323.
40. Butterbeans, *A Married Man's a Fool*, May 1924, Okeh 8180.
41. Roark Bradford, op. cit., pp. 84 and 219.
42. Bessie Smith, *Preachin' the Blues*, 17 February 1927, Columbia 14195D, Philips BBL 7049.
43. Danny Barker, quoted in Robert Goffin, *Horn of Plenty, The Story of Louis Armstrong*, Allen Towne & Heath 1947, p. 157.
44. Big Bill Broonzy, *Preaching the Blues*, 6 February 1939, Vocalion 05096.
45. Roy Brown, *Judgement Day Blues*, c. 1948, De Luxe 3212.
46. Robert Johnson, *Preaching Blues*, 27 November 1936, Vocalion 04630, CBS 62456.
47. Robert Johnson, *Me and the Devil Blues*, 30 June 1937, Vocalion 04108, CBS 62456.
48. Arthur Huff Fauset, *Black Gods of the Metropolis*, University of Pennsylvania Press 1944, p. 108.
49. Lightnin' Hopkins, *Unkind Blues*, c. 1947, Gold Star 664, Fontana 688 803 ZL.
50. J. T. Funny Paper Smith—the Howling Wolf, *Fool's Blues*, c. July 1931, Vocalion 1674.
51. Tommy Griffin, *Dying Sinner Blues*, part 2, 1 October 1936, Bluebird BB B-6834.
52. Mississippi Mudder (Papa Charlie), *Please Baby*, 7 January 1935, Decca 7822.
53. Country Paul, *Mother, Dear Mother*, 1952, King 1473, Post-War Blues, vol. 3.
54. Bert Mays, *Oh-Oh Blues*, November 1927, Paramount 12632, Riverside RM 8809.
55. Kaiser Clifton, *Teach Me Right from Wrong*, 30 May 1930, Victor V-38600.
56. Blind Willie McTell, *Broke Down Engine*, 18 September 1933, Vocalion 02568.
57. Blind Willie McTell, *Southern Can Mama*, 21 September 1933, Vocalion 02622.
58. Walter Davis, *Lifeboat Blues*, 2 August 1933, Victor 23418.
59. John Lee Hooker, *Burnin' Hell*, November 1948, Sensation 21.
60. Doctor Clayton, *Angels in Harlem*, 7 August 1946, Victor 20-1995, RCA RCX-7177.
61. Full details of these and other recordings listed, falling between the

years 1921 (Excelsior Quartet) and 1942, may be found in Robert M. W. Dixon and John Godrich, *Blues and Gospel Records 1902–1942*, Brian Rust 1963.
62. Harlem Hamfats, *Hallelujah Joe Ain't Preachin' No More*, 14 January 1937, Chicago, Decca 7299, Ace of Hearts AH77.
63. Robert Pete Williams, interview with the author, 27 September 1966.
64. Paul Oliver, *Conversation with the Blues*, pp. 168–70.
65. Sippie Wallace, interview with the author, 28 September 1966.
66. Curtis Jones, 'The Curtis Jones Story,' part 4, *R & B Monthly*, no. 4.
67. Dan Mahony, *Columbia 13/14000–D Series*, Record Handbook 1, Walter C. Allen 1961.
68. Arnold Rose, op. cit., pp. 279–80.
69. Wright Holmes, *Alley Blues*, c. 1947, Gotham 511, Blues Classics BC 7.
70. Arnold Rose, op. cit., p. 280.

THE FORTY-FOURS

1. Little Brother Montgomery, in Paul Oliver, *Conversation with the Blues*, p. 70.
2. Little Brother Montgomery, *Vicksburg Blues*, in collection *Conversation with the Blues*, Decca LK 4664. This is a re-creation of the original recording, *Vicksburg Blues*, c. September 1930, Paramount 13006, Riverside RLP 8009, Decca LK 4664 recorded 14 July 1960.
3. Paul Oliver, op. cit., p. 70.
4. Gayle Dean Wardlow, *Biographical Notes* for Origin OJL's 2, 5 and 8.
5. Charley Taylor, *Louisiana Bound*, c. March 1930, Paramount 12967.
6. Paul Oliver, op. cit., p. 70.
7. Ibid.
8. Lee Green, *Number Forty-Four Blues*, c. August 1929, Vocalion 1401.
9. Lee Green, *44 Blues*, 24 August 1934, Decca 7016.
10. Roosevelt Sykes, in Oliver, op. cit., p. 71.
11. Roosevelt Sykes, *Forty-Four Blues*, 16 July 1960, collection *Conversation with the Blues*, Decca LK 4664. This is a re-creation of the original recording '*44*' *Blues*, Okeh 8702, Historical 5, recorded 14 June 1929.
12. James Boodle-It Wiggins, *Forty-Four Blues*, 12 October 1929, Paramount 12860.
13. Mae Glover, *Forty-Four Blues*, 24 February 1931, Champion 16351.
14. Mississippi Matilda, *Happy Home Blues*, 15 October 1936, Bluebird B6812.

15. Johnny Temple, *New Vicksburg Blues*, 12 November 1936, Decca 7244.
16. Jazz Gillum, *5 Feet 4*, 26 February 1945, Bluebird 34–0730.
17. Willie Kelly, *32–20 Blues*, 12 June 1930, Victor V–38619, French RCA 86–431.
18. Samuel Charters, *The Bluesmen*, Oak Publications 1967, p. 72.
19. Ibid.
20. Skip James, *22–20 Blues*, *c.* February 1931, Paramount 13006.
21. The text of Arthur Big Boy Crudup's *Give Me a 32–20* is quoted in Paul Oliver, *Blues Fell This Morning*, p. 253.
22. Big Maceo Merriweather, *Maceo's 32–20*, 5 July 1945, Victor 20–2028. Fuller text in Oliver, op. cit., p. 201.
23. Arthur Big Boy Crudup, *Crudup's Vicksburg Blues*, 9 April 1947, Victor 22–0029.
24. Cat-Iron, *Got a Girl in Ferriday, one in Greenwood Town*, Natchez 1950s, Folkways FA2389.
25. Karl Gert zur Heide has confirmed that Montgomery was in Ferriday in 1922 when the town was flooded to a depth of eight feet. Montgomery has also explained this in interview in *Eureka*, vol. 1, no. 5, p. 19.
26. Scott Dunbar assisted by Celeste and Rose Dunbar, *Vicksburg and Natchez Blues (Goin' Back to Vicksburg)*, *c.* 1955, Folkways FA2659.
27. Frederic Ramsey Jr, *Been Here and Gone*, Cassell 1960, pp. 125–6.
28. Butch Cage and Willie Thomas, *Forty-Four Blues*, 7 August 1960, Arhoolie F 1005.
29. Butch Cage and Willie Thomas, *44 Blues*, *c.* 1959, Folk-Lyric FL 111.
30. Pete Welding, Notes to *Big Joe Williams/Back to the Country*, Testament 2205, Bounty BY 6018.
31. Big Joe Williams, *Ain't Gonna Be Your Lowdown Dog*, *c.* 1965, Testament 2205, Bounty BY 6018.
32. Muddy Waters, *Louisiana Blues*, *c.* 1951, Chess lp 1427, London LTZ-M 15152.
33. Hambone Willie Newbern, *Roll and Tumble Blues*, 14 March 1929, Okeh 8679, CBS (M) 63288.
34. Sleepy John Estes, *The Girl I Love, She Got Long Curly Hair*, 24 September 1929, Victor V–38549, RBF 8.
35. Robert Johnson, *If I Had Possession over Judgement Day*, 27 November 1936, and *Travelling Riverside Blues*, 20 June 1937, both Columbia CL–1654, CBS 62456.
36. Baby Face Leroy, *Rollin' and Tumblin'*, part 2, *c.* 1950–1, Parkway 501, Blues Classics BC 8.
37. Sunnyland Slim, *Goin' Back to Memphis*, 1954, Blue Lake 105, Blues Classics BC 16.
38. Doctor Ross, *Illinois Blues*, *c.* 1964, Testament 2206, Bounty BY 6020.

39. Junior Brooks, *Lone Town Blues*, *c.* 1951, RPM 343, Post-War Blues pwb2.
40. Woodrow Adams, *Wine Head Woman*, *c.* 1955, Meteor 5018, Blue Horizon 45–1001.
41. Howling Wolf, *Forty-Four*, 1955, Chess 1584, Chess lp 1434.
42. Otis Spann, *Vicksburg Blues*, *c.* 1966, Testament T 2211, Bounty BY 6037.

POLICY BLUES

1. St Clair Drake and Horace R. Cayton, *Black Metropolis*, Harcourt, Brace 1945, pp. 485–6.
2. James Weldon Johnson, *Black Manhattan*, Alfred A. Knopf 1930, p. 217.
3. Hurtig's and Seamon's playbill reproduced in 'The Story of Louie Metcalf', *Record Research*, issue 46, October 1962. Quotation from Louie Metcalf on p. 7 of this issue.
4. Charlie Jackson, *Four-Eleven-Forty-Four*, *c.* May 1926, Paramount 12375.
5. Drake and Cayton, op. cit., p. 470.
6. James D. Horan, *The Mob's Man*, Robert Hale 1960, pp. 107–8.
7. Elvira Johnson, accompanied by The Birmingham Darktown Strutters, *Numbers on the Brain*, 17 June 1926, Gennett 3337.
8. Yodelling Kid Brown, *Policy Blues*, August 1928, Vocalion 1205.
9. Drake and Cayton, op. cit., p. 472.
10. Jim Jackson, *Policy Blues*, 14 February 1928, Victor 21268.
11. Brother John Sellers, 'Their Only Hope', Paul Oliver, *Conversation with the Blues*, p. 145.
12. Horan, op. cit., p. 109.
13. The texts of Jimmy Gordon's *Number Runner's Blues*, Decca 7536; Ollie Shepard's *The Numbers Blues* and John Lee Hooker's *Playing the Races* may be found in Paul Oliver, *Blues Fell This Morning*, pp. 147–9.
14. Bumble Bee Slim, *Policy Dream Blues (You Better Get On It)*, 4 April 1935, Vocalion 03090, CBS (M) 63288.
15. Walter Vincson, *Rosa Lee Blues*, 1 August 1941, Bluebird BB B–8963.
16. Kokomo Arnold, *Policy Wheel Blues*, 15 July 1935, Decca 7147.
17. From material gathered by workers of the Workers Project Administration (WPA), Louisiana Writers' Project in 'Nickel Gig, Nickel Saddle', in Lyle Saxon, Edward Dreyer, Robert Tallant (ed.), *Gumbo Ya-Ya*, Riverside Press 1945, pp. 124–5 and 136.
18. Tommy Griffin, *Dream Book Blues*, 16 October 1936, Bluebird B–6756.
19. Cripple Clarence Lofton, *Policy Blues*, December 1943, Session 10–014, Vogue (E) LDE 122.

20. Reported in *Louisiana Weekly*, 9 January 1937.
21. Saxon, Dreyer, Tallant, op. cit., pp. 121-2.
22. Albert Clemens, *Policy Blues* (*You Can't 3-6-9 Me*), 12 April 1935, Bluebird B-5930.
23. E. Franklin Frazier, *Black Bourgeoisie*, The Free Press 1957, chapter 4.
24. Louisiana Johnny, *Policy Blues* and *Three-Six-Nine Blues*, 8 January 1938, Vocalion 02980.
25. Drake and Cayton, op. cit., p. 479. Table 22 gives a 'Financial Analysis of Three Policy Companies For One Week: 1938'—the Interstate Company; the East & West Company (see Bumble Bee Slim, *Policy Dream Blues*, no. 14 above) and the Monte Carlo Company.
26. Roi Ottley, *Inside Black America*, Eyre and Spottiswoode 1948, p. 121.
27. James Banister, *Gold Digger*, c. 1954, States 141, Highway 51 H100.
28. Arbee Stidham and His Orchestra, *Mister Commissioner*, c. 1952, Checker 751.
29. *Forward Times*, Houston, Texas, 9 October 1965, 'White "Wife" Gets Most of Policy King's Fortune'.
30. Lightnin' Hopkins, *Policy Game*, 29 July 1953, Decca 28841.

JOE LOUIS AND JOHN HENRY

1. Roi Ottley, *Black Odyssey*, John Murray 1949, p. 262.
2. Joe Pullum, *Joe Louis Is the Man*, 13 August 1935, Bluebird B-6071.
3. Gay Talese, 'The King as a Middle-Aged Man', *Esquire*, June 1962.
4. Memphis Minnie, *He's in the Ring* (*Doin' the Same Old Thing*), 22 August 1935, Vocalion 03046, CBS (M) 63288.
5. Quoted in Ottley, op. cit., p. 262.
6. Carl Martin, *Joe Louis Blues*, 4 September 1935, Decca 7114.
7. Paul Oliver, *Blues Fell This Morning*, p. 297.
8. Leroy's Buddy, *Champ Joe Louis* (*King of the Gloves*), 23 June 1938, Decca 7476.
9. Sonny Boy Williamson, *Joe Louis and John Henry*, 21 July 1939, Bluebird B-8403, Blues Classics BC 3.
10. Gay Talese, op. cit.
11. Quoted in Walter White, *How Far the Promised Land?*, Viking Press 1956, p. 116.
12. Paul Robeson accompanied by Count Basie and His Orchestra, *King Joe*, parts 1 and 2, 1 October 1941, Okeh 6475, Parlophone R 2966.
13. Ike Smith, *Fighting Joe Louis*, c. 1935, Champion 50040.

Notes

THE BLUE BLUES

1. Cecil Sharp, *Folk-Songs from Somerset 1904–09*, quoted in James Reeves, *The Idiom of the People*, Heinemann 1958, p. 114.
2. Cecil Sharp, *English Folk-Songs, Some Conclusions*, 1907, 4th ed., Mercury Books 1963, pp. 128–9.
3. Exceptions are the Vance Randolph Collection deposited in the Library of Congress and certain songs of cowboys collected, but not published, by John A. Lomax.
4. James Reeves, op. cit., and James Reeves, *The Everlasting Circle*, Heinemann 1960.
5. Gates Thomas, publications of the Texas Folk Lore Society, vol. 5, 1926, 'South Texas Negro Work Songs', p. 155.
6. Ibid., p. 164.
7. Howard Odum and Guy B. Johnson, *The Negro and His Songs*, University of North Carolina, Chapel Hill 1925, p. 166.
8. John A. Lomax and Alan Lomax, *Our Singing Country*, note to *Stavin' Chain*, Macmillan 1941, p. 305.
9. Dr Alain Locke, *The Negro and His Music*, the Associates in Negro Folk Education, Washington DC 1936, p. 87.
10. Ibid., p. 88.
11. Frederic Ramsey Jr and Charles Edward Smith, *Jazzmen* 1939, pp. 12–13.
12. William L. Grossman and Jack W. Farrell, *The Heart of Jazz*, Vision Press 1958, p. 70.
13. Bud Scott, quoted in Nat Shapiro and Nat Hentoff, *Hear Me Talkin' To Ya*, Peter Davies, 1955, pp. 45–6.
14. Buddy Bottley, quoted in Danny Barker, 'A Memory of King Bolden', *Evergreen Review*, no. 37, September 1965, p. 68.
15. Ibid., p. 70.
16. Ibid., p. 70.
17. Sigmund Spaeth, *A History of Popular Music in America*, Random House 1948, p. 385.
18. Bottley, op. cit., p. 70.
19. Alan Lomax, *Mister Jelly Roll*, Cassell 1952, p. 60.
20. Ibid., p. 47 fn.
21. Ibid., p. 48.
22. Ibid., p. 48 fn.
23. Jelly Roll Morton, *Winin' Boy Blues*. Full text from the Library of Congress recording. In the block of titles Library of Congress 1667–72, two only, *The Murder Ballad* and *Winin' Boy Blues* were issued in part, on Riverside RLP 9008. The notes explained, '*The Murder Ballad* is the only issuable portion of a very long composition . . . perhaps the day will come when a more tolerant and adult society will permit of its complete issue.' *Winin' Boy Blues* was similarly truncated but four versions, partially expurgated, have appeared on Swaggie S1213.

24. Lomax, op. cit., p. 48 fn.
25. Mance Lipscomb, *Stavin' Chain*, c. 1960. In collection. *The Un-expurgated Folk Songs of Men*, compiled by Mack McCormick, Raglan LP 51.
26. Brian Rust, *Jazz Records 1897–1931*, Brian Rust 1962.
27. Milton (Mezz) Mezzrow and Bernard Wolfe, *Really the Blues*, Secker and Warburg, 1957, pp. 45–6.
28. Full discographical details of blues recordings made up till 1942 will be found in Robert M. W. Dixon and John Godrich, *Blues and Gospel Records 1902–1942*, Brian Rust 1964.
29. James Stump Johnson and Dorothea Trowbridge, *Steady Grindin'*, 2 August 1933, Bluebird B–5159.
30. Thomas A. Dorsey, quoted in note to *Georgia Tom and Friends*, c. 1965, Riverside RLP 8803.
31. The Hokum Boys, *Beedle-um-Bum*, December 1928, Paramount 12714, also on Riverside RLP 8803.
32. Mrs Bartlett in Dorothy Scarborough, *On the Trail of Negro Folk Songs*, Harvard 1925, p. 277.
33. Jim Jackson, *I'm Wild about My Lovin'*, 27 August 1928, Victor V–38525, also on Victor X-Vault LVA 3032.
34. Bo Carter, *All Around Man*, 20 February 1936, Bluebird BB B–6295, Melodeon MLP 7324.
35. Archie Green, letter to Paul Oliver, 25 August 1966.
36. W. C. Handy, *A Treasury of the Blues*, Charles Boni 1926, 1949. Notes to the collection by Abbé Niles, pp. 243–4.
37. Claude McKay, *Home to Harlem*, Harper 1928, pp. 36–7.
38. Mezzrow and Wolfe, op. cit., p. 26.
39. Iain Laing, *Jazz in Perspective*, Hutchinson 1946, p. 122.
40. May Alix with Jimmy Noone and His Orchestra, *My Daddy Rocks Me with One Steady Roll*, 24 June 1929, Vocalion 2779.
41. Joe Turner, *Cherry Red*, 30 June 1939, OK 4997, Parlophone R–2717.
42. Rex Harris, *Jazz*, Penguin Books 1952, pp. 36–7.
43. Rudi Blesh, *Shining Trumpets*, Cassell 1949, pp. 112–13, 130.
44. Martin Williams, 'Recording Limits and Blues Form', in *The Art of Jazz*, Cassell 1959, p. 91.
45. Samuel Charters, *The Poetry of the Blues*, Oak Publications 1963, pp. 83–4.
46. Sara Martin, *Kitchen Man Blues*, December 1928, QRS R–7043, also on Riverside RLP 12–130.
47. Sara Martin, *Mean Tight Mama*, QRS R–7043, Riverside RLP 12–130.
48. Bessie Smith, *Empty Bed Blues*, 20 March 1928, Columbia 14312.
49. Samuel Charters, op. cit., p. 84.
50. Rudi Blesh, op. cit., p. 130.
51. Lizzie Miles, *My Man o' War*, 27 January 1930, Victor 23281, RCA RD–7840.

52. Odum and Johnson, op. cit., p. 166.
53. Mack McCormick, 'The Damn Tinkers' in *American Folk Music Occasional*, ed. Chris Strachwitz, 1964, p. 7.
54. Ibid., p. 8.
55. Dixon and Godrich, op. cit., p. 3.
56. Whistling Alex Moore, *Blue Bloomer Blues*, 18 February 1937, Decca 7288.
57. Texas Alexander, *The Risin' Sun*, 15 November 1928, Okeh 8673.
58. Kokomo Arnold, *Sissy Man Blues*, 15 January 1935, Decca 7050.
59. Robert Johnson, *Stones in My Passway*, 19 June 1937, Vocalion 03723, CBS 62456.
60. Robert Johnson, *Phonograph Blues*, 23 November 1936, unissued test pressing, CBS (M) 63288.
61. Robert Johnson, *Terraplane Blues*, 23 November 1936, Vocalion 03416, CBS 62456.
62. Walter Davis, *I Think You Need a Shot*, 3 April 1936, Bluebird BB 6498, *Down with the Game* vol. 2, DWG 201. Other erotic blues by Walter Davis are discussed in Neil Slaven, 'The Doctor's Candy Stick Got the Needle' in *Jazzbeat*, September 1966, pp. 16–17.
63. Dobby Bragg, *We Can Sell That Thing*, August 1930, Paramount 13004.
64. Peetie Wheatstraw, *What's That?* 28 August 1940, Decca 7823.
65. Bo Carter, *What Kind of Scent Is This?* 24 October 1931, Okeh 8923.
66. Mississippi Sheiks with Bo Carter, *Crackin' Them Things*, 10 June 1930, Okeh 8810.
67. Sam Hill from Louisville, *You Got to Keep Things Clean*, 27 January 1931, Brunswick 7216.
68. Robert Johnson, *They're Red Hot*, 27 November 1936, Vocalion 03563, Kokomo K 1000.
69. Gates Thomas, op. cit., p. 166.
70. Clara Smith, *It's Tight Like That*, 26 January 1929, Columbia 14398, CBS (M) 63288.
71. Lightnin' Slim, *Rooster Blues*, c. 1956, Excello 2169.
72. Gates Thomas, op. cit., pp. 157–8.
73. Oscar Papa Celestin, *Oh Didn't He Ramble*, June 1951, Bandwagon 11.
74. Old Ced Odum with Lil Diamonds Hardaway, *In Derbytown*, 30 September 1936, Decca 7241.
75. Whistling Rufus, *Who's Gonna Do Your Sweet Jelly Rollin'?*, 11 December 1933, Bluebird B–5306.
76. Papa Charlie Jackson, *All I Want Is a Spoonful*, September 1925, Paramount 12320, Heritage RE100.
77. Charley Patton, *A Spoonful Blues*, 14 June 1929, Paramount 12869, Origin OJL–7.
78. Mack McCormick, notes to Arhoolie F1001 below.

79. Mance Lipscomb, *Just a Spoonful*, July 1960, Arhoolie F1001.
80. Mississippi John Hurt, *Coffee Blues*, 1966, Vanguard VRS 9220, Fontana TFL 6079.
81. Papa Charlie Jackson, op. cit.
82. Charley Patton, *Shake It and Break It (Don't Let It Fall, Mama)*, 14 June 1929, Paramount 12869, Origin OJL-7.
83. Louise Johnson, *On the Wall*, 28 May 1930, Paramount 13008, Riverside RLP 8809.
84. Pinetop Burks, *Fannie Mae Blues*, 25 October 1937, Vocalion 04107.
85. Eddie Miller, *I'd Rather Drink Muddy Water*, 12 November 1936, Melotone 7-02-60.
86. James P. Johnson in Tom Davin, 'Conversations with James P. Johnson', *Jazz Review*, July 1957, p. 11.
87. Cripple Clarence Lofton, *I Don't Know*, 1939, Solo Art 12009, Vogue LDE 122.
88. Willie Mabon, *I Don't Know*, c. 1952, Chess 1531, Chess CRL 4003.
89. W. T. Kirkeby assisted by Sinclair Traill, *Ain't Misbehavin'*, Peter Davies, 1966, p. 41.
90. Ibid., p. 73.
91. Willie (the Lion) Smith with George Hoefer, *Music on My Mind*, MacGibbon & Kee 1965, pp. 55-6.
92. Rudi Blesh and Harriet Janis, *They All Played Ragtime*, Sidgwick & Jackson 1958, pp. 191-2.
93. Smith and Hoefer, op. cit., p. 26.
94. James P. Johnson, op. cit., p. 16.
95. Ibid., p. 13.
96. Perry Bradford, *Born with the Blues*, Oak Publications, New York 1965, p. 154 et seq.
97. Smith and Hoefer, op. cit., p. 42.
98. Mary Dixon, *All Around Mama*, 20 March 1929, Columbia 1442.
99. Tampa Red's Hokum Jug Band, vocal by Frankie Jaxon, *She Can Love So Good*, August 1930, Vocalion 1540, Melodeon MLP 7324. Another version made on this date was not issued.
100. Ethel Waters, *His Eye Is on the Sparrow*, W. H. Allen 1951, pp. 7, 22-3.
101. Billie Holiday, *Lady Sings the Blues*, Barrie Books 1958, pp. 7-8.
102. Bertha Idaho, *Down on Pennsylvania Avenue*, 25 May 1929, Columbia 14437, CBS (M) 63288.
103. Grossman and Farrell, op. cit., pp. 70-1.
104. Clara Smith, *Jelly, Look What You Done Done*, 10 May 1928, Columbia 14319.
105. S. Charters, op. cit., p. 83.
106. Victoria Spivey, *My Handy Man*, 12 September 1928, Okeh 8615. For slight variations see also Paul Oliver, *Blues Fell This Morning*, p. 102; Paul Oliver, *Conversation with the Blues*, p. 151.

107. St Louis Bessie (Bessie Mae Smith), *Meat Cutter Blues*, 6 November 1930, Vocalion 1615.

108. Victoria Spivey, *Black Snake Blues*, 5 May 1926, Okeh 8338. Full text in Oliver, *Conversation with the Blues*, p. 113.

109. For discussions on sexual symbols and metaphors in the blues, see Oliver, *Blues Fell This Morning*, chapter 4. Also Samuel Charters, *The Poetry of the Blues*, Oak, chapter 7.

110. Wynonie Harris, *Lovin' Machine*, 2 July 1951, King 4485, Vogue V 2111.

111. Blind Blues Darby, *Spike Driver Blues*, 30 April 1937, Decca 7816.

112. Mose Andrews, *Ten Pound Hammer*, 30 March 1937, Decca 7338.

113. See Dr Ernest Dichter, *The Strategy of Desire*, Boardman & Co. 1960, appendix 11, pp. 295–320, 'Excerpts from a Motivational Research Study on the Plymouth Car conducted by Ernest Dichter 1939–40'.

114. Bertha Chippie Hill, *Sport Model Mama*, 14 May 1927, Okeh 8473.

115. Cleo Gibson, *I've Got Ford Engine Movements in My Hips*, 14 March 1929, Okeh 8700, Parlophone PMC 1177.

116. Bessie Smith, *Yellow Dog Blues*, 6 May 1925, Columbia 14075-D, CBS BPG 62379. See notes by George Avakian to the latter album for a full description of the text.

117. Virginia Liston, *Rolls-Royce Papa*, 29 May 1926, Vocalion 1032, Historical Jazz vol. 4.

118. Lightnin' Slim, *My Starter Won't Work*, c. 1950s, Excello 2142, Stateside SL 10135.

119. Dixon and Godrich, op. cit., note p. 335.

120. Brunswick matrix listing from file cards, unpublished manuscript by Robert M. W. Dixon.

121. Oliver, *Conversation with the Blues*, Edith Johnson, p. 111.

122. Edith North Johnson, *Honey Dripper Blues*, 7 September 1929, Paramount 1283.

123. Doctor Clayton, *Honey Stealin' Blues*, 27 March 1942, Bluebird 34–0702.

124. This view is advanced in Samuel Charters, *The Country Blues*, Michael Joseph 1960, pp. 166–7 and pp. 212–13 for instance.

125. Curley Weaver, *Sweet Patunia*, 26 October 1928, Columbia 14386, CBS (M) 63288.

126. Willie Baker, *Sweet Patunia Blues*, 11 March 1929, Gennett 6751.

127. Lucille Bogan, *Sweet Patunia*, March 1927, Paramount 12459.

128. Little David (David Alexander), *Original Sweet Patuni* (*Patootie Blues*), 2 August 1936, Decca 7211.

129. Jesse James, *Sweet Patuni*, c. June 1936, Decca unissued, Post 439 as by 'Hooker Joe' and titled *Ram Rod*.

130. Big Bill Broonzy, interview with Paul Oliver, spring 1955.

131. R. Blesh, op. cit., p. 126.

132. Ma Rainey, *Shave 'Em Dry*, c. August 1924, Paramount 12222.

133. Papa Charlie Jackson, *Shave 'Em Dry*, February 1925, Paramount 12264.

134. James Boodle-It Wiggins, *Gotta Shave 'Em Dry*, January 1930, Paramount 12916.

135. Lil Johnson, *New Shave 'Em Dry*, 19 November 1936, Vocalion 13428, CBS (M) 63288.

136. E. Franklin Frazier, *The Negro Family in the United States*, Dryden Press New York, 1951, pp. 221–2.

137. Lucille Bogan, *Shave 'Em Dry*, 5 March 1935, Perfect 0332.

138. Lucille Bogan, *Shave 'Em Dry*, probably same or near date as above, unissued test pressing, CBS (M) 63288.

139. Memphis Minnie, *Dirty Mother For You*, 10 January 1935, Decca 7048.

140. Leadbelly, *Noted Rider*, c. 1944, Asch 560–3, Melodisc 512.

141. Leadbelly, *The Bourgeois Blues*, 1938. Library of Congress recording, Electra EKL 301/2.

142. *Monologue* (dialogue with Alan Lomax), *Dance Calls, Dance Steps*, Electra, EKL 301/2.

143. Roosevelt Sykes, *Dirty Mother For You*, 18 February 1936, Decca 7160.

144. Shufflin' Sam and His Rhythm, *Dirty Mother For You*, 16 September 1936, Vocalion 03329.

145. Shorty Bob Parker, *Ridin' Dirty Motorsickle*, 6 June 1938, Decca 7488.

146. Mack McCormick, Notes to *The Unexpurgated Folk Songs of Men*, 1965, Raglan LP51, pp. 8–9.

147. Sam Chatman, *God Don't Like Ugly*, July 1960, Arhoolie F1006.

148. Gilda Gray, interview in *Current Opinion*, September 1919.

149. Chris Smith, *Don't Slip Me in the Dozen*, c. April 1924, Ajax 17004.

150. Dr Roger Abrahams, *Deep Down in the Jungle*, 'Negro Narrative Folklore from the Streets of Philadelphia', Folklore Associates 1964, p. 51.

151. Bottley, op. cit., p. 68.

152. Ramsey and Smith, op. cit., p. 18.

153. Paul Chevigny, 'A Rough Old Country' in *The Village Voice*, 23 September 1965, p. 17, col. 3.

154. Oliver, *Conversation with the Blues*, transcript of interview with Speckled Red, August 1960, p. 61.

155. Kay Shirley and Frank Driggs, *The Book of the Blues*, Crown Publishers 1963, pp. 227–9.

156. Speckled Red, *The Dirty Dozens*, 2 September 1956, unissued Delmark recording. Verses from the original expurgated recording of *The Dirty Dozen* are given in Oliver, *Blues Fell This Morning*, pp. 128, 130.

157. Memphis Minnie, *New Dirty Dozen*, July 1930, Vocalion 1618, Blues Classics BC 13.

158. Dirty Red (Nelson Wilborn), *Dirty Mother Fuyer, c.* 1946, Aladdin 194, Melodeon MLP 7324. See also Oliver, op. cit., p. 290.
159. One String Sam (Eddie Jones), *Dirty Dozens, c.* 1962, Portents 2 c.f. Newman I. White, *American Negro Folk Songs*, Harvard UP 1928, Folklore Associates 1965, p. 136.
160. Lightnin' Hopkins, *Dirty Dozens, c.* 1961 in collection *The Unexpurgated Folk Songs Of Men*, Raglan R1001.
161. Howard W. Odum, *Wings On My Feet*, Bobbs-Merrill 1929, pp. 93–4. This couplet was collected in Alabama 1915–16. See also Newman I. White, op. cit., p. 365.
162. Sweet Pease Spivey, *Double Dozens (You Dirty No-Gooder)*, 12 August 1936, Decca 7204.
163. R. Abrahams, op. cit., p. 57.
164. Ibid., p. 52.
165. *Statute of Federal Crimes and Criminal Procedure*, 1948, chapter 71, especially section 1461, title 18, USCA sections 1461–4.
166. *New York Penal Law*, section 1141, sub-division 1 as amended, Laws, 1950, chapter 624.
167. Uncle Skipper, *Cutting My ABCs*, 29 March 1937, Decca 7353, cf. Peg 'n Whistle Red, *A to Z Blues, c.* 1950, Realm RM 209.
168. R. Abrahams, op. cit., p. 56.
169. Ibid., p. 56, n.
170. Mike Desilets, 'Blues at the Club 47, Cambridge, Mass. and at Newport R. I.', in *Blues Unlimited*, no. 37, October 1966, p. 10.
171. Charles S. Johnson, *Patterns of Negro Segregation*, Gollancz 1944, p. 315.
172. Lawrence Gellert and Elie Seigmeister, *Negro Songs of Protest*, American Music League, n.d.
173. Joseph Himes, 'Changing Social Roles in the New South', in *Southwest Social Science Quarterly*, December 1956, p. 241.
174. Howling Wolf, *Spoonful*, 1960, Chess 1772, lp 1469.
175. Lewis Killian and Charles Grigg, *Racial Crisis in America*, Spectrum 1964, p. 143.
176. Dr Abram Kardiner and Dr Lionel Ovesey, *The Mark of Oppression: Explorations in the Personality of the American Negro*, World Publishing Co., 1962, pp. 340–1.
177. Ibid., p. 34.

Some of the examples quoted in the text appear on a long-playing record entitled *Screening the Blues* issued by CBS Records on CBS (M) 63288.

INDEX OF BLUES AND SONG TITLES

Index

Index

Index

NAME INDEX OF SINGERS AND MUSICIANS

The following abbreviations are used:

bjo:	banjo	sax:	saxophone
clt:	clarinet	tam:	tambourine
dms:	drums	tmb:	trombone
gtr:	guitar	tpt:	trumpet
hca:	harmonica	vln:	violin
mand:	mandolin	vo:	vocal
pno:	piano	wbd:	washboard

Abney, Peg Leg Ben, pno, vo, 211
Adams, Woodrow, gtr, vo, 123, 124
Alexander, Alger (Texas), vo, 14, 47–8, 49, 61, 77, 86, 184, 186–7
Alexander, Bob, *see* Black Bob
Alexander, Little David, pno, vo, 222–3
Alexander, Ora, vo, 220
Alix, May, vo, 176
Allen, Fulton, *see* Fuller, Blind Boy
Amerson, Rich, vo, 6
Ammons, Albert, pno, 222
Anderson, Jelly Roll, 208
Andrews, Mose, gtr, vo, 213
Andy Boy, pno, vo, 151
Anthony, Eddie, *see* Macon Ed
Arnold, James (Kokomo), gtr, vo, 6, 44, 55, 73, 92, 93, 134, 137, 138, 187, 189, 240

Baby Face Leroy (Leroy Foster), gtr, vo, 121
Bailey, Buster, clt, 130
Baker, Willie, gtr, vo, 220
Banister, James, gtr, vo, 145
Barbecue Bob (Robert Hicks), gtr, vo, 22, 78, 220
Barker, Danny, gtr, vo, 67
Basie, Count, pno, 161
Bates, Deacon L. J., *see* Blind Lemon Jefferson
Beatty, Josephine, vo, 205
Bechet, Sidney, clt, sax, 65

Bell, Alfred, tpt, 228
Berry, Charles Chuck, gtr, vo, 85
Bessemer Blues (Jazz) Singers, vo, 80
Big Maceo (Merriweather), pno, vo, 4, 93, 111
Birmingham Jubilee Singers, vo, 80
Black Ace (B. K. Turner), vo, gtr, 35, 81
Black Bob (Bob Alexander), pno, 152, 228, 235
Blackwell, Frank Scrapper, gtr, vo, 101
Blind Blake (Arthur Phelps), gtr, vo, 33
Bo Diddley (Ellis McDaniel), gtr, vo, 184
Bogan, Lucille (Bessie Jackson), vo, 85, 221–2, 230–2, 241
Bolden, Buddy, tpt, vo, 167, 168, 238
Bollin, Zu Zu, gtr, vo, 165
Boogie Woogie Red (Vernon Harrison), pno, 13
Bonds, Son, gtr, vo, 22, 83, 84
Bottley, Buddy, tpt, 167–8, 238
Bracey, Ishman, gtr, vo, 79, 101
Bradford, Perry, pno, 204
Bragg, Dobby (Roosevelt Sykes and/or Wesley Wallace), pno, vo, 190
Bridey, Rufus (Whistling Rufus), pno, vo, 195–6

Index

Other titles of interest

BIG BILL BLUES
William Broonzy's Story
as told to Yannick Bruynoghe
176 pp., 4 drawings, 15 photos
80490-5 $10.95

BLUES: AN ANTHOLOGY
Edited by W. C. Handy
228 pp., 14 illus.
80411-5 $15.95

THE BLUES MAKERS
Samuel Charters
New preface and new
chapter on Robert Johnson
416 pp., 40 illus.
80438-7 $16.95

THE BOOKS OF AMERICAN
NEGRO SPIRITUALS
Two volumes in one
James Weldon & J.R. Johnson
384 pp.
80074-8 $15.95

CHICAGO BLUES
The City and the Music
Mike Rowe
226 pp., 147 photos
80145-0 $13.95

THE DEVIL'S MUSIC
A History of the Blues
Second Edition
Giles Oakley
306 pp., 36 illus.
80743-2 $14.95

FATHER OF THE BLUES
W. C. Handy
Edited by Arna Bontemps
317 pp., 3 illus.
80421-2 $13.95

I SAY ME FOR A PARABLE
The Oral Autobiography of
Mance Lipscomb, Texas Bluesman
as told to and compiled by
Glen Alyn
Foreword by Taj Mahal
508 pp., 45 illus.
80610-X $16.95

I'D RATHER BE THE DEVIL
Skip James and the Blues
Stephen Calt
400 pp., 13 pp. of illus.
80579-0 $14.95

THE LEGACY OF THE BLUES
Art and Lives of Twelve
Great Bluesmen
Samuel B. Charters
192 pp., 15 photos
80054-3 $9.95

LISTEN TO THE BLUES
Bruce Cook
New introd. by the author
404 pp., 12 photos
80648-7 $13.95

LOVE IN VAIN
A Vision of Robert Johnson
Alan Greenberg
New foreword by Martin Scorsese
272 pp., 9 photos
80557-X $13.95

MEETING THE BLUES
Alan Govenar
248 pp., over 250 illus.
80641-X $17.95

PORTRAIT OF THE BLUES
America's Blues Musicians in
Their Own Words
Paul Trynka
160 pp., $9^1/_2 \times 11$, 123 photos
80779-3 $25.00

THE ROOTS OF THE BLUES
An African Search
Samuel Charters
151 pp., 9 photos
80445-x $10.95

BIG ROAD BLUES
Tradition and Creativity
in the Folk Blues
David Evans
396 pp., many illus.
80300-3 $15.95

BLACK TALK
Ben Sidran
New foreword by Archie Shepp
228 pp., 16 photos
80184-1 $10.95

BLUES FROM THE DELTA
William Ferris
New introduction by Billy Taylor
226 pp., 30 photos
80327-5 $13.95

BLUES OFF THE RECORD
Thirty Years of
Blues Commentary
Paul Oliver
132 pp., 17 photos
80321-6 $13.95

BLUES WHO'S WHO
Sheldon Harris
775 pp., 450 photos
80155-8 $35.00

THE COUNTRY BLUES
Samuel B. Charters
288 pp., 45 illus.
80014-4 $12.95

Available at your bookstore

OR ORDER DIRECTLY FROM

DA CAPO PRESS, INC.

1-800-321-0050